SPAIN'S
BEST-LOVED
DRIVING
TOURS

Hungry Minds, Inc.

New York, NY ■ Indianapolis, IN ■ Cleveland, OH

Written by Mona King

Revised fifth edition published 2002
Revised second edition 1996, published in this format 1998
First published 1992

Edited, designed and produced by AA Publishing.

Published by AA Publishing

Published in the United States by
Hungry Minds, Inc.
909 Third Avenue, New York, NY 10022

Find us online at Frommers.com

Frommer's is a registered trademark of Arthur
Frommer. Used under license.

ISBN 0-7645-6591-5
ISSN 1520-9938

Color separation: Daylight Colour Art, Singapore

Printed and bound by G. Canale & C. S.P.A.,
Torino, Italy

Right: *Templo de la Sagrada Família, Barcelona*

CONTENTS

ABOUT THIS BOOK

This book is not only a practical guide for the independent traveller, but is also invaluable for those who would like to know more about the country.

It is divided into 5 regions, each containing between 3 and 6 tours which start and finish in major towns and cities which we consider to be the best centres for exploration.

Each tour has details of the most interesting places to visit en route, plus panels catering for special interests – for those whose interest is in history, wildlife or walking, and those who have children. There are also panels which highlight scenic stretches of road along the route and which give details of special events, crafts and customs. The route directions are accompanied by an easy-to-use map at the beginning of each tour, along with a simple chart showing intermediate distances in kilometres and miles. This can help you to decide where to take a break and stop overnight, for example. (All distances quoted are approximate.)

Before setting off it is advisable to check with the tourist information centre (addresses are given after the symbol [i] at the end of town entries) at the start of the tour for recommendations on where to break your journey and for additional information on what to see and do, and when best to visit.

Tour Information
See pages 166–73 for addresses, telephone numbers and opening times of the attractions mentioned in the tours, including the telephone numbers of tourist offices.

Hotels and restaurants
See pages 159–65 for a list of recommended hotels and restaurants en route for each tour.

Business Hours
Banks: savings banks, mostly offering exchange facilities, are called *cajas*. They are generally open: Monday–Friday 9–2, Saturday (October–May, main branches only) 9–1.
Exchange facilities are also available outside these hours at airports.
Post offices: generally open Monday–Saturday 9–2, but major branches have longer hours. Mail can be sent addressed to you at *Lista de Correos*. You will need to take personal identification with you when collecting. Post boxes are yellow and some have different sections for different destinations. *Sellos* (stamps) can also be bought at *estancos* (tobacconists).
Shops: open Monday–Saturday 9.30–1, 4–8 (large stores 10–9).

Credit Cards

Major credit cards are widely accepted, but check first for the card sign. Cash can be obtained from banks and certain cash dispensers. Note your credit card numbers and emergency telephone numbers in case of loss. Advise the company immediately if your card is lost or stolen.

Currency

The Euro (€) will start circulating on 1 January, 2002. Both the peseta and the Euro will then be in use until 28 February 2002, after which only the Euro will be accepted.
There are 100 cents to 1 Euro (€). Coin denominations will be: 1, 2, 5, 10, 20 and 50 cents. Notes will be of: €5, €10, €20, €50, €100, €200 and €500.

Customs Regulations

Visitors from EU countries can bring in items for their personal use without paying any duty. For tobacco products, alcohol and perfume, officials have guidelines as to what is an acceptable amount for personal use. Customs duties are leviable on amounts exceeding their limits. Wines, spirits and cigarettes are generally cheaper in Spain than in many countries.

Electricity

220 volts AC 50HZ and 110/125 in some bathrooms and older buildings. Plugs have two round pins, so an adaptor is required.

Embassies

Australia: Plaza Descrubidor Diego de Ordás 3, Madrid, tel: 91 441 93 00.
Canada: Edificio Goya Calle Nuñez de Balboa 35, Madrid, tel: 91 4314300.
UK: Calle de Fernando el Santo 16, Madrid 4, tel: 91 700 82 00.
US: Serrano 75, 28006 Madrid, tel: 91 5774000.

Emergency Telephone Numbers

General Emergencies 112
Policia Nacional 091

These 24-hour numbers may not connect you with the nearest station but will get your message relayed. Describe the nature of the emergency (*urgencia*), your location and the services required.
Bomberos (Fire) 080
Medical Emergencies 061
Madrid: Ambulance Red Cross (Cruz Roja) 91 522 2222
Barcelona: Ambulance Red Cross (Cruz Roja) 93 300 2020

Entry Regulations

You must have a valid passport to enter Spain. Nationals of EU countries, Norway, Iceland, Cànada, the USA and Japan do not need a visa for stays of up to 90 days. If in doubt check with the Spanish Tourist Office.

Health

Residents of EU countries are entitled to some free medical treatment on production of form E111 (obtain this from your post office before departure). However, it is wise to obtain a comprehensive travel insurance policy which provides full health cover.

Motoring

For information on motoring in Spain, see pages 158–9.

Public Holidays

1 January – Año Nuevo
6 January – Día de los Reyes (Epiphany)
Good Friday – Viernes Santo
1 May – Día del Trabajo (May Day)
15 August – Asunción
12 October – Día de la Hispanidad
1 November – Todos los Santos (All Saints' Day)
6 December – Constitucíon
8 December – Immaculada Concepción
25 December – Navidad (Christmas Day)

Telephones

All telephone numbers in Spain have a nine-digit system, starting with 9 and incorporating the area code.

International access codes are as follows: to call Spain from Australia, dial 00 11; New Zealand 00; UK 00; US and Canada 011 (followed in each case by 34 for Spain, then the subscriber's number). Country codes are: Australia 61; Canada 1; New Zealand 64; UK 44; US 1. Public phone booths are plentiful. They will be adjusted to take Euro (€) coins, but phone cards are often more convenient.

Time

Spain is two hours ahead of GMT in the summer and one hour ahead in the winter.

Tourist Offices

Spanish National Tourist Offices:
UK: 22/23 Manchester Square, London W1M 5AP. Tel: 020 7486 8077.
US: 666 Fifth Avenue, New York, NY 1013. Tel: (212) 265-8822.

Useful Words

The following words and phrases may be helpful.
English   *Spanish*
hello   *hola*
goodbye   *adiós*
good morning   *buenos días*
good afternoon   *buenas tardes*
good evening and goodnight   *buenas noches*
do you speak English?   *¿habla usted inglés?*
yes/no   *sí/no*
please   *por favor*
excuse me, I don't understand   *perdón, no entiendo*
thank you (very much)   *(muchas) gracias*
I am/my name is...   *soy/me llamo*
how are you?   *¿como está?*
very well   *muy bien*
where is ... ?   *¿dónde está ...?*
open/closed   *abierto/cerrado*
I would like ...   *me gustaría ...*
do you have ... ?   *¿tiene ... ?*
how much is ... ?   *¿cuánto es/vale/cuesta ... ?*
1 to 10   *uno, dos, tres, cuatro, cinco, seis, siete, ocho, nueve, diez*

CATALUNYA, THE LEVANT & THE BALEARICS

This region offers a variety of panoramas, bound together by its long sweep of Mediterranean coastline and a common language. It includes three of Spain's best-known tourist areas – the Costa Brava, the Costa Blanca and Mallorca.

The capital of Catalunya is Barcelona, a thriving commercial centre. To the north are the eastern Pyrenees, which separate the Iberian peninsula from the rest of Europe. This is a sparsely populated area dominated by rugged mountains and green valleys irrigated by the rivers Ter, Llobegrat and Segre, together with tributaries of the Ebro. To the east, the rugged coastline of the Costa Brava features high cliffs, rocky coves and sandy beaches.

The Levant, including the Valencia region, famous for rice-growing, extends to the palm groves south of Alicante. The coast flattens out into long stretches of sandy beaches broken up by rocky promontories. This is the region of the *huertas*, fertile cultivated lands, irrigated by water from the Turia and Jacar rivers, that produce a rich harvest of oranges, lemons, olives, vegetables and flowers. Inland, in the south lie desolate areas, reminiscent of lunar landscapes.

Opposite the Levant lies Mallorca, the largest of the Balearic Islands. Between the Sierra de Tramuntana in the west and the gentler slopes of the Sierra de Levante in the east is a plain of orchards, fields and windmills. Known for the beauty of its coast, pinewoods and olive groves, the island is at its best in spring when the almond blossom is in bloom.

Numerous invasions and occupations have shaped the culture. Phoenicians, Greeks, Carthaginians, Romans and Moors have all played their part and left testimonies to their presence.

The official language is Catalan. Following periods of suppression it is again widely spoken in Catalunya and street names and place names are written in Catalan. A variant of the language is spoken in Valencia as a result of its conquest in the 13th century by King Jaime I of Aragón. Mallorca has its own version, known as Mallorquín.

Sunflowers throw back the light of the sun all over Spain

Tour 1

Scenery is the emphasis of this itinerary, which takes you into the heartland of the eastern Pyrenees. This provides wonderfully varied landscapes, from mighty mountain ranges to green valleys, rivers and lakes. Along the route are little Pyrenean towns and castles dating back to medieval or even Roman times, along with churches built in the typical Catalan Romanesque style. A highlight is undoubtedly the visit to Spain's most sacred sanctuary in the spectacular setting of the great Montserrat massif.

Tour 2

The once desolate Costa Brava ('wild coast') has long since become one of Spain's most popular holiday areas. Parts are still very attractive, however, with picturesque little fishing villages set in sandy coves surrounded by pine-clad hills. The drive offers stretches of stunning beauty, as steep cliffs drop sharply into the sea. The vivid blues and greens of the Mediterranean and purple shades of the mountains,

coupled with the fragrance of the pines, are a part of its attraction. Visits to ancient Greek and Roman ruins, inland towns and a beautiful old monastery provide cultural interest.

Tour 3

The first part of the journey takes you down the Costa Dorada (golden coast), named for its splendid sandy beaches. The route passes through attractive scenery, where stretches of twisting hair-pin bends give way to more relaxed driving through rolling hills and valleys. Along the way there are picturesque resorts, old towns and one of Spain's greatest Roman cities. Travelling inland along part of the old Cistercian Route, the tour visits three beautiful monasteries in lovely surroundings.

Tour 4

The route begins with Valencia and continues along part of the Costa Blanca ('white coast'), known for its beaches of fine white sand, holiday resorts and mild winter climate. Dramatic rock formations provide impressive landscapes along the route.

The coast of Mallorca near the charming mountain village of Deià

Inland is a sharp contrast in scenery and interest, with several fascinating old towns.

Tour 5

A visit to a unique palm forest is followed by a drive down Spain's southeastern coast, where the Costa Blanca leads to the Costa Cálida ('warm coast'). The tour combines wild, rugged mountain scenery inland with beautiful stretches of coastal road. The area of the Mar Menor, with its large saltwater lagoon and tourist development, is an interesting part of the country.

Tour 6

There are two Mallorcas: that of mass tourism, and the Mallorca of fine mountain scenery, almond trees and olive groves. This tour visits some of its best features: monasteries, Roman remains, spectacular caves and picturesque fishing villages. There are beautiful stretches of coastline, with rocky coves and sandy beaches, the essence of this very Mediterranean island.

The Catalan
Pyrenees

Barcelona is the capital of Catalunya, Spain's second city and its principal port. Its medieval past lives on in the old Barri Gòtic, while the elegance of the 19th century, shown in the Plaça Reial, contrasts with the unique flamboyance of Gaudí-designed buildings.

2/3 DAYS • 492KM • 305 MILES

The monastery of Montserrat, spectacularly set high up in the Montserrat mountains

ℹ️ *Plaça de Catalunya, 17–S*

▶ *From Barcelona, take the **A2** towards Lleida/Lérida. Leave at junction 22 near Martorell for the **NII**, travelling north-west, and after a few kilometres turn right on to the **C1411** towards Manresa. At Monistrol village follow the road up the mountain to the monastery car-park.*

❶ Montserrat, Barcelona
Set among wild rock formations and jagged peaks is the Monestir de Montserrat, which contains Catalunya's most sacred sanctuary. Vast numbers of pilgrims gather each year to venerate the Black Virgin, patron of Catalunya, who is kept here. The origins of the monastery, one of Spain's major tourist attractions, centre on the legend of the miracle-working statue of the Virgin, supposedly found in a cave near by in 880. A chapel dedicated to her was erected, and in 976 monks of the Benedictine order founded a monastery that steadily grew in size and importance.

The church was rebuilt by Philip II, who greatly favoured the place. The monastery was fortified by the Catalans during

---

RECOMMENDED WALKS

Montserrat has several short walks in stunning scenery to places such as Sant Miquel and Sant Joan.

Above: the medieval castle of Cardona on its hilltop is now a *parador* (hotel). The view from the fortifications, with their pepper-pot turrets, is stunning (left).

altar is the polychrome statue of the dark-faced Virgin. It can be reached by a staircase and may be touched through a circle cut in the glass. The library

SPECIAL TO...

When you visit the Monestir de Montserrat, it is worth making the effort to hear the Escolanía. This is one of the oldest boys' choirs in Europe, dating back to the 13th century. The boys are brought up in the monastery and receive a religious education. The singing is dedicated to the Virgin of Montserrat. The choir performs daily at 1pm and sometimes at 6.45pm (except for July and Christmas).

the Peninsular Wars, but in 1812 it was sacked by the French, with the result that most of the present structure is from the 19th century, with some parts completed only after World War II. Before entering the monastery, stop for a moment on the observation platform to have a look at the dramatic surroundings. The most important part of the building is the Basilíca, built between 1560 and 1592 in the Renaissance style, and restored in the 19th century. The interior is a vast dark area lit by a mass of tiny lights. In a glass niche above the high

The Catalan Pyrenees

contains an impressive collection of books, and there are several museums.

A short ride by funicular takes you on an awe-inspiring journey to the Sant Joan ridge, where an observation terrace affords spectacular views of the great Montserrat massif.

▶ *Rejoin **C1411** and continue north to Manresa. Turn left on to the **C1410** and continue northwest to Cardona.*

2 Cardona, Barcelona
A final turn in the road reveals the magnificent sight of the old medieval castle of Cardona. Rising from a great brown rock cone, it looms over the little village below, offering magnificent views. The castle is made up of a group of buildings that were constructed between the 10th and 19th centuries. It has now been converted into an attractive *parador*, however you can still visit its fine collegiate church, Colegiata de Sant Vincenc, and crypt below, which have been well preserved.

▶ *Continue on the **C1410** for 20km (12 miles) to Solsona.*

3 Solsona, Lleida/Lérida
Solsona is a picturesque little town with quaint streets, old houses and the remnants of medieval ramparts. There are ruins of a 12th- to 13th-century castle at the top of the hill. Near the bridge is the cathedral. Erected in the 12th century and rebuilt between the 14th and 15th centuries, it shows a combination of Romanesque and Gothic styles. The Diocesan Museum in the Palau Episcopal has a good collection of paintings, frescos and fine altar-fronts, while the exhibits in the salt museum are fashioned out of blocks of salt from Cardona.

▶ *Follow the **C1410** west. At Bassella take the **C1313** north to La Seu d'Urgell (Seo de Urgel).*

4 La Seu d'Urgell, Lleida/Lérida
Serving as a natural gateway to the tiny republic of Andorra, La Seu d'Urgell lies in a typical Pyrenean valley, surrounded by high wooded mountains. It is the centre of a bishopric and has a fine Romanesque cathedral dating back to the 12th century, with later additions. The Diocesan Museum has an interesting display of religious art. Other buildings of note are the 11th-century Romanesque Chapel of Sant Miguel and the 15th-century Casa de la Ciutat, built in Gothic style.

[i] *Avenida Valls d'Andorra 33*

▶ *Continue east on the **N260** to Puigcerdá.*

5 Puigcerdá, Girona/Gerona
Puigcerdá has a cosmopolitan atmosphere typical of border towns. It is attractively situated on a hilltop overlooking the Cerdanya, a district that is split between Spain and France. A bridge connects the town to Bourg-Madame in France. The main buildings of interest are the 15th-century Ajuntament, the 13th-century church of Sant

Domenéc and the church of Santa Maria, which is also 13th century. The town is a pleasant place to explore, with its lively main square, busy little streets and pretty houses with balconies. The boating lake to the north is a favourite resort, both in summer and winter. You can take a short side trip to Llívia, about 5km (3 miles) northeast. This little medieval town is a Spanish enclave within France and has a small museum displaying items from its pharmacy, apparently one of the earliest in Europe.

[i] *Querol 1*

▶ *Take the **N152** east for 49km (30 miles) to Ribes de Freser.*

6 Ribes de Freser,
Girona/Gerona

This popular resort lies on the River Freser in an attractive setting of green forests. It is the starting point for a funicular ride up to Núria. The journey takes about 45 minutes and passes through mountains and pine forests. The Núria Sanctuary is a famous pilgrimage centre and the place is also a popular winter sports resort.

[i] Plaça de l'Ajuntament 3

▶ Continue south for 14km (9 miles) on the **N152** to Ripoll.

7 Ripoll, Girona/Gerona

Although the town is essentially industrial, stop here to visit the Antiguo Monestir de Santa Maria which stands in the square. Founded in the 9th century, it was subsequently destroyed – first by an earthquake, then by fire – and later restored. It has a richly carved Romanesque door and a cloister with a fine collection of capitals depicting religious scenes.

[i] Plaça de l'Abat Oliba s/n

▶ Take the **C151** northeast to Sant Joan de les Abadesses (San Juan de las Abadesas).

8 Sant Joan de les Abadesses, Girona/Gerona

As you arrive you will see the lovely 12th-century bridge over the River Ter. In the centre of the town stands the magnificent Abbey of Sant Joan. It was founded in the 9th century and belonged originally to the Benedictines. During the course of time it suffered severe damage and had to be rebuilt several times. The impressive Romanesque church and the magnificent Gothic cloister are fine examples of the architecture of these periods. In the central apse above the high altar is a beautiful 13th-century carving in wood of the Descent from the Cross.

[i] Plaça de l'Abadía 9

▶ Take the **C151** northeast for 14km (9 miles) to Camprodon.

9 Camprodon,
Girona/Gerona

Camprodon lies in the heart of the Pyrenees, surrounded by mountains and woods. Attractive houses with red-tiled roofs and balconies look down on narrow, winding streets and squares. A familiar sight is the lovely 16th-century arched bridge that spans the river. Buildings of special interest include the Romanesque Monestir de Sant Pere (St Peter's), the parish church and the Ajuntament (town hall). Many Spanish families come to Camprodon in the summer to enjoy the healthy mountain air and good walking in beautiful surroundings.

[i] Plaça d'Espanya 1

▶ Return south, join the **C153** and continue southeast to Olot.

10 Olot, Girona/Gerona

Olot is famed for the painted and carved figures that are used for the Nativity performances. It is also known for its 'Olot School' of 19th-century Catalan painters. Many of these works, along with some fine sculptures and examples of modernistic art, can be seen in the Museu Comarcal de la Garrotxa, as well as exhibits which trace Olot's development as a textile centre.

The town is in a volcanic region and evidence of old craters still remain all around, although they are mostly covered by vegetation. The small museum, Casals dels Volcans, located within the botanical garden, Jardí Botànic, on the outskirts of town, has an interesting display of photographs, manuscripts and exhibits on the subject. A detour of some 7km (4 miles) east along the C150 will take you to the black basalt village of Castellfollit de la Roca, which is perched on a clifftop looking over the River Fluvià.

[i] Lorenzana 15

▶ Take the **C152**, turning right on to the **C153** south for 64km (40 miles) to Vic.

RECOMMENDED WALKS

There is a lovely walk from Olot that takes you through the magnificent Fageda d'en Jordà beech forest to the large crater of the Volcà de Santa Margarida (Santa Margarida volcano). Another route from Olot follows the River Fluvià down the Vall d'En Bas, passing through several charming villages.

⓫ Vic, Girona/Gerona

The old episcopal town of Vic
lies at the confluence of the
rivers Méder and Gurri. Its two
main attractions are the Plaça
Major (main square) and the
cathedral, which is situated on
the edge of town. Founded in
the 11th century and restored
in the 18th, it features a handsome Romanesque bell tower.
Inside, look out for the richly
ornate 15th-century marble
altar and the elegant cloister,
which is graced by a splendid
monument to Jaime Balmes,
counsellor to Pope Pius IX.
The adjoining Museu
Episcopal has an impressive
collection of Romanesque art,
works from the Gothic period
and Roman relics.

The heart of the old town is
the large and lively Plaça Major,

*Wall paintings by Sert of the
Stations of the Cross in the 18th-
century cathedral at Vic*

which is lined with arcades and
handsome buildings. This central square is surrounded by an
area of narrow streets, winding
alleys and little hidden squares.
Among them you will find the
Casa Consistorial (town hall), a
fine building of Gothic origin,
with more recent additions.
Near by are the remains of a
Roman temple dating back to
the 2nd or 3rd century AD, and
medieval walls.

ⓘ *Ciutat 4*

▶ *Take the N152 south. By
Tona take unclassified roads
southeast to Santa Fé del
Montseny.*

⓬ Santa Fé del Montseny

The Sierra del Montseny is a
magnificent range of mountains
luxuriantly covered by green
forests. There are several routes
through the Sierra that you
could take on your homeward
journey, all passing through
attractive country. The
suggested drive takes you
through some exceptionally
beautiful scenery to the Ermita
de Santa Fé del Montseny,
which stands at an altitude of
1,100m (3,610 feet) and offers
wonderful views of the area.
The tiny village here provides
an excellent base for mountaineering in the area, or for
those who want to walk.

▶ *Continue southeast and
then return to Barcelona
on the A7.*

The Costa
Brava

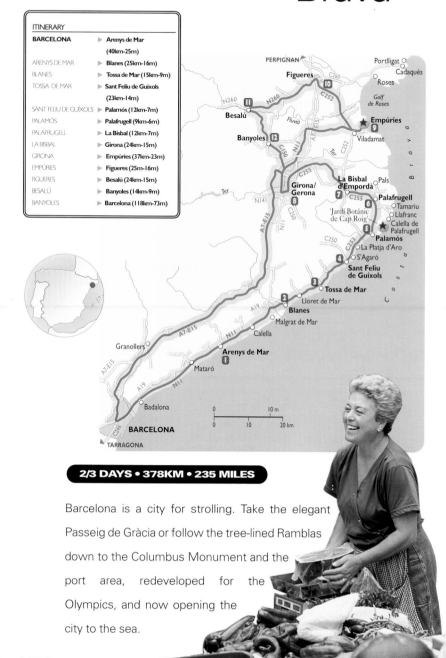

2/3 DAYS • 378KM • 235 MILES

Barcelona is a city for strolling. Take the elegant Passeig de Gràcia or follow the tree-lined Ramblas down to the Columbus Monument and the port area, redeveloped for the Olympics, and now opening the city to the sea.

up, the Church of Santa Maria looks down on the roof-tops. A climb up to the top of the Sa Palomera, southwest of the harbour, provides a good view of the sandy bay of Blanes.

> ℹ️ *Plaça Catalunya s/n*

> ▶ *Follow the road through Lloret de Mar to Tossa de Mar*

❸ Tossa de Mar
Girona/Gerona

Tossa de Mar was called 'The Blue Paradise' by the French artist, Marc Chagall, who produced many paintings of the town in the 1930s. Some of his works are exhibited in the Museu de la Vila Vela, along with other paintings and a mosaic from the Roman settlement here. The old town is picturesque, with its narrow streets and medieval houses contained within massive walls and turrets from the 12th century. There is also a splendid view from the lighthouse.

> ℹ️ *Avenida Pelegrí 25, Ed Terminal*

SCENIC ROUTES

The route between Tossa and Sant Feliu is particularly beautiful. Its tortuous bends take you high over mountain tops and down among the pine forests, with magnificent views of cliffs. The stretch between Besalú and Banyoles on the C150 also offers some splendid mountain scenery.

> ▶ *Continue northeast to Sant Feliu de Guíxols.*

❹ Sant Feliu de Guíxols,
Girona/Gerona

This large, cheerful town is considered to be the capital of the Costa Brava. Its busy port and lack of a good, sandy beach

---

> ℹ️ *Plaça de Catalunya, 17–S*

> ▶ *Leave Barcelona from the Plaça Glòries Catalanes and take the A19 coast road east. Turn right at Badalona and join the NII through Mataró to Arenys de Mar.*

❶ Arenys de Mar,
Girona/Gerona

The main attractions in Arenys are its pretty little port and its reputation for excellent seafood. The fishing harbour is fun to explore and is full of activity when the catch comes in. The large marina is now an international regatta centre.

The Church of Santa María (begun in 1584 by the French) is worth a visit to see the magnificent 18th-century retable (decorated panels above the altar) by the artist Pablo Costa.

Arenys has a long tradition of white bobbin lace-making and you may still see some of the local women,

known as *puntaires*, sitting out on their doorsteps practising their ancient skills.

> ▶ *Continue on the NII coastal road. At Malgrat branch off northeast to Blanes.*

❷ Blanes, Girona/Gerona

Blanes, the start of the Costa Brava, is a popular resort in an attractive setting. After exploring the harbour you can stroll along the promenade to the old town which has a Gothic fountain in the main square. Further

---

BACK TO NATURE

Just beyond the harbour of Blanes is the Botanical Garden of Mar y Murtra (sea and myrtle), where you will find hundreds of species of plants, largely from the Mediterranean area. The garden is beautifully laid out on an original design by the German Karl Faust.

gives it a different ambience to some of its neighbours. The 11th-century Porta Ferrada (iron gate) and the adjoining church are the remains of a Benedictine monastery.

The Ermita de Sant Elm, on the outskirts of town, offers a splendid view of the coast.

[i] *Plaça Monestir 54*

▶ *Take the **C253** to Palamós.*

8 Palamós, Girona/Gerona
Palamós's main attractions are its beautiful setting in a wide

---

FOR CHILDREN

Children will enjoy a visit to Water World, a lively water park located near Lloret de Mar.

---

curved bay and its lively port and yacht harbour. A major fishing centre, it is one of the most important towns in the region. Colourful fish auctions take place in a hall called the Lonja.

In the old part of the town is the 14th-century Gothic Church of Santa Maria amid the original narrow streets.

[i] *Passeig del Mar s/n*

▶ *Take the **C255** inland for 9km (6 miles) to Palafrugell.*

9 Palafrugell,
Girona/Gerona
Palafrugell is a busy commercial and shopping town. A few remains of Moorish walls can be seen and there is the little Gothic Church of San Martí. This is a good spot for a detour to some of the Costa's most delightful resorts. A short drive

through pine woods leads to Tamariu and another road takes you to the resorts of Calella de Palafrugell and Llafranc. There is a stunning view of the bays from the lighthouse below the Ermita de Sant Sebastià, poised on top of the hill.

[i] *Carrilet 2*

▶ *Continue northwest on the **C255** for 12km (7 miles) to La Bisbal d'Empordà.*

BACK TO NATURE

In season a mini-train runs from the centres of Llafranc and Calella de Palafrugell to the attractive Botanical Garden (Jardí Botànic de Cap Roig), which features rare plants and Mediterranean shrubs.

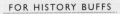

The River Onar runs through the city of Girona

brown and yellow. While here, visit the large 14th-century Romanesque castle, once the seat of the ruling Bishops of La Bisbal d'Empordà, the parish church and the old bridge.

i *Aigüeta, 17*

▶ *Continue west to Girona.*

8 Girona, Girona/Gerona
Founded by the Iberians, Girona was occupied by the Romans, the Moors, and retaken by Charlemagne in 785, later to form part of the kingdom of Catalunya and Aragon. The River Onar separates the new town from the old, which is located on the east bank and best explored on foot.

The old town is a step right back into the Middle Ages. You find yourself among dark, secretive streets, picturesque houses and hidden squares. The cathedral appears unexpectedly, rising majestically from a flight of steps. This impressive building, one of the finest cathedrals in Catalunya, dates back to the 14th century. The huge 12th-century embroidered 'Tapestry of the Creation' is a unique exhibit among many treasures in the museum. The adjoining 12th-century cloister is noted for its carved capitals. Other historic buildings are the former Iglesia Colegiata de Sant Feliu, with its tall tower, the old Episcopal Palace, which is now the Art Museum, and the 12th-century Banys Àrabs (Arab Baths). Interesting by day, the floodlit old town is magical by night.

Pleasant areas in the new town are the Plaça de la Independencia, surrounded by attractive arcades, and the Parque de la Dehesa.

i *Rambla de la Llibertat 1*

▶ *Take the NII north and after 21km (13 miles) make a right turn to Empúries.*

The remains of the Roman town at Empúries, overlooking Roses Bay

9 Empúries, Girona/Gerona
This impressive archaeological site is one of the most important in Spain and has both Greek and Roman ruins. It was originally founded by the Greeks in the 6th century BC and known as 'Emporion' which means market. The place flourished and produced coins which were used in the region. In the 2nd century BC the Romans arrived to fight the Carthaginians, and built on to the existing town. Some of the most valuable pieces that have been excavated from the site can be seen in the Archaeological Museum in Barcelona. Empúries (Ampurias) became a bishopric under the Visigoths, but was destroyed during the conflicts with the Moors. The museum

RECOMMENDED WALKS

One very attractive walk is along the 'Avinguda de Mar', a cliff path that links the two pretty little resorts of Calella de Palafrugell and Llafranc. The route has beautiful views over each of the bays in turn.

7 La Bisbal d'Empordà,
Girona/Gerona
La Bisbal d'Empordà is renowned for ceramics and has an Escola de Ceràmica (School of Ceramics). The tradition goes back to the Middle Ages, and contemporary work has been influenced by the designs of the Arabs, French and Italians. The pottery is to be seen all over the town and is recognisable by its dominant colours of green,

The fortifications on the medieval bridge, gateway to Besalú

has a collection of archaeological finds from the area, along with reconstructions of Greek and Roman life. A detour northeast to the coast takes you to the delightful whitewashed village of Cadaqués and nearby Portlligat, where Salvador Dalí lived for many years.

▶ *Return to Viladamat and then take the **C252** northwest to Figueres (Figueras).*

⑩ Figueres, Girona/Gerona
Figueres is a major town of the Empurdà region. Buildings of historical interest include the 14th-century Church of Sant Pere, with a fine Romanesque tower, and the Castell de Sant Fernand, an impressive 18th-century fortress. The exhibits in the Museu de l'Empordà, on the town's tree-lined Rambla, include items from Empúries.

FOR CHILDREN

The Toy Museum in Figueres, Museu de Joguets, has a large collection of dolls from different countries and periods of history.

The real interest in Figueres, however, is the great Salvador Dalí, surrealist artist and eccentric, who was born here in 1904. The extraordinary Teatre-Museu Dalí (Dalí Museum), with its distinctive dome, topped by curious egg shapes, is not only a feature of the town, but a big attraction in Spain. Here, some of Dalí's works are presented in a most exciting and imaginative way.

ⓘ *Plaça del Sol*

▶ *Take the **N260** southwest for 24km (15 miles) to Besalú.*

⑪ Besalú, Girona/Gerona
A splendid old fortified bridge over the River Fluvià serves as the main entrance to the ancient town of Besalú. Once capital of the Garrotxa region, the town is a medieval treasure, with its narrow streets and old houses. Handsome buildings surround the Plaça Major, which is lined with attractive doorways. The massive Monestir de Sant Pere and the churches of Sant Vicenç and Santa Maria, are all from the 12th century.

ⓘ *Plaça de la Llibertat 2*

▶ *Take the **C150** southeast to Banyoles (Bañolas).*

⑫ Banyoles, Girona/Gerona
The popular lakeside town of Banyoles has a good beach, offering facilities for bathing and watersports. On the Plaça del Font (Fountain Square) is the Museu Arqueològic Comercal which displays antiquities from the area. In the 10th-century Church of Sant Esteve (St Stephen), later rebuilt in the classical style, is a 15th-century retable, the work of the stone mason, Joan Antigo.

ⓘ *Passeig Industria 25*

▶ *Continue on the **C150**, then join the **A7** back to Barcelona.*

SPECIAL TO...

The *sardana* is an important part of Catalan folklore. The dance's origins are not clear, but it is thought to have roots in the Cerdanya region. It is danced all over Catalunya, at weekends or on festival days. Anyone may take part (but do try to learn some of the steps before joining in). The participants join hands and dance in a constantly moving circle to the accompaniment of the local *cobla* (band).

Roman Relics &
Golden Beaches

Barcelona's hills, Montjuïc and Tibidabo, are great places for entertainment. Museums, from modern art to archaeology, and the Olympic Stadium are on Montjuïc with the old fishermen's quarters below, now rejuvenated. Tibidabo has a funfair and stunning panoramic views. Below lies the amazing Gaudí creation of Parc Güell.

2/3 DAYS • 597KM • 373 MILES

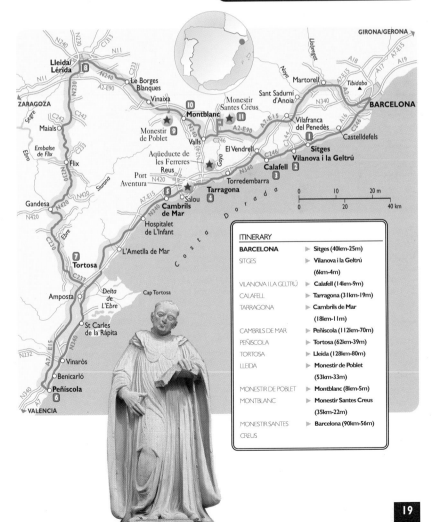

ITINERARY

BARCELONA	▶ Sitges (40km-25m)
SITGES	▶ Vilanova i la Geltrú (6km-4m)
VILANOVA I LA GELTRÚ	▶ Calafell (14km-9m)
CALAFELL	▶ Tarragona (31km-19m)
TARRAGONA	▶ Cambrils de Mar (18km-11m)
CAMBRILS DE MAR	▶ Peñíscola (112km-70m)
PEÑÍSCOLA	▶ Tortosa (62km-39m)
TORTOSA	▶ Lleida (128km-80m)
LLEIDA	▶ Monestir de Poblet (53km-33m)
MONESTIR DE POBLET	▶ Montblanc (8km-5m)
MONTBLANC	▶ Monestir Santes Creus (35km-22m)
MONESTIR SANTES CREUS	▶ Barcelona (90km-56m)

The cathedral at Tarragona, built over a period of time in a mixture of Romanesque and Gothic styles.

i Plaça de Catalunya, 17–S

▶ *Leave Barcelona from the Plaça Espanya and take the C246 southwest to Sitges.*

SPECIAL TO...

Penedès, southwest of Barcelona, is a major wine area, with production ranging from sparkling wines (*cavas*) to fine wines and liqueurs. It is known for its wines of high alcoholic content. On your return to Barcelona you might go via Vilafranca del Penedès and visit the Museu del Vi (Wine Museum), which presents a history of wine.

---

❶ Sitges, Barcelona

Sitges is a traditional resort that lured Spanish families long before it became an international tourist centre. As well as its splendid sandy beach and shallow waters, Sitges is a picturesque little town with great charm. The local church, with its rose-coloured façade, adds to the picture. The Cau Ferrat Museum, once home of the painter Santiago Rusinyol (1861–1931), houses a collection of his paintings, together with works by El Greco, Picasso, Utrillo and others.

i Sinia Morera 1

▶ *Take a minor road southwest for 6km (4 miles) to Vilanova i la Geltrú (Vilanueva y Geltrú).*

FOR CHILDREN

The spectacular theme park of Port Aventura offers a variety of exotic amusements. Located just outside Salou, this is a must for children of all ages.

---

❷ Vilanova i la Geltrú, Barcelona

This is an industrial town and a resort, with a fine sandy beach and picturesque fishing harbour. It has two museums of interest: the Museu Romàntic Can Papiol, which is housed in an elegantly furnished town house and devoted to life in the early 1800s; and the Biblioteca Museu Balaguer, which is noted for its fine collection of antiquities and Catalan paintings.

> [i] *Passeig del Carme (Parc de Ribes Roges)*

> ▶ *Continue down the **C246** coast road to Calafell, 14km (9 miles).*

8 Calafell, Barcelona
The small fishing village of Calafell is another favourite summer resort with a long sandy beach, suitable for a quiet stop and a look at the Romanesque parish church and the ruins of the 12th-century castle.

> ▶ *Continue on the **C246** to El Vendrell and join the **N340** to Tarragona.*

4 Tarragona, Tarragona
The route passes through El Vendrell, the birthplace of the famous Spanish cellist, Pablo Casals (1876–1973).

A lovely Roman town, Tarragona was founded by Publius Cornelius Scipio during

The well-preserved Roman Aqueduct near Tarragona

the Second Punic War of 218 BC. A stroll along the attractive tree-lined Rambla Nova leads to the observation platform 'Balcó del Mediterrani', which offers a sweeping view of the coast. Below is the harbour and the Parc del Miracle, where you can see the remnants of a 2nd- or 3rd-century BC Roman amphitheatre, once the venue for combats between man and beast. The Museu National Arqueològic has mosaics, ceramics and antiquities from the region. A climb from the centre of town takes you to the cathedral, which was built between the 12th and 14th centuries. It shows a harmonious blending of Romanesque and Gothic styles, with a fine façade and lovely rose window in the centre. The Passeig Arqueologic is a pleasant shaded walk along the foot of the massive city ramparts, which extend for some 1,000m (1,100 yards) and up to 10m (33 feet) in parts.

Statue of Pablo Casals, the cellist, in his home town of El Vendrell

The Museu Paleocristina, on the outskirts of the town, has a fine display of tombs, mosaics and jewellery. Adjoining it is an old Christian cemetery dating back to the 3rd century.

> [i] *Fortuny 4, Bajos*

> ▶ *Continue on the **N340** south to Cambrils de Mar.*

5 Cambrils de Mar, Tarragona
Cambrils de Mar is a picturesque little port with a maritime tradition. The

RECOMMENDED WALKS

Leave Tarragona from the Rambla Nova and drive 4km (2½ miles) north to the Roman aqueduct, the Acueducto de les Ferreres (El Pont del Dimoni or Devil's Bridge). A pleasant walk of about 30 minutes takes you through a lovely area of pines to the base. Part of the structure has long disappeared but two tiers of arches still stand and are an impressive sight.

harbour is dominated by an ancient church tower, originally a Roman defence fortification. The port becomes a hive of activity when the fishing fleet comes in, and has a reputation for good eating.

▶ *Continue south down the coastal road (N340) for 112km (70 miles) to Peñiscola.*

⑥ Peñiscola, Castellón

This is a veritable jewel of a place, rising like a fortress from a rocky peninsula that juts out to sea. The town was taken from the Moors in 1233 by King Jaime I. Its main feature is the castle, an impressive structure built by the Knights Templars. Later, the deposed antipope, Benedict XIII (Pope Luna), took refuge in the castle and spent his last years here until his death in 1422. The castle offers magnificent views of the coastline. Within the surrounding walls is the old town, a labyrinth of tiny winding streets – strictly for pedestrians only.

▶ *Drive inland to join the A7 north, turning off after 46km (29 miles) on the C237 to Tortosa.*

⑦ Tortosa, Tarragona

The episcopal town of Tortosa holds a commanding position over the delta of the River

SCENIC ROUTES

The drive from Barcelona down the eastern coast of Spain has some particularly scenic sections. After Castelldefels the C246 runs along the coast to Sitges, offering splendid sea views. Be prepared for countless curves and bends in the road. There are attractive stretches before Calafell, between Torredembarra and Tarragona; after Salou, on the N340; and between Tortosa and Lleida (N230).

FOR HISTORY BUFFS

During the Spanish Civil War (1936–9), Tortosa was the scene of an important battle. On 24 July, 1938, the Republicans, who were in control of Catalunya at the time, attacked the advancing Nationalist forces. They crossed the River Ebre but were unable to advance further and had to remain in trenches until their ultimate defeat. The victory of the Nationalists is commemorated by a monument rising from the river.

Ebre. The cathedral was begun in 1347 and built over a long period of time. The naves are 14th-century Gothic, while the façade and the chapel to the Mare de Deu de la Cinta (the Virgin), patron saint of the city, are baroque. Other buildings of note are the 14th-century Palau Episcopal and the Colegio de Sant Lluis, which was founded in 1544 by Emperor Charles V for converts from the Moorish faith, and has an elegant courtyard with some fine decoration. Many splendid old palaces from the 15th and 16th centuries can be seen, as well as remains of the city walls.

ⓘ *Plaça del Bimil*

▶ *Take the C230 north to Gandesa, then turn right on to the N420 before turning left back on to the N230 to Lleida.*

⑧ Lleida, Lleida/Lérida

Originally an Iberian settlement, Lleida came under the Romans in the 2nd century BC and was the scene of numerous battles and sieges over the years. It was the birthplace of Enrique Granados (1867–1916), famed for his classical guitar compositions.

Enclosed within the city walls is the Seu Vella (old cathedral), which is dominated

The ancient town of Tortosa is now a fascinating blend of old and new.

by a tall 14th-century octagonal tower. Built between the 12th and 15th centuries, it shows the transition from Romanesque to Gothic. During the 18th century the cathedral was used as a garrison and has been undergoing restoration for some years. It has a fine Gothic cloister, noted for its tall, graceful arches.

Lleida also has a new cathedral. The Seu Nova was built in the 18th century in neo-classical style, and was the first of its kind in Catalunya. Other sights of interest include the 13th-century town hall, known as the Palau de la Paería, attractive courtyard

10 Montblanc, Tarragona
Montblanc is an impressive sight, with its massive medieval ramparts and towers and narrow entrance gates. Overlooking the town is the Church of Santa María begun in the 14th century and never fully completed.

▶ *Continue on the N240 southeast to Valls. Turn left on to the C246, then left again on a minor road, crossing the A2 to Santes Creus.*

11 Monestir Santes Creus, Tarragona
The Santes Creus monastery rises grandly over the forest around it. It is a fine example of the Cistercian style and is, like Poblet, among Catalunya's most important monasteries.

Founded in 1157, the monastery was occupied by Cistercian monks from France. It long enjoyed the favour of the Kings of Aragon but, like Poblet, it suffered damage during the wars of the 19th century, and is also under restoration. The church is 12th-century Romanesque and contains the royal tombs of former kings of Catalunya including that of Pedro III.

▶ *Return south to the A2 and join the A7 back to Barcelona, 90km (56 miles).*

---

and the churches of Sant Llorenç and Sant Martín. The 15th-century hospital of Santa María now houses the Museu Arqueològic, with Iberian and Roman relics from the area. Lleida is an excellent centre for excursions into the Pyrenees.

ℹ️ *Major 3/bis*

▶ *Take the N240 southeast towards Tarragona. Shortly after going under the A2 (motorway) turn right to the Monestir de Poblet.*

9 Monestir de Poblet, Tarragona
Tucked away on the lower slopes of the Prades Mountains, the Monastery of Santa María de Poblet was founded in 1149 by Ramón Berenguer IV as a token of thanks to God for the regaining of Catalunya from the Moors. The following year 12 Cistercian monks, sent from Fontfroide (near Narbonne in France), began building the monastery which is a fine example of Cistercian art. The monks benefited from the patronage of the Aragon kings, for whom the monastery became a favourite stopping place for royal journeys. The lovely Gothic cloister and adjoining chapter house contain a number of abbots' tombstones in the pavement.

▶ *Rejoin the N240 and continue for 8km (5 miles) to Montblanc.*

BACK TO NATURE

The delta of the River Ebre attracts huge numbers of birds, both migrants from northern areas and residents, so the Parc Natural del Delta de L'Ebre, west of Tortosa was created to protect them. Among the many species that can be seen are plovers, avocets, black-winged stilts and red-crested pochards. Flamingos gather on the Salinas marshes, although their presence and numbers are rather unpredictable. Other inhabitants include otters, the stripeless tree frog and terrapins.

The Costa
Blanca

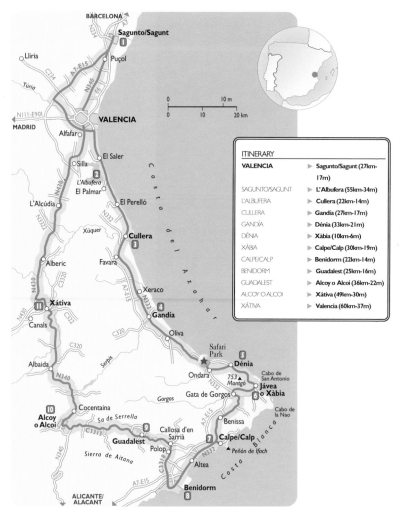

ITINERARY

VALENCIA	▶	**Sagunto/Sagunt (27km-17m)**
SAGUNTO/SAGUNT	▶	**L'Albufera (55km-34m)**
L'ALBUFERA	▶	**Cullera (22km-14m)**
CULLERA	▶	**Gandía (27km-17m)**
GANDÍA	▶	**Dénia (33km-21m)**
DÉNIA	▶	**Xàbia (10km-6m)**
XÀBIA	▶	**Calpe/Calp (30km-19m)**
CALPE/CALP	▶	**Benidorm (22km-14m)**
BENIDORM	▶	**Guadalest (25km-16m)**
GUADALEST	▶	**Alcoy o Alcoi (36km-22m)**
ALCOY O ALCOI	▶	**Xátiva (49km-30m)**
XÁTIVA	▶	**Valencia (60km-37m)**

Valencia, Spain's third city **2/3 DAYS • 396KM • 247 MILES**
and a busy port, is graced with many fine buildings such as the
Catedral (1262–1482), a mixture of Romanesque, Gothic and
baroque styles, La Lonja, built in 1483 as the Silk Exchange, and
the Iglesia de Santa Catalina with its hexagonal belfry.

ℹ *Calle de la Paz, 48*

▶ *From Valencia, take the N340 north to Sagunto.*

❶ Sagunto/Sagunt, Valencia

The original *Saguntum* was founded by the Iberians but was later allied to Rome. The town was attacked by the great Carthaginian general, Hannibal, in 218 BC. Abandoned by Rome, the citizens resisted for several months until the city finally fell to the enemy, sparking off the Second Punic War. Five years later the Romans recaptured the town and rebuilt it. Later, it was under Moorish occupation.

On one side of the Plaza Mayor (main square) stands the 14th-century Gothic Iglesia de Santa María, which has an 18th-century gilded altar with a fine cross in mother-of-pearl. From the road up the hillside, you can see stone arches over some of the streets, which once framed the old gates leading to various parts of the town. A highlight is the Teatro Romano (Roman Theatre). Dating back to the end of the 2nd century AD, it has a diameter of 50m (165 feet), with a capacity for some 6,000 spectators. There is a small museum alongside.

The road winds up to the Castillo de Sagunto, which has sweeping views over the coast and the town. The ruins of the fortress, spread over the hillside, show evidence of Iberian, Carthaginian and Roman occupation; the walls are mainly from the Moorish period.

ℹ *Plaza Cronista Chabret*

▶ *Return southwest on the A7/E15 for 6km (4 miles). Join the A7 heading southwest around Valencia. After 20km (12 miles) turn left off the A7, travelling south of Valencia, and join the coastal road south to El Saler and L'Albufera.*

Moorish walls surround the medieval castle spread over the hill at Sagunto but earlier it was a strongpoint for Iberians, Carthaginians and Romans too

---

BACK TO NATURE

The large freshwater lagoon of L'Albufera is a nature park of great ecological importance, and is a paradise for birdwatchers. Among the species of birds that breed here are red-crested pochards, purple herons, black-winged stilts and numerous warblers. Little egrets are often seen feeding in the water and, in the autumn, thousands of wildfowl, lapwings and golden plover arrive to spend the winter. The arrival of these migratory birds can be watched from the village of El Palmar, on the lagoon. The flight of the ducks is a famous sight in L'Albufera.

❷ L'Albufera, Valencia

A short drive south beyond Valencia's El Saler beach will bring you to L'Albufera, Spain's largest lagoon (the name derives from the Arabic for 'small sea'). The lagoon is surrounded by rice fields and separated from the sea by a sand bar known as La Dehesa. Three channels carry fresh water into the sea.

▶ Continue south to Cullera.

❸ Cullera, Valencia

The effects of tourism have taken their toll on Cullera, like many other places, once a tiny fishing village and now characterised by high-rise blocks. The place still retains some of its old charm, however, and it is worth

going up the hill to the Ermita de Nuestra Señora del Castillo, which contains a venerated image of the Virgen del Castillo, patron saint of the town. Near by are the ruins of an old castle and a splendid view of the coast and surrounding rice fields.

⊡ *Carrer del Riu 38*

▶ *Join the **N332** and travel south for 27km (17 miles) to Gandía.*

❹ Gandía, Valencia

Gandía was formerly the seat of a dukedom given to the Borja family in 1485 by Ferdinand the Catholic. Of major interest is the Palacio de los Duques (Ducal Palace), a handsome

Fishing boats gather in the harbour at Gandía, the town from where the Borjas set out for Italy

SCENIC ROUTES

The coastal road from Gandía to Dénia is very pleasant, with long sandy beaches broken up by dramatic rock formations. There are many areas of lush vegetation with palm forests, orange groves and beautiful oleander and cypress trees. The road south of Xàbia to Benidorm, the route to Guadalest, inland on the C3313, and the section from Alcoy to Xátiva on the N340 are particularly scenic.

Renaissance building notable as the birthplace and residence of Francisco Borja (1510–72), who became the 4th Duke of Gandía. He was the superior of the Jesuit Order, and was canonised as Saint Francis Borja in 1671. The building has seen considerable alterations since the 16th century and is now a Jesuit college. The state apartments are richly decorated and the patio is attractively adorned with coats of arms. The flooring is laid out to represent the four elements of the Creation and bordered by lovely ceramic tiles.

Close to the Palace are the 18th-century Ayuntamiento (town hall) and the Iglesia de Santa María, which is a good example showing the transition from Gothic to Renaissance architecture.

[i] *Marqués del Campo*

▶ *Continue on the N332 south. At Ondara take a left turn to Dénia.*

5 Dénia, Alicante

The original Dénia is thought to have been colonised by the Greeks before the 8th century BC and known as *Hemero-skopeion*. Under the Romans it became *Dianium*, after the temple of Diana. It flourished as a port during the time of the Moors (715–1253), and at one time it controlled the island of Mallorca. Today it is principally a seaside resort and port.

The town is crowned by the remains of the old fortress, which provides a fine view of the surroundings. The area around the fishing port is fun to explore. Take a look at the small 18th-century Iglesia de Santa María and the 17th-century Ayuntamiento.

The Sierra del Montgo towers over the southern end of the town, rising to a height of 753m (2,470 feet). The climb to the top is arduous, but the views from the summit are superb. On a clear day you can see the outline of Ibiza, more

than 100km (65 miles) away to the east.

[i] *Plaza del Oculista Buigues, 9*

▶ *Take the regional road down the coast for 10km (6 miles) to Xàbia (Jávea).*

FOR CHILDREN

Between Ondara and Oliva, just off the N332, is the Safari Park Vergel, which features free roaming animals, a dolphinarium and a funfair, among other attractions for children.

---

6 Xàbia (Jávea), Alicante

The small fishing port of Xàbia spreads along a wide bay between two pine-covered rock masses, which descend sharply to the sea. The pretty setting, combined with a lively yacht marina and fine sandy beaches, makes it an appealing resort. It has a late Gothic church shaped like a ship's hull. In spring Xàbia is filled with the scent of lemon and orange blossom.

At one end of the resort is the great rock of Cabo de la Nao, with some caves in its steep cliff face. Opposite is the tiny island of Portichol. Visit the lighthouse on Cabo de San

Antonio for great views of the coast towards Xàbia and Cabo de la Nao.

[i] *Plaza Almirante Bastarreche, 11*

▶ *Return westwards to the N332 and continue south for 30km (19 miles) to Calpe.*

7 Calpe/Calp, Alicante

Your approach to Calpe is heralded by the magnificent sight of the Peñón de Ifach – a famous landmark of the Costa Blanca – rising majestically from the sea. Nestling beneath this great volcanic mass is Calpe, whose dramatic setting features among its main attractions.

It is another in the long line of popular resorts to be found down this coast, with a fine

---

RECOMMENDED WALKS

The fit and energetic should enjoy a walk up a good path to the summit of the Peñón de Ifach (about 1½ hours), from where there is a panoramic view of the Costa Blanca.

The Peñón de Ifach towers over the resort of Calpe. This landmark rock is 332m (1,089 feet) high

sandy beach and busy fishing harbour. In the old part of town is a small Gothic-Mudejar church and a 16th-century tower, all that remains of the fortified walls.

ⓘ *Avenida Ejércitos Españoles, 66*

▶ *Continue along the N332 for 22km (14 miles) to Benidorm.*

8 Benidorm, Alicante
Benidorm is the Costa Blanca's most famous resort, attracting multitudes of visitors each year. The place has changed beyond recognition since the days when it was a sleepy little fishing village. It is now an inter-national fun city, crammed with bars, shops and nightspots that provide non-stop entertain-ment, which holds particular appeal for the younger set. Tall hotels and apartment blocks dominate the skyline all along the bays.

Whatever your thoughts about Benidorm in season, its setting is dramatic, with its two splendid bays of golden sands and high-rise blocks silhouetted against the high mountains. Steer clear of the tourist area and explore the old fishing quarters, which have narrow streets and a pretty church with a blue dome. A rather elegant look-out terrace near by offers a sweeping view of the bay and the little island of Plumbaria. If you have time, take a boat trip to the island and enjoy a swim.

ⓘ *Avenida Martinez Alejos, 16*

▶ *Take the C3318 north past Polop, then turn left on to the C3313 to Guadalest.*

FOR CHILDREN

Terra Mítica is a spectacular new theme park where children and families alike can have fun in five different settings – Egypt, Greece, Rome, Iberia and the islands.

---

9 Guadalest, Alicante
A drive through some spectacu-lar scenery will bring you to the dramatic sight of Guadalest, a tiny village with a Moorish castle, perched on top of a lofty mountain crag. Most of the village was destroyed by an earthquake, but you can clam-ber up to the fortress, known as the Costa Blanca's 'eagle's nest' for its impregnable position and superb views over the surround-ing landscapes.

▶ *Continue on the C3313 west for 36km (22 miles) to Alcoy o Alcoi.*

10 Alcoy o Alcoi, Alicante
The town of Alcoy lies in a setting of olive groves and vine-yards against a backdrop of the Sierra de Montcabre, presenting an attractive picture as you approach it. Alcoy is famous for its *peladillas*, a very popular sweet in Spain, made of sugar-coated almonds. The town has

The Costa Blanca

The ruins of the Moorish castle at Guadalest in an impregnable position on a crag above the village

two fine churches, the Iglesia de Santa María and the Iglesia de Santo Sepulcro, which has attractive tile decorations. The Museo Arqueológico (Archaeological Museum) houses an extensive collection of Iberian pottery and Greek tablets found in the area.

ⓘ *Ayuntamiento (Town Hall)*

SPECIAL TO...

The festival of the Moors and Christians is celebrated all over Spain, but is especially colourful in Alcoy where it takes place between 22 and 24 April, and centres on St George's Day, 23 April. For three days an image of St George (to whom the village had appealed for help in times of need) is carried through the streets and around the walls of a great cardboard castle. Mock battles are fought between the Moors and the Christians, inevitably ending in victory for the Christians. This is all accompanied by bell-ringing, fireworks and jollity.

▶ *Take the N340 north to Xátiva (Játiva).*

❶ Xátiva (Játiva), Valencia
The ramparts of Xátiva are apparent from some distance, rising from twin peaks. Set among olive groves and vineyards, Xátiva is an attractive little town of fountains and trim trees, with a number of interesting monuments. Some fine old palaces and fountains can be seen on and around Moncada Street, which is a very picturesque area. The Colegiata (Collegiate Church) is an excellent example of the 16th-century Renaissance style and the municipal hospital opposite has a fine 16th-century Plateresque façade. Allow time for a visit to the

---

FOR HISTORY BUFFS

A short detour of about 8km (5 miles) on a minor road southwest of Xátiva takes you to the small village of Canals. The castle here is famed as the birthplace of Alonso Borja. The Borja family came to Canals from Aragón in the 14th century and Alonso, who was born here in 1378, later became Pope Calixtus III. His nephew, Rodrigo Borja (1431–1503), or Borgia as the name was written in Italian, became Pope Alexander, notorious for his scandalous behaviour and father of Lucretia and Cesare Borgia.

Museo Municipal, which has an extensive collection of antiquities, including the Pila de los Moros, a Moorish basin dating from the 11th century with, unusually for a Muslim work of art, decorations that depict human figures.

There are good views from the cypress-planted Calvary and the Ermita de San Feliu (hermitage of St Felix). A further climb up the hill takes you to El Castillo, a 16th-century castle built on Iberian and Roman foundations, from which there is a magnificent view of the surrounding countryside.

ⓘ *Alameda Jaime 1–50*

▶ *Return to Valencia on the N430.*

SPECIAL TO...

Those with an interest in musical bands should make a point of visiting Liria, a short distance northwest of Valencia. Known as the 'City of Music', it has an international reputation for its bands of musicians. It is said great rivalry exists between the bands, who jealously guard their own territory.

RECOMMENDED WALKS

Many of the antiquities displayed in the museum in Alcoy were found in the nearby Sierra Sereta. A steep climb of about half an hour will take you to the top, where there are magnificent views of the surrounding mountainous landscapes.

TOUR
5

Palm Forests & Rugged Peaks

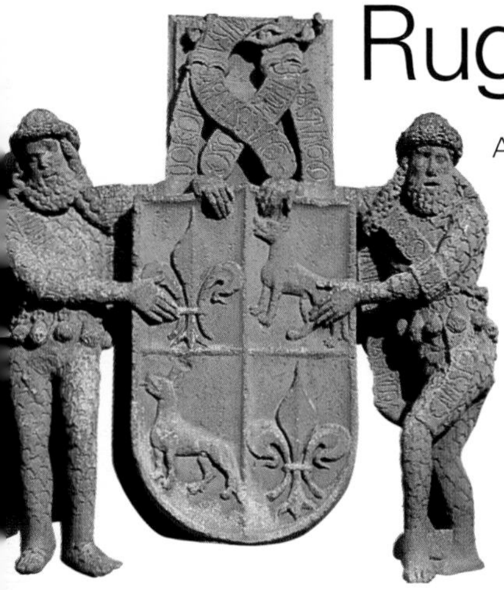

Alicante, or Alacant, main gateway to the Costa Blanca, is a pleasant southern city. Attractions include its palm-lined esplanade, new marina and the picturesque old quarters of Barrio Santa Cruz. See also the Town Hall, the cathedral, Iglesia de Santa María and the panoramic view from the Castillo de Santa Barbara.

ITINERARY	
ALICANTE	▶ **Elche o Elx (24km-15m)**
ELCHE O ELX	▶ **Orihuela (33km-21m)**
ORIHUELA	▶ **Murcia (24km-15m)**
MURCIA	▶ **Alhama de Murcia (32km-20m)**
ALHAMA DE MURCIA	▶ **Aledo (21km-13m)**
ALEDO	▶ **Totana (9km-6m)**
TOTANA	▶ **Lorca (20km-12m)**
LORCA	▶ **Águilas (39km-24m)**
ÁGUILAS	▶ **Marazzón (46km-29m)**
MARAZZÓN	▶ **Cartagena (39km-24m)**
CARTAGENA	▶ **La Unión (11km-7m)**
LA UNIÓN	▶ **Alicante (98km-61m)**

2/3 DAYS • 396KM • 247 MILES

ALBACETE
'Fort West'
Vinalopó
ALICANTE/ ALACANT
A7-E15
N332
N330
Crevillente
N340
C3317
Elche o Elx
1
Santa Pola
Albatera
C3223
A7-E15
2
Orihuela
Guardamar del Segura
Segura
Mula
C415
N340
3
Murcia
C3321
Alcantarilla
Torrevieja
Santuario de la Fuensanta
RESERVA NACIONAL DE SIERRA DE ESPUÑA
N340-E15
Guadalentín
Sierra de Carrascoy
N301
Sierra de Espuña
4
Alhama de Murcia
Aledo
5
Totana
6
Ermita de Sta Eulalia
C3211
N340
C3315
C3319
San Pedro del Pinatar
San Javier
Mar Menor
Costa Blanca
Lorca
7
N332
N301
La Manga del Mar Menor
La Unión
11
Cabo Negrete
C3211
Sierra de Almenara
Mazarrón
9
Cartagena
10
Puerto de Mazarrón
Golfo de Mazarrón
Costa Blanca
C3211
8
Cabo Cope
Águilas
N332
ALMERÍA
0 10 20 m
0 10 20 30 km

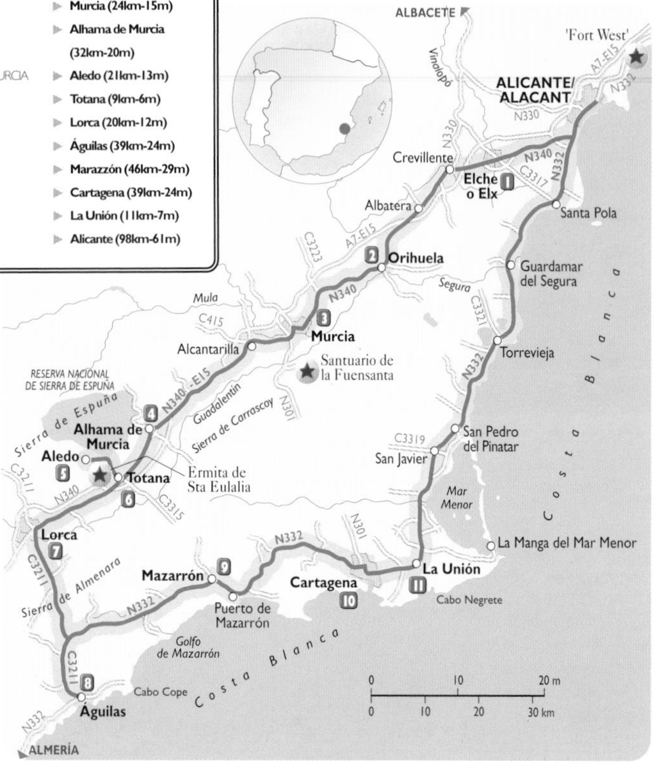

The Explanada de España, with wavy multicoloured pavings, extends along the seafront at Alicante. *Left:* the harbour

which are thought to be at least 150 years old and have seven stems that grow out from the main trunk. The dates are cut in winter from the female palms, while some of the male trees are bound to bleach the fronds. These are then sold for Palm Sunday processions.

i Parque Municipal

---

i Rambla Méndez Nuñez 23

▶ Take the **N340** southwest for 24km (15 miles) to Elche o Elx.

0 Elche o Elx, Alicante
The main attraction of Elche is the unique palm forest which surrounds the town, adorning its parks and gardens and shading its streets. There is an excellent view over the town and palm grove from the tower of the 17th-century baroque Santa María Basílica. The Palacio de Altimira near by was built in the 1400s as lodgings for the kings

of Spain. In the Museo Arqueológico there is a copy of the *Lady of Elche* sculpture, thought to be from the 4th or 3rd century BC, found in the vicinity and now in the Archaeological Museum of Madrid.

The Palmeral de Europe (Palm Forest of Europe), the largest date palm grove in Europe, lies to the east of the town and was originally planted by the Moors. Many of the palms reach a height of 25m (82 feet). In the Huerto del Cura (Priest's Orchard) you can see the impressive trees of the 'Palmera Imperial' species,

---

SPECIAL TO...

The *Misteri d'Elx (Mystery of Elche)* is a play about the Assumption of the Virgin. It takes place on the Feast of the Assumption in the Basílica of Santa María, with spectacular performances on 14 and 15 August. The actors are local and the music medieval.

The Renaissance belfry of the Cathedral at Murcia

▶ Continue on the **N340** for 33km (21 miles) to Orihuela.

2 Orihuela, Alicante
Orihuela lies on the banks of the River Segura, which provides irrigation for the surrounding orange and lemon groves. The Cerro de Oro (Hill of Gold) rises in the background. The name of the town is thought to be derived from the Roman *Aurariola*. The town suffered severe damage from an earthquake in 1829. Among the few old buildings to survive are the El Salvador cathedral, built in the 14th and 15th centuries, with fine Gothic vaulting; the late-Gothic Santiago Church,

---

SCENIC ROUTES

Particularly attractive stretches include the approach to Elx and on to Orihuela through a palm and orange grove; the Leyva Valley, between Alhama de Murcia and Aledo, high up in the mountains of the Sierra de España; Puerto de Mazarrón to Cartagena; and La Unión back to San Javier both on the N332 west of the large saltwater lagoon of the Mar Menor.

---

and the Santo Domingo College, former home of the University of Orihuela, founded in the 16th century.

ℹ *Francisco Díaz, 25*

▶ Continue for 24km (15 miles) on the **N340** south-west to Murcia.

3 Murcia, Murcia
Capital of its province, Murcia spreads along both sides of the Río Segura, in the heart of the *huerta* (a fertile, irrigated region). Murcia is the seat of a bishopric and a university town. The cathedral, built in the 14th century with later Renaissance and baroque additions, features an impressive façade and splendid 18th-century belfry. Inside are lavish Renaissance decorations in the Capilla de los Junterones and the rich late-Gothic of the Chapel of los Velez. One of several museums in Murcia, the Museo Salzillo displays a striking collection of figures carved by the 18th-century sculptor Francisco Salzillo that are carried in the Holy Week processions.

ℹ *San Cristóbal, 6*

▶ Take the **N340** southwest to Alhama de Murcia.

FOR HISTORY BUFFS

Just south of Murcia is the Santuario de la Fuensanta, a pilgrimage centre overlooking the *huerta*. Consecrated at the end of the 17th century, it has a fine façade, crowned with two towers.

---

4 Alhama de Murcia, Murcia
On the way to Alhama de Murcia, stop at Alcantarilla, 9km (6 miles) out of Murcia, to visit the Museu de Tradiciones y Artes Populares. Amongst the exhibits is a huge old waterwheel called a *noria*, which the Moors used for irrigation.

Continue through orange and lemon groves, then by cornfields to a large, craggy rock topped by the tower of an old Moorish fort. Below lies the ancient spa town of Alhama de Murcia, which is known for its warm, medicinal sulphur springs, and still has traces of Roman occupation.

▶ Continue along the **N340**. At Totana take a right turn and drive to Aledo.

5 Aledo, Murcia
At the southern end of the Sierra de España is the small medieval town of Aledo, famous for its old castle, which was held for a long period by the Knights of the Calavatra (1085–1160) during the Moorish occupation.

BACK TO NATURE

The natural park of the Sierra España is Murcia's largest nature reserve with rugged mountains and high peaks. Among its inhabitants are wild sheep (moufflon), wild cats, boar and foxes; eagles, owls and partridges are some of the birds to be seen here.

▶ Return on the same road to Totana, 9km (6 miles).

6 Totana, Murcia
Totana was a town of some importance under the Romans. The 16th-century Iglesia de Santiago (St James) has a fine 17th-century baroque portal and Mudejar coffered ceiling. Some 7km (4 miles) away is the Ermita de Santa Eulalia, the town's patron saint, famed for its Mudejar roof and 16th-century murals.

▶ Take the **N340** south to Lorca.

7 Lorca, Murcia
At the entrance to the Valley of El Guadalentín lies the town of Lorca, an important agricultural centre. Lorca was a bishopric

under the Visigoths, called *Ilurco* by the Romans, and *Lurka* by the Moors. Above the town are the remains of the old Moorish castle, built between the 13th and 15th centuries, and the medieval churches of Santa María, San Juan and San Pedro.

Further down the hill is the Iglesia de San Patricio, with a Renaissance tower and baroque doorway, and the elegant Ayuntamiento.

[i] *López Gisbert, 12 (Palacio Guevara)*

▶ *Take the C3211 south to Águilas.*

8 Águilas, Murcia
The seaside town of Águilas dates back to the 17th century and is comparatively unchanged. Its two most impressive buildings are the Mudéjar-style Ayuntamiento and the Iglesia de San José. A climb up to the Castillo de San Juan de las Aguilas on top of the hill provides a fine view of the bay and distant mountains.

▶ *Take the C3211 north, then at the N332 turn right to Mazarrón.*

9 Mazarrón, Murcia
The main features in this small inland town are the Castillo de los Vélez, with the remains of an old watch tower, and the Iglesia de San Andrés, which has a fine 16th-century Mudéjar coffered ceiling. A short drive leads to Puerto de Mazarrón, which lies in a splendid bay.

[i] *Avenida Doctor Meca, 20, Puerto de Mazarrón*

▶ *Continue on the N332 north-east to Cartagena.*

> ### RECOMMENDED WALKS
>
> The Sierra de Espuña offers many lovely walks in pine forests and mountain terrain.

10 Cartagena, Murcia
Cartagena is Spain's major naval base and a big commercial port. Founded by the Carthaginians in the 3rd century BC, it became the region's capital under the Romans. It declined under the Moors but rose to importance during the 16th century. Worth visiting are the Iglesia de Santa María la Vieja, the Roman Torre Ciega (literally, blind tower) and the Ayuntamiento. On the main quay of the port is the world's first submarine, launched by Isaac Peral in 1888.

[i] *Plaza Bastarrache s/n*

▶ *Take the N332 east to La Unión.*

11 La Unión, Murcia
La Unión emerged as an important centre for lead mining a century ago. The Mercado (market) and the Casa del Piñon are two examples of early 20th-century architecture, making full use of wrought-iron. The August festival of the 'Cante de las Minas' (mining songs) is held in the market-place.

East is the modern resort of La Manga del Mar Menor with golf, tennis and watersports.

▶ *Return to Alicante on the northeast coast road (N332).*

The ornate doorway of the Church of San Patricio, Lorca, is a fine example of baroque carving

The Magic of
Mallorca

Although for many it is just a gateway to beach resorts, Palma has charm and it is well worth exploring its historic buildings – the Gothic Cathedral with its landmark spire, the Ajuntament, and La Lonja, the former Exchange, as well as the lively Passeig de Borne, crammed with shops and bars. West of Palma, the 14th-century Castell de Bellver, built on a hill by Mallorcan kings and now a museum, has fine views of Palma Bay from its commanding postion.

FREDERIC CHOPIN

3 DAYS • 358KM • 223 MILES

Fishing boat with floats in the harbour at Port Andratx

Plaça de la Reina 2

▶ *From Palma take the C719 southwest to Port d'Andratx.*

❶ Port d'Andratx, Mallorca
From a tiny fishing village, Port d'Andratx has become one of Mallorca's most prominent yachting centres, with sailing vessels of all shapes and sizes moored in the harbour. The town is set in an attractive bay surrounded by hills and has a pleasant seafront promenade lined with bars and restaurants. The yachting set provides an international atmosphere during the season.

▶ *Take the C710 and branch off right to Valldemossa.*

❷ Valldemossa, Mallorca
To many, the name of Valldemossa conjures up visions of Chopin, music and romance. The Polish composer Frédéric Chopin spent the winter of 1838 to 1839 here with the French

authoress George Sand. The Reial Cartuoxa (Royal Carthusian Monastery) where they stayed is the main feature of the village. After the monks were expelled in 1835 the place served as lodgings for travellers. The apartments, or rather cells, where the couple stayed are furnished in the style of the period, and include the piano on which the great master composed some of his best-known works. In the cloister is a very old pharmacy. First

SCENIC ROUTES

The road along the magnificent Serra de Tramuntana, across the northwest of the island, is outstanding. The corniche from Andratx to Sóller is one of the most beautiful drives in Mallorca. There are spectacular views of the coast from look-out posts such as the Mirador Ricardo Roca and Ses Animes, and around Banyalbufar.

Terrace at Valldemossa monastery where Chopin stayed

FOR CHILDREN

There are a number of amusement parks near Palma. At Costa d'en Blanes, north of Palma Nova, Marineland has spectacular shows of performing dolphins and sea lions. Along the Autovía Palma-El Arenal is the huge Aquacity, another popular water park. By Magaluf, south of Palma Nova, are two further attractions, Aquapark and Wester Park, a Wild West theme park offering lively shows and thrilling water rides.

established by the monks as early as 1723, it looks much the same as it must have done then. Take a look, too, at the small museum in the monks' library.

▶ *Rejoin the **C710** for 10km (6 miles) to Deià (Deyà).*

3 Deià (Deyà), Mallorca
Deià has long been a favourite haunt for writers and artists, such as the poet and writer Robert Graves who spent some time here after World War II. The village consists of a delightful cluster of red houses on top of a hill, idyllically set among almond trees and groves of oranges, lemons and olives. Behind the parish church is the cemetery where Graves is buried. There is a wonderful view from here of the surrounding mountains and rocky coves below. A somewhat precipitous climb down the hill takes you to the sea.

▶ *Continue on the **C710**. Take a left turn to Port de Sóller.*

> RECOMMENDED WALKS

Mallorca has so many attractive areas for walking that you can more or less make a choice anywhere along the route. The Serra de Tramuntana in the northwest of the island offers countless hikes in magnificent scenery. Booklets can be obtained from the local tourist office.

4 Port de Sóller, Mallorca
The route from Deià passes through the small hamlet of Lluc Alcari, where Pablo Picasso lived for a time. The picturesque old fishing port of Port de Sóller is now a popular tourist spot. It has an attractive harbour, framed by the pine-covered hills of the Serra de Tramuntana, and an excellent sandy beach. The Santuario de Santa Catalina, by the old fishing quarter, provides a fine view of the resort. Five

The mellow village houses of the mountain village of Deià set among olive groves and almonds

kilometres (3 miles) inland is Sóller town, linked to Port de Sóller by a narrow-gauge railway or by road, where the Convent de Sant Francesc (St Francis) is worth a visit, along with the handicrafts centre in the local museum.

ⓘ *Canonge Oliver 10*

▶ *Rejoin the **C710** and branch off left to the Monestir de Lluc.*

5 Monestir de Lluc, Mallorca
Situated on one of the highest points of the island is Mallorca's principal monastery and pilgrimage centre. The entrance is lined with houses and doorways, which once provided shelter for pilgrims who arrived here to venerate the Virgin of Lluc, patron saint of the island. Inside the monastery is a

Back in the town, other places worth a visit are the Gothic chapel of Roser Vell, which has a fine altarpiece, the church of Montision (both 18th-century), and the baroque-style Convent de Sant Domènech. There is a Roman bridge just outside town.

Port de Pollença, some 6km (4 miles) away, is an attractive little fishing port set in a wide bay framed by the dramatic silhouette of the Sierra de Sant Vincenc (San Vincente mountains). It is a very popular, fast-developing resort and yachting centre.

If you have time, continue northeast into the Formentor peninsula, one of the most scenic parts of the island. A drive to the lighthouse at the end of Cap de Formentor offers magnificent views of this superb coastline.

▶ *From Port de Pollença take the coast road for 15km (9 miles) to Alcúdia.*

> ### RECOMMENDED WALKS
>
> A pleasant stroll can be taken in Port de Pollença along the seafront promenade, which starts from the northern end of town and follows the sea, shaded by trees and lined with villas and open-air cafés and restaurants.

7 **Alcúdia,** Mallorca
The little medieval town of Alcúdia is encircled by some impressive old ramparts dating back to the 14th century. Inside are small narrow streets and handsome mansions, mainly from the 16th and 17th centuries. The town had quite a sizeable Roman population and the local museum has exhibits of Roman times as well as prehistoric artefacts. A colourful market takes place on Tuesdays and Sundays just outside the old city walls.

wooden statue of the Virgin encrusted with jewels. There is also a 17th-century church, and a small museum with a collection of paintings, ceramics and religious items. Mass is celebrated each day, when you can hear the stirring singing of the famous boys choir of Lluc.

▶ *Continue on the C710 for 21km (13 miles) to Pollença (Pollensa).*

6 **Pollença,** Mallorca
Pollença's crowning glory is the Calvari (Calvary), which stands at the top of an impressive flight of 365 steps. Those who make it to the top will find a little white 18th-century chapel with an old crucifix and a good view over the bays of Alcúdia, Pollença and even as far as Cap de Formentor. On Good Friday there is a service in the chapel followed by a torchlit procession down the steps.

Steps lead up through the village of Pollença to the Calvary

standing some 35m (115 feet) high, overlooking the sea. They consist of a vast number of caverns and are noted for the extraordinary, sometimes grotesque shapes of the stalactites and stalagmites.

Artà itself features some attractive mansions, churches and the Almudain, a medieval fortress containing a sanctuary. Near by, the Ermita de Betlem (Sanctuary of Betlem) stands high on a hill with a fine view of the bay of Alcúdia.

▶ *Take the C715 southwest for 29km (18 miles) to Manacor.*

9 Manacor, Mallorca
Manacor has a long tradition of furniture-making dating back to the 17th century, when it became a centre for wood craftsmen. Its main claim to fame, however, lies in the production of pearls, an important industry in Mallorca and internationally known. You can visit the factory and see how the pearls are produced in a simulated process that resembles the natural one.

A Roman theatre about 1.5km (1 mile) south is situated in some fields. The theatre was carved from rock, and items uncovered here are to be seen in the museum in the Castell de Bellver, Palma.

▶ *Take the C712 southeast to Artà. Continue southeast on a minor road to the Coves d'Artà (Caves of Artà), 45km (28 miles).*

8 Coves d'Artà, Mallorca
On the beach of Canyamel are the caves of Artà. The largest known caves on the island, they are said to have provided the inspiration for Jules Verne's famous story *Journey to the Centre of the Earth.* They are reached by a huge opening in the cliff,

Recent development at Porto Cristo has changed the little port but not spoilt its character

BACK TO NATURE

Birdwatchers should stop at S'Albufera, a partly dried-up lagoon in swamp lands southwest of Alcúdia, where you can see many species of birds. Look for black-winged stilts, stone curlews and little egrets. In the south of the island Sa Marina de Llucmayor is an area of strange rock formations that are of geological interest, with extensive views from the top. The rocks and lagoons are also a natural habitat for sea birds and marine plants.

FOR HISTORY BUFFS

Petra (northwest of Manacor) is the birthplace of the Franciscan, Fray Junípero de la Serra (1713–84), famous for his mission work in California and Mexico. San Francisco, San Diego and Santa Barbara are three of his former missions that grew into large towns. Junípero's home is now the museum of the Casa Museu Fray Junípero de la Serra, and his statue stands in the town.

Other places of interest include the church of the Virgin of the Sorrows, noted for its large domed ceiling and unusual Christ figure, and the Museo Arqueológico, which is housed in the Torre dels Enegistes.

▶ *Take the road east to Porto Cristo.*

🔟 Porto Cristo,
Mallorca
The attractive little port of Porto Cristo is one of the oldest anchorages on the island, confirmed by the discovery of a sunken Roman ship in the area. In the Middle Ages the port flourished for it was the main entry point for the island's imports. As with so many other seaside villages and towns in mainland Spain and in the Balearics, it has developed over recent years into a popular holiday destination, which has inevitably changed its old character. Nevertheless it still remains a picturesque little resort with considerable charm.

▶ Near by are the Coves del Drac.

Giant saguaro cacti flourish in Mallorca's warm climate

Post boxes in Mallorca are easy to spot – their bright yellow paint enlivens the street scene

🔟 Coves del Drac, Mallorca
The caves of Drac are the best known in Mallorca, and no tourist trip is complete without a visit here. They stretch for some 2km (1½ miles) and visitors travel through a wonderland, over bridges and past a series of underground pools. Lago Martel (Lake Martell) is the largest underground lake in Europe and its transparent waters reflect the weird and wonderful shapes of the rock formations. In summer, concerts are held aboard a small vessel which floats on the lake. If you want to see more caves, the Coves dels Hams (Caves of Hams) near by are also magnificent, noted for the pure white of the stalactites, and lovely underground lakes.

▶ Return to Manacor and take the **C714** south to Felanitx.

🔟 Felanitx, Mallorca
The old town of Felanitx dates back to the 13th century. Visit the Convent de Sant Augustín and the parish church, which has a fine Gothic façade. Felanitx is the birthplace of the

---

artist Miguel Barceló who still keeps a studio here.

South of Felanitx is the old convent of Castillo de Santueri, perched on a huge rock mass.

▶ Continue for 16km (10 miles) on the **C714** south to Santanyi (Santani).

🔟 Santanyi, Mallorca
A massive gateway, known as Porta Murada, still remains from the town fortifications. These were built as a defence against piracy, which was once a recurrent problem in this part of the island. The parish church has an excellent rococo organ, and there is a fine Romanesque–Gothic oratory in the Roser's chapel. Near by are the remains of some prehistoric sites and fortifications.

▶ Take the **C717** for 51km (32 miles) back to Palma.

ANDALUCIA

To many people the image of Spain is the reality of Andalucia: dazzling white villages perched on mountain tops silhouetted against brilliant blue skies. Forming a sharp contrast are the sun-soaked beaches and high-rise blocks lining its southern shores. Its past has included some 600 years of Roman domination and almost 800 years of Moorish occupation. This brought the region rich cultures and some unique monuments, of which the Alhambra in Granada, the Mosque of Córdoba and the Alcázar in Sevilla are the finest examples.

The region is renowned for its song and dance, from the gypsy lament of the flamenco to the twirling rhythms of the Andalucian dances known as *sevillanas*. It is also famed for its festivals. Sevilla's Holy Week Processions and Spring Fair are outstanding.

Andalucia is a vast region made up of the provinces of Huelva, Cádiz, Sevilla, Córdoba, Jaén, Almería, Granada and Málaga, with Sevilla as its capital. Its long coastline, which stretches from Portugal in the west to Almería in the east, is washed by both the Atlantic Ocean and the Mediterranean. These coasts are divided into sections knows as the Costa de Heulva, Costa de la Luz (Light), Costa del Sol (Sunshine), Costa Tropical and Costa de Almería.

In the north is the Sierra Morena, while the land further south is dominated by the Andalucian Mountains, incorporating the beautiful snowcapped peaks of the Sierra Nevada including Spain's highest peak, the Mulhacén, 3,482m (11,424 feet).

Around the basin of the River Guadalquivir olive groves and cereals create patterns of green and gold, and forests of cork-oaks flourish. Further south are sugar-cane and banana plantations and cotton fields, while important wine-growing regions lie around Jerez de la Frontera, Málaga and south of Córdoba. In the southwest is a great expanse of salt marshes and fenland, called the 'Marismas', which contains one of Spain's most important nature parks.

Take some carriage exercise from the Plaza de Espana, Sevilla; a pleasant way to sightsee

Tour 7

This tour of eastern Andalucia takes you off the beaten track through a sparsely populated area of rugged mountains, deep valleys and vast plains, a veritable journey into the unknown. Further north is one of Spain's best-known nature parks in a magnificent setting of high mountain peaks, fresh green forests and rivers. Dotted about the landscape are historically interesting little towns. Old cave dwellings also add interest to the journey through this unusual part of Spain.

Tour 8

On this tour you travel through some of the most impressive scenery to be found in southern Andalucia, combining beautiful mountain roads, woods and valleys, with a drive along one of the most attractive parts of the coast. The highlight of the trip is a visit to one of Spain's most important Moorish legacies. Added to this is the splendid setting with the snowcapped mountains of the Sierra Nevada in the background.

Tour 9

The sun-soaked coastline of Spain's southern coast with its familiar skyline of modern high-rise blocks contrasts sharply with the magnificent mountain landscapes and charming Andalusian villages of the hinterland. Two special features on this tour are the view of the coast's famous landmark, the rock of Gibraltar, and one of Spain's best-known bridges.

Tour 10

This drive through the basin of the River Guadalquivir goes through cornfields and groves of old twisted olive trees, and past small farmhouses. There are wine-growing areas among the gentle hills, and views of distant mountains. The villages are Moorish in appearance – square white houses, red-tiled roofs and little old streets. The highpoint is Spain's Moorish Mosque, magnificent in its entirety.

A 'cortijo' or farm deep in the countryside near Cazorla

Tour 11

The first part of the tour leads through the forested mountains of the Sierra Morena, and then down, passing through olive groves and fig plantations. These, in turn, lead to the shores of the Atlantic. In the southwest corner, close to the Portuguese border, is the area referred to as the 'cradle of new civilisations'. It was from here that many expeditions by Spanish explorers set sail across the Atlantic in the 15th and 16th centuries to the lands of golden promise.

Tour 12

Andalucia's 'white towns' are famous and several of these have been included on this route. You will find that the names of many of these towns are followed by 'de la Frontera', an appellation dating from the 200 years of fighting between the Moors and Christians, when these towns determined changing frontiers, until Granada, last stronghold of the Moors, fell to the Christians. The tour also explores the coastline of sandy beaches and pine-woods, and several of Andalucia's ports and holiday resorts. A trip into Andalucia's foremost wine-growing region culminates in a visit to its renowned sherry-producing area.

Lunar Landscapes of the South

Almería was a flourishing Roman port; to the Moors it was Al-Mariyya – 'mirror of the sea'. The Alcazába (fortress) overlooks the city, and the cathedral, rebuilt in the 16th century on the site of a former mosque, also resembles a fortress, to counter raids by Barbary pirates.

2/3 DAYS • 645KM • 402 MILES

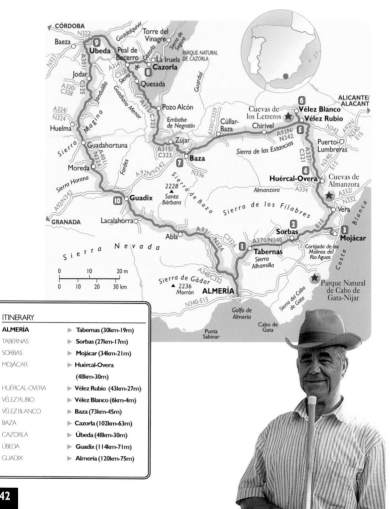

i *Parque Nicolás Salmerón, Esq Martínez Campos*

SCENIC ROUTES

Areas of outstanding scenery include the stretch north of Almería through the 'Wild West' mountains around Tabernas to Sorbas (A370/N340); the area around Mojácar; Mojácar north up to Vélez Rubio (N340, C321 and A327); the approach to the Sierra de Cazorla; from Jódar (south of Úbeda) down to Moreda and beyond (C325 and N401/N324); and Guadix southeast on the A921/N324 nearly all the way to Almería.

▶ *Take the* **A92** *north and join the* **A370** *northeast for 30km (19 miles) to Tabernas.*

❶ Tabernas, Almería

The little town of Tabernas has a definite Moorish look, but has Roman origins. Tucked away at the foot of a hill, it lies on a vast plain between the Sierra de los Filabres and the Sierra de Alhamilla. There are remains of an old Moorish castle, and the church has a fine Mudéjar coffered ceiling. The area's wild, barren landscapes were the setting for many 'spaghetti Westerns' during the 1960s and '70s, and parts of *Lawrence of Arabia* were shot in an area to the northeast.

▶ *Continue northeast on the* **A370/N340** *for 27km (17 miles) to Sorbas.*

❷ Sorbas, Almería

Sorbas rates as one of the most picturesque towns in the region. A cluster of white houses is perched on top of a high cliff that descends sharply down to the River Aguas and other small streams. The remains of an old Moorish castle form part of the skyline. Sorbas is noted for pottery and some of its workshops can be visited. There are also cave dwellings in the area.

▶ *Continue north on the* **A370/N340**. *Branch off right to Mojácar.*

Fortifications of the 16th-century Moorish Alcazába which still dominates Almería

❸ Mojácar, Almería

A few kilometres from the sea is the stunning little Moorish town of Mojácar. Its flat white buildings sprawl up a steep hill, and it holds a commanding position over the coast and surrounding plains. Its former name of Meschech-Masstia is

---

BACK TO NATURE

A road southeast of Sorbas leads to the Cortijada de los Molinos del Río Aguas, a good point from which to explore the River Aguas, where you may find tortoises and a wonderful range of colourful flowers typical of this area. Near by are some caves in crystallised gypsum with an inner lagoon. Further along is the Parque Natural de Cabo de Gata-Nijar, situated in the volcanic mountain range of the Sierra del Cabo de Gata.

one of the oldest known names in Spain. Of Carthaginian origin, the town was of some importance during Roman times, and strong influences remain from the Moorish occupation. Steep, winding streets lead to the top of the village, with fine views of the sea and countryside.

> *i* Plaza Nueva, s/n

> ▶ *Return to the N340 and continue north to Huércal-Overa, making a short detour to see the Cuevas de Almanzora cave dwellings just north of Vera.*

4 **Huércal-Overa,** Almería
Huércal-Overa is an important agricultural centre. Formerly inhabited by the Moors, the town became deserted when they were driven out of Spain. It was gradually repopulated during the 16th century. The most notable buildings in the town are the Iglesia de Nuestra Señora de la Asunción (Church of Our Lady of the Assumption) with a fine altar, the Ayuntamiento and the Plaza de Toros (bullring), which dates back to the beginning of this century. Embroidery features among the traditional crafts practised here.

> ▶ *Take the A327/C321 north and join the N342 west to Vélez Rubio.*

5 **Vélez Rubio,** Almería
Right in the middle of a wild, barren landscape lies Vélez Rubio, capital of the area since the beginning of the 18th century. The Convento de San Francisco, the parish church and the Iglesia de Nuestra Señora del Carmen (Church of Our Lady of Carmen) are all fine examples of baroque architecture. The old hospital and the Ayuntamiento are also notable buildings, and there are many

The flat-topped, white houses of the Moorish village of Mojácar can be seen for many miles

elegant private mansions from earlier centuries.

> ▶ *Take the A317 north for 6km (4 miles) to Vélez Blanco.*

6 **Vélez Blanco,** Almería
Built on the slopes of a mountain, Vélez Blanco has a rich heritage, with Roman origins. Buildings of special interest include the Iglesia de Santiago (Church of St James), with a fine Mudejar ceiling, and the Convento de San Luís, both showing Mudejar and Renaissance styles. Its chief splendour, however, is the magnificent Renaissance castle on top of the hill overlooking the town and offering panoramic views of the surrounding landscape. The flamboyantly decorated 16th-century courtyard, however, is now in the Metropolitan Museum in New York.

On the outskirts of town is the Cueva de los Letreros, with neolithic cave paintings.

> ▶ *Rejoin the A92N/N342 and continue on this road west to Baza.*

7 **Baza,** Almería
The old Iberian settlement of Baza lies in the valley of Baza, in the heart of a fertile plain surrounded by rather barren mountains. The discovery of an Iberian stone figure, the Dama de Baza (Lady of Baza), excavated here in 1971, was a find of

---

SPECIAL TO...

An unusual celebration takes place between Guadix and Baza on 6 September in honour of Nuestra Señora de la Piedad, patron saint of Baza. A character from Guadix (known as 'El Cascamorras') has to travel to Baza to take possession of the statue of the Virgin, enduring insults and all sorts of abuses from the people of Baza during the course of the journey.

---

some importance. Buildings of note include the 16th-century Iglesia Colegiata, built in the Renaissance style; the Iglesia de Santiago, also from the 16th century, with elegant Mudejar coffered ceilings; and the Iglesia de San Juan y Los Dolores (Church of St John and the Sorrows). The Iglesia de Santo Domingo has fine cloisters. In the Iglesia de la Merced is the image of Nuestra Señora de la

The Santa María fountain in Baeza

Piedad, the town's patron saint. The Moorish Baths in the town centre have been preserved as a National Monument.

> ▶ *Continue on the N342 for a short distance before turning right on to the A315/C323 north. At Peal de Becerro take the regional road east to Cazorla.*

8 **Cazorla,** Jaén
Capital of the area, Cazorla is dominated by the mighty mountain ranges of the Sierra de Cazorla and Sierra de Segura. Its two attractive main squares are surrounded by fine mansions. The ruins of the Iglesia de Santa María show the Plateresque style, and the two castles, Castillo de las Cinco Esquinas (Five Corners) and La Yedra, are both medieval. The

designated a nature park and provides excellent walks for serious hikers and a wonderful area for nature-lovers. There are good views of the area from here over the Valley of the Guadalquivir.

i Juan Domingo, 2

▶ *Return to Peal de Becerro and rejoin the A315 north-west. Take the N322 west to Úbeda.*

🅾 **Úbeda,** Jaén

Úbeda has some great palatial buildings and many fine churches. The Sacra Capilla del Salvador (Sacred Chapel of St Salvador) was built in an elaborate Renaissance style in the 16th century, and has a superb sculpture of the *Transfiguration* by Alonso Berruguete. The Iglesia de Santa María was begun in the

13th century and not completed until several centuries later. Of note inside are its lovely cloister and splendid grilles. The 13th-century Iglesia de San Pablo (Church of St Paul) boasts a fine portal.

From Úbeda the view is stunning, out over the ranks of olive groves to the distant hills

town is particularly lovely in spring, when the purple blossoms of the many Judas trees are out.

Just north of Cazorla is the tiny village of La Iruela, perched on a high cliff, with a castle at the top. Just beyond this is the gateway to the Sierra de Cazorla and the Sierra de Segura. The area has been

A few of the cave dwellings carved out of the soft tufa rock near Guadix are still inhabited

The heart of the old town is the Plaza Vázquez de Molina, an attractive square surrounded by elegant buildings. The Ayuntamiento is in the Palacio de las Cadenas (House of Chains), named after the iron chains that were once placed around the courtyard. It is a graceful building, flanked by arcades and with an unusual 16th-century fountain built into the wall.

Other buildings worth a mention are the Montiel Palace, Bishop Canastero's Mansion (note the coat-of-arms on the outside) and the Palacio de los Marqueses de Mancera, formerly the property of the Viceroy of Peru. In the centre of the old Plaza del Mercado is a monument to San Juan de la Cruz (St John of the Cross), famous poet and mystic. He died here in the Oratory, near the Plaza, in 1591.

i *Plaza Baja del Marqués 4*

FOR CHILDREN

Children are sure to be thrilled by a visit to Mini Hollywood, one of three theme towns where some of the old Westerns were filmed. Typical cowboy-style entertainment includes mock gunfights, jail breaks and hangings. (Located off Carretera Nacional, some 10km/6 miles west of Tabernas.)

▶ *Take the **301** south, joining the **340** before turning east onto the **A92** and south to Guadix.*

🔟 Guadix, Jaén

The Renaissance cathedral is the most prominent building of the town and features a massive tower and a baroque portal. The churches of Santiago (St James) and Santa Ana (St Anne) have fine Mudéjar coffered ceilings. In the upper part of the town is the Alcazába (Moorish palace), and other buildings of note are the Palacio Episcopal and the Palacio Peñaflor. The main square, Plaza Mayor, is a fine example of Renaissance architecture and offers an attractive view over the rooftops.

Cave dwellings, hollowed out of the soft tufa rock, are one of Guadix's most interesting features. They are in the Barrio Santiago, beyond the Iglesia de Santiago, and some are quite spacious, with two storeys; many are comfortably fitted out with running water, electricity and television. The conical chimneys protrude from the pathways above, creating a strange spectacle.

i *Avenida Mariana Pineda*

▶ *Return to Almería on the A92/N324, 120km (75 miles).*

Spain's
Moorish Legacy

Málaga is the 'capital' of the Costa del Sol, the main gateway to its famous resorts. Founded by the Phoenicians, it was held by the Moors from 711 until 1487, and the Alcazába (Moorish palace), stands as a legacy of the past. A new attraction is the Picasso Museum, which will house a collection of works by the artist, a native of Málaga.

2/3 DAYS • 347KM • 217 MILES

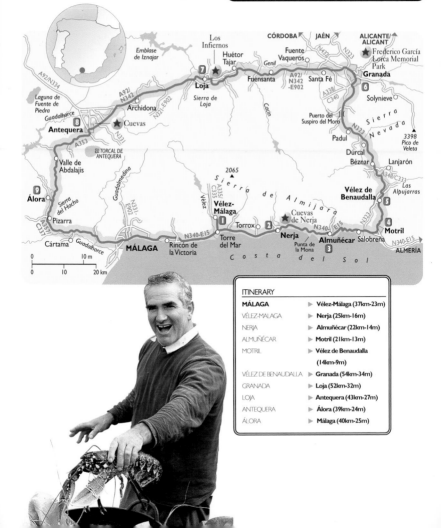

Above: the Balcon de Europa at Nerja. *Left:* looking down from the Balcon, over the beach and the town to the mountains beyond

ℹ️ *Pasaje de Chinitas, 4*

▶ *From Málaga take the N340 east. At Torre del Mar turn north on to the C335 to Vélez-Málaga.*

1 Vélez-Málaga, Málaga
Lying towards the end of a valley among subtropical vegetation is the little white town of Vélez-Málaga. On top of the hill stands the old Moorish Alcázar, or castle. Take a look at the Iglesia de Santa María la Mayor (St Mary Major), the Iglesia de San Juan (St John) and the Ayuntamiento. Thursday is market day, always a colourful event.

▶ *Return south and continue on the N340 to Nerja.*

FOR CHILDREN

Located in the residential area of El Tomillar, between Torre del Mar and Vélez-Málaga, is Aquavelis, a splendid aquapark for children, which offers 11 sorts of aquatic delights, including a large swimming-pool, waterchutes and fast kamikaze slides. There is also a spiral slide and a children's playground.

2 Nerja, Málaga
Its clifftop setting is one of Nerja's main attractions, with lovely views of the rocky coves below. Near the main square is a terrace with the famous Balcón de Europa (Balcony of Europe)

lookout point over the Mediterranean, so named by King Alfonso XII when he came here in 1885.

About 2km (1½ miles) away, near the village of Maro, are the impressive Cuevas de Nerja. They were discovered in 1959 and contain paintings from palaeolithic times.

ℹ️ *Puerta del Mar*

▶ *Continue on the N340 for 22km (14 miles) to Almuñécar.*

3 Almuñécar, Granada
This attractive little town is a cluster of whitewashed houses sprawling up a steep hill, crowned by the remains of an old Moorish castle. The ancient aqueduct and the Torre del Monje (Tower of the Monk) are Roman. Also of interest is the Cueva de los Siete Palacios (Cave of Seven Palaces, or

Vaults). The beaches of La Herradura and Punta del Mar have contributed to the growth in tourism. The nearby Punta de la Mona is a wonderful lookout point for views over the Mediterranean.

ℹ️ *Avenida Europa Palacete la Najarra*

▶ *Continue east to Motril.*

4 Motril, Granada

Make a brief stop here before continuing on the next lap of your journey. Among the town's most important buildings are the Iglesia Colegiata de la Encarnación (Collegiate Church of the Incarnation) and the Santuario de Nuestra Señora de la Cabeza, said to have been the home of the mother of Boabdil, the last of the Moorish kings of Granada.

▶ *Take the regional road north to Vélez de Benaudalla.*

5 Vélez de Benaudalla, Granada

Vélez de Benaudalla is a typical Andalucian village of white houses and red-tiled roofs clustering below a large hexagonal tower and with beautiful mountains around it. A good place for a break before you continue the next stage which is quite a drive.

Granada, the Alhambra. *Left:* intricate decoration in the Mexuar Court. *Inset: an* overall view

▶ *Continue north on the regional road for a short distance, then turn right on to the N323 north for 54km (34 miles) to Granada.*

6 **Granada,** Granada

The city of Granada is built on three hills: the Alhambra, the Albaicín and the Sacromonte, dominated by the beautiful snowcapped mountains of the Sierra Nevada. It is thought to have been founded by the Iberians. The Romans and the Visigoths were here later, and in 711 it was conquered by the Moors. The town was called Gharnatha and a fortress was erected on the Alhambra Hill. During the Reconquest it became the last stronghold of

the Moors until 2 January, 1492, when the Moorish Caliph, Emir Abdallah Mohammad XI, known to the Spaniards as Boabdil, the Boy King, was deposed and Moorish domination of Spain came to an end.

You can either walk up the hill to the Alhambra or take the longer route by car. The entrance is through the Puerta de las Granadas (Gateway of the Pomegranates), built by the Habsburg Emperor Charles V. A short walk up a pathway lined by elm trees (planted by the Duke of Wellington) leads to the Puerta de la Justicia (Gate of Justice). On the west side of the square stands the oldest

The Italian-style gardens, refreshed with fountains, at the Generalife Palace, once the summer residence of the Moorish kings.

structure of all, the Alcazába. Dating back to the 9th century, only its outer walls remain.

To the east is the Palacio de Carlos V (Palace of Emperor Charles V). Begun in 1526 and never completed, it was built in classical Renaissance style, in sharp contrast to the style of architecture which characterises the Alhambra. Many beautiful treasures can be seen in the two museums here, the Museo Provincial de Bellas Artes (Museum of Fine Arts) and the Museo Hispano-Musulmán (Museum of the Alhambra), noted for its priceless Alhambra Vase, which dates back to 1320.

To the north is the masterpiece itself, the Alcázar, or Casa Real (Royal Palace). Started in 1334 and completed in 1391, it is a remarkable architectural achievement, characterised by rich and elaborate decorations. Entrance is through the Patio del Mexuar (Mexuar Court), formerly the council chamber and later used as a chapel, which leads to the lovely Patio de los Arrayanes (Court of the Myrtle Trees). Adjoining this is the Sala de los Embajadores (Hall of the Ambassadors). Originally used as a throne room for the Moorish kings, it is noted for its rich decorations and magnificent domed ceiling.

The Mozárabes Gallery leads to the splendid Patio de los Leones (Court of Lions), a main feature of the palace and the old heart of the harem. Chambers leading from here include the Sala de los Abencerrajes (Abencerrajes Gallery) to the south, with an impressive stalactite ceiling and a marble fountain; and the Sala de los Reyes (King's Chamber) to the east, noted for its alcove paintings of historical scenes. The Sala de

The white houses of Andalucia set off the flowers the Spanish love to tend; here, in Antequera

las dos Hermanas (Hall of the Two Sisters), on the north side, features an intricately decorated honeycomb dome. This leads, in turn, to the Sala de los Ajimeces (Ajimeces Gallery) and on to the Mirador de Daraxa, a charming little look-out balcony. The Patio de Daraxa (Daraxa Courtyard) is a lovely inner courtyard with cypresses and orange trees.

More galleries and patios may be visited before you make your way to the Generalife, on the Cerro del Sol (Hill of the Sun). The Palacio del Generalife was completed in 1319 and served as the summer residence of the Moorish kings. The Patio de la Acequia (Canal Court) is planted with roses, laurels and orange trees and the surrounding gardens are laid out in Italian style.

Allow time to explore the town itself. The heart of the city is the large square Plaza de Isabel la Católica, where a monument stands to commem-orate the Santa Fé Agreement of 1492 made between Isabel la Católica and Columbus. The 19th-century Ayuntamiento stands in the smaller Plaza del Carmen. Near by is the 18th-century Palacio Arzobispal (Archbishop's Palace). A little further on is the Catedral de Santa María de la Encarnación (St Mary of the Incarnation). Begun in 1523 and consecrated in 1561, it stands as a memorial to the victory of Christianity in Spain. It has a richly decorated interior and a fine Capilla Mayor (Main Chapel), which is noted for its high dome and beautiful stained-glass window. Other buildings of interest include the Carthusian Monastery, the Audiencia (Law Court), the 16th-century Iglesia de Santa Ana and the Casa de Castríl, which houses the Museo Arqueológico (Archaeological Museum). On the right bank of the Darro

ravine is the Albaicín, the old Moorish quarter, where a wander around its narrow, cobblestoned streets and hidden corners recaptures the past. Behind the Albaicín is the Sacromonte Hill, where the gypsies live in caves and put on flamenco shows.

Beware when the bullfight is on. All streets become one-way, leading right to the bull-ring, where you might find yourself inadvertently spending the rest of the day!

[i] *Plaza Mariana Pineda, 10*

▶ *Take the A92/N342 west to Loja.*

7 Loja, Granada
Located in the west of the province of Granada, Loja is dominated by the ruins of an old Moorish castle. Buildings of interest in the town include the 15th-century Iglesia de la Encarnación, the 16th-century Iglesia de San Gabriel and the Convento de Santa Clara

(Convent and Church of Santa Clara), which has a fine Mudejar ceiling. Take a look also at the Ayuntamiento, the Granary, the Hospital de la Misericordia and the old Alcazába (fortress) that over-looks the town.

In the vicinity are two lovely waterfalls, the Colas de Caballo (Horsetail Falls), and Los Infiernos (Hell), which cascade into the River Genil.

SPECIAL TO...

The Renaissance Palacio de Carlos V (Palace of Emperor Charles V) provides a beautiful setting for the Festival of Music and Dance, which is held here annually at the end of June/ beginning of July and is recog-nised as an important inter-national event. The programme includes concerts, ballet, guitar recitals and other events, with performances by famous artists and orchestras.

▶ Take the **A92** west and branch off left to Antequeia, soon after passing Archidona.

8 **Antequera,** Málaga
The presence of prehistoric dolmen caves in the area indicates this market town's ancient origins. The old castle on top of the hill was the first fortress to be taken by the Christians (in 1410) during the reconquest of the Province of Granada, although it was later recaptured by the Moors. There is a fine view across the plains from its well-preserved ramparts. Close to the castle is the 16th-century Colegiata de Santa María la Mayor, noted for its Mudejar ceiling. The churches of San Sebastián and St Augustín feature Mudejar belfries and the churches of El Carmen and los Remedios have fine baroque interiors. If you visit the Museo Municipal, look for the bronze statue of a Roman boy called Efebo.
The dolmen caves

are to the left of the Granada road. These prehistoric caves served as burial places in neolithic times and have great historical significance.

ℹ️ *Plaza San Sebastian, 7*

▶ Take the **A353** south-west for 39km (24 miles) to Álora, which lies slightly off the road.

9 **Álora,** Málaga
Alora stands high above the River Guadalhorce in an area of olive and citrus groves. This charming town has a ruined castle, a 17th-century church with an unusual wooden roof and a few fine buildings.

▶ Continue on the **A353** and join the **357** back to Málaga.

The large and dramatic tower of the cathedral at Málaga

The Sun Coast
& Medieval Villages

Pleasant features of Málaga are its lively harbour and the seafront promenade, or Paseo Marítimo. In the old part of town is the Market Hall (Mercado Atarazanas) which teems with life and, dotted around the narrow twisting streets, are plenty of old *bodegas* (wine vaults); Málaga is known for its production of sweetish wines from the muscatel grape.

3 DAYS • 403KM • 250 MILES

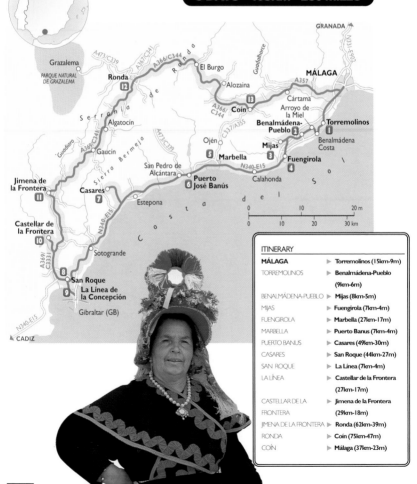

i Pasaje de Chinitas, 4

▶ Take the **N340** to Torremolinos. Turn left into town.

❶ Torremolinos, Málaga
This is the start of the most developed part of the Costa del Sol. One of the first resorts in the area to cater for mass tourism, it still retains a certain charm, with life centering around the pedestrianised Calle San Miguel. Steps leads down to the beaches and a seafront esplanade, which links the resort to the picturesque district of La Carihuela.

i Plaza de las Comunidades Autónomas s/n (Bajondillo Beach)

▶ Continue along the coast road to Benalmádena Costa. Turn right for 4km (2½ miles) to Benalmádena-Pueblo.

❷ Benalmádena-Pueblo, Málaga
Benalmádena Costa offers good beaches, a casino, golf club and the marina (Puerto Marina). A short drive inland leads to Benalmádena-Pueblo, a delightful Andalucian village dating back to the time of the Phoenicians, with relics of the Romans and Moors. At Arroyo de la Miel, near by, there are the ruins of a Roman arch, once the entrance to a building known as El Tribunal (Tribune).

i Avenida Antonio Machado, 12

▶ Continue on the regional road northwest for 8km (5 miles) to Mijas.

❸ Mijas, Málaga
The little town of Mijas is so picturesque that it was quickly 'discovered' by tourists, with all the inevitable changes that result. It is still appealing, however, with pretty whitewashed houses, tiny winding streets and flowers everywhere. There are wonderful views down to the coast. Renowned as

The view from Mijas

a crafts centre, it specialises in ceramics and basket weaving.

i Plaza de la Virgen

▶ Take the regional road south for 7km (4 miles) to Fuengirola.

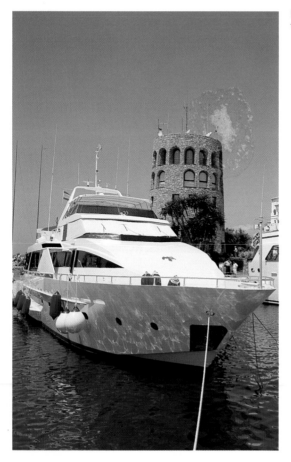

Boats of many nationalities crowd the marina at Puerto José Banús

flower-decked balconies. These open out on to the Plaza de los Naranjos (Square of Oranges), an enchanting square edged with orange trees and surrounded by restaurants and boutiques. A walk along the old fortifications overlooks the area, with the old Moorish castle way above.

The town of Ojén, 8km (5 miles) inland, is reached by a winding road. It has a pleasant 16th- to 18th-century church, a beautifully laid-out Andalucian cemetery, and is well known for its pottery.

i Plaza de la Fontanilla

▶ *Continue for a short distance along the coast road. Branch off to Puerto José Banús, 7km (4 miles).*

6 Puerto José Banús, Málaga
This short stretch between Marbella and Banús, known as the Golden Mile, is one of the most attractive parts of the Costa del Sol, with luxurious properties set in lovely gardens. The area is lush and green, with tropical flowers and vegetation, framed by the dramatic silhouette of the mountains in the background. Puerto José Banús was created as a marina for Marbella, and is an Andalucian-type village of white houses lining a yacht harbour. Bars, restaurants and boutiques sprang up and it became a very fashionable resort.

▶ *Continue along the **N340** coast road. Just past Estepona take a right turn to Casares, 20km (12 miles).*

7 Casares, Málaga
This part of the tour takes you inland to the Sierra Bermeja and, although it means returning to the coast by the same road, you will not regret it when you catch your first glimpse of Casares on the hill high above.

4 Fuengirola, Málaga
Fuengirola has also changed beyond recognition, from a sleepy fishing port to a resort of high-rise blocks. It has extensive beaches, bars, restaurants, lively evening entertainment, and attracts the crowds in the summer. It has also become a favoured winter retreat for retired people. Culture is minimal here, though there are the ruins of a 10th-century castle.

i Avenida Jesús Santos Rein 6

▶ *Continue on the **N340** for 27km (17 miles) to Marbella.*

5 Marbella, Málaga
Marbella is the centre of the Costa del Sol. The description

'playground of the rich' refers to the jetsetters and pop stars who stay in luxurious surroundings and frequent the smart restaurants and nightspots to be found along this part of the coast. The appearance of tall, modern blocks over the years has inevitably changed Marbella's skyline and character. However, it has some attractive areas, including its busy harbour and a seafront promenade with bars and restaurants.

On a clear day Africa is faintly visible, while at the western end of the scene is the unmistakable outline of the Rock of Gibraltar. Marbella's hidden delight, however, is the old town behind the main street, with its narrow streets, whitewashed houses and

The medieval village of Casares overlooked by a Moorish castle

This medieval village is one of the most attractive in the area. A gentle stroll up the steep, winding streets leads to the ruins of its Moorish castle. There are two 18th-century churches, the parish church and the Iglesia de San Sebastián, and a beautifully laid-out cemetery adorned with flowers.

▶ *Return to the **N340** and continue to San Roque.*

8 San Roque, Cádiz
San Roque was founded in the 18th century by the Spanish inhabitants of Gibraltar, who left after it was taken by the British in 1704. The town is situated on a low hill, with pleasant views. Places of interest include the Iglesia de Santa María and the Palacio de los Gobernadores.

▶ *Take the **A383** for 7km (4 miles) to La Línea de la Concepción.*

9 La Línea, Cádiz
La Línea de la Concepción stands at the foot of the Rock of Gibraltar and is the border town between Spain and the British colony of Gibraltar. Closed for many years, the frontier is now open for travel between the two countries. Whether or not you decide to visit, it is worth making the drive to get a close look at this gigantic piece of rock silhouetted against the sky, an impressive sight and the landmark of the whole coast.

▶ *Return to San Roque and take **N340** west for 3km (2 miles); turn right on the **A369/C331** to Castellar de la Frontera, 7km (4 miles) along an unclassified road.*

FOR HISTORY BUFFS

The Cuevas de la Pileta, some 27km (17 miles) southwest of Ronda, shelter paintings of animals in shades of red and black and drawings of huge fish, believed to date back some 25,000 years. The paintings resemble those in the Altamira Caves in northern Spain.

Bridge over the gorge of the River Guadalevín which divides Ronda

10 Castellar de la Frontera, Cádiz

Your route now takes you into the hinterland of southern Spain, where you can enjoy superb mountain scenery and visits to some of Andalucia's famous white towns.

Castellar de la Frontera is one of these lovely old walled cities, crowned by a large Moorish castle. Its white houses, red-tiled roofs and surrounding forests all add to its attractions. Ancient walls dating back to the 13th century enclose the old part of town, which has tiny streets and pretty squares.

▶ *Return to and continue north on the A369/C331 for 29km (18 miles) to Jimena de la Frontera.*

11 Jimena de la Frontera, Cádiz

This little town is also an attractive cluster of whitewashed houses built up a hillside. It was under Moorish occupation for a considerable time and has a well-preserved castle from that period, reached through a triple-arched gateway.

▶ *Take the A369/C341 northeast for 62km (39 miles) to Ronda.*

12 Ronda, Málaga

Ronda is well known for its spectacular setting, in particular the dramatic view of the bridge over the gorge of the River Guadalevín, which splits the town in two. It lies on the edge of the Serranía de Ronda, against a backdrop of sheer rock. Its unique situation, together with its attractive old quarter and historic interest, makes it a fascinating place to visit. It is one of the oldest towns in Spain and was for a long time capital of an independent Moorish kingdom, conquered by the Catholics in 1485. In the new part of town is one of the oldest bullrings in Spain.

There are magnificent views from here of the deep river valley and rugged splendours of the Serranía de Ronda. Across the famous Puente Nuevo bridge is La Ciudad, the old part. The bridge was built between 1775 and 1793 and is an outstanding architectural achievement. The old town is a maze of narrow, twisting streets and houses. Buildings of note include the Colegiata de Santa María la Mayor, built on the site of a former mosque, and the Palacio de Mondragón, which combines Mudéjar and Renaissance styles of architecture. Follow the nearby flight of steps down the hillside for a classic view of the bridge and the houses perched on the clifftop

ℹ️ *Plaza de España 1*

▶ *Take the A369/C344 to Coín.*

A typical Ronda house with doorway carvings and balcony

13 Coín, Málaga

Coín is a good place for a break on the last part of the return journey to Málaga. Set in the Valley of Orange Blossoms, this is a typical Andalucian market town of whitewashed houses and pretty squares, known for its colourful Saturday market.

▶ *Take the A366 eastwards and turn on to the A355 which leads to the A357 back to Málaga, a distance of 37km (23 miles).*

TOUR

10

The Great
Mosque &
Moorish Towns

The capital of Andalucia, Sevilla stands on the River Guadalquivir, with the 13th-century Torre del Oro, built to guard the river, as a landmark. The town was ruled by the Moors from 712 to 1248 and the Giralda, minaret of the Great Mosque, is Sevilla's most prominent feature. The Palace of the Alcázar was built by Pedro the Cruel (1350–69) on a 12th-century Moorish fortress.

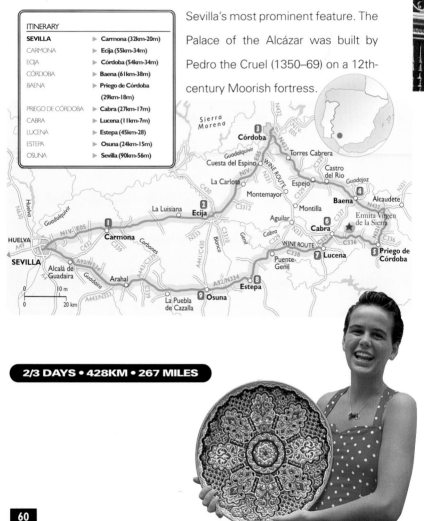

ITINERARY	
SEVILLA	▶ **Carmona (32km-20m)**
CARMONA	▶ **Ecija (55km-34m)**
ECIJA	▶ **Córdoba (54km-34m)**
CÓRDOBA	▶ **Baena (61km-38m)**
BAENA	▶ **Priego de Córdoba (29km-18m)**
PRIEGO DE CÓRDOBA	▶ **Cabra (27km-17m)**
CABRA	▶ **Lucena (11km-7m)**
LUCENA	▶ **Estepa (45km-28)**
ESTEPA	▶ **Osuna (24km-15m)**
OSUNA	▶ **Sevilla (90km-56m)**

2/3 DAYS • 428KM • 267 MILES

ℹ *Avenida de la Constitución, 21B, Sevilla*

▶ *From Sevilla take the **NIV/E5** east for 32km (20 miles) to Carmona.*

❶ Carmona, Sevilla

The town of Carmona stands on the highest point of a flat plain. It has a Moorish fortress, which holds a commanding position and offers good views of the countryside. This delightful little town has two old entrance gates, known as the Córdoba Gate and Sevilla Gate.

SCENIC ROUTES

The first part of the journey takes you through the fertile plains of the Guadalquivir valley, with patches of yellow and green fields relieved by olive groves and gently rolling hills, offering pleasant rather than remarkable scenery. There is a very scenic stretch between Priego de Córdoba and Cabra on the C336, and some attractive scenery round Lucena.

The Iglesia de Santa María de la Asunción is 15th-century late Gothic, and you can see the patio of the Great Mosque on whose foundations the church was erected. The Santuario (1525–51) has a notable retable while Roman mosaics decorate the Ayuntamiento.

West of the town is a Roman necropolis. This network of underground tombs was arranged in groups, with a crematorium at the front. Look out for the tomb known as El Elefante for its unusual carving of a young elephant.

▶ *Continue east on the **NIV** for 55km (35 miles) to Ecija.*

❷ Ecija, Sevilla

The ancient town of Ecija lies beside a small basin on the River Genil. Thought to date back to Greek times, it was known to the Romans as *Astigi*, and pottery, mosaics and other items found during excavations have given some insight into its early history. Its baroque belfries, decorated with colourful tiles, are an attractive feature of the town. The

Delicate stonework ornaments the Renaissance façade of Sevilla's splendid Ayuntamiento

Iglesia de Santiago, entered through an 18th-century patio, has Mudejar windows from a previous building, and an elaborate Gothic retable. There are several handsome 18th-century palaces in the town including the Palacio Benamej, the Palacio Peñaflor, decorated with paintings on the outside, and the Palacio Valdehermoso, which has a fine Renaissance exterior.

▶ *Continue on the **NIV** northeast for 54km (34 miles) to Córdoba.*

RECOMMENDED WALKS

A detour north of Ecija takes you to the village of Hornachuelos, which is on the edge of a large game-hunting area. This stretches away to the north of the region and offers some excellent walking.

8 Córdoba, Córdoba

Córdoba, a town of narrow streets and alleyways, is situated on a plain between the Sierra de Córdoba and the River Guadalquivir. Córdoba suffers from extremes of climate, with very hot summers and cold winters.

Already quite prominent when the Romans arrived, the town continued to flourish and

materials, designed to catch the light, forming a myriad of colours. The columns are topped by capitals and crowned with striking red-and-white-striped arches, typical of Moorish art. An important feature of a mosque is the mihrab, a sacred niche hollowed out from the wall. They are always built to face Mecca in the east, although

The red-and-white striped arches in the mosque at Córdoba

this one points more south than east, owing to a miscalculation. From 1436, when Córdoba was taken by the Christians, the mosque became the cathedral. The Patio de los Naranjos

(Court of Orange Trees) is particularly attractive in spring when it is filled with the scent of orange blossom. Through the Puerta del Perdón (Gate of Forgiveness) a flight of steps leads up to the baroque Campanario (bell tower). It provides a superb view of the rooftops of Córdoba and the sweep of the River Guadalquivir.

The Museo Arqueológico has interesting exhibits of sculptures and Roman antiquities, and the Museo de Bellas Artes has a fine collection of paintings. Those with an interest in bullfighting should visit the Museo Municipal Taurino (Museum of Bullfighting). A statue of the famous Spanish bullfighter, Manolete, stands in the Plaza San Marina de las Aguas.

The Zoco (from the old Arab souk) has displays of handicrafts and occasional flamenco performances.

in 152 BC became the capital of Hispana Ulterior.

It developed into a prosperous city under the Moors and was an important cultural and artistic centre. The town was conquered by the Catholic King Ferdinand in 1436, having long been used by Christian leaders as a centre for plotting the retaking of Granada from the Moors. It was in Córdoba that Christopher Columbus was granted the commission by Queen Isabella for his first exploratory expedition to the New World.

The great Mezquita (mosque) was constructed by the Moors between the 8th and 10th centuries. It is one of the largest mosques in the world and is a remarkable achievement of Moorish architecture. Its beauty lies in its interior. As you enter you are confronted by hundreds of columns made of onyx, marble and other

---

FOR CHILDREN

Córdoba's zoo, located on Avenida Linneo (in front of the Jardín Botánico), has a wide variety of animals, with an unusual black lion. Another treat for children could be a tour around town in an elegant horse-drawn carriage. Aquatic parks near Córdoba include the Guadalpark, located at Poligono Aeropuerto-Sevilla-Este (open May to September) and Aquasierra in Villafranca de Córdoba.

FOR HISTORY BUFFS

On the N432 between Córdoba and Baena is the small town of Castro del Río, where Spain's famous author, Miguel Cervantes, was imprisoned for a time in 1592. You can take a look at his old prison, which is housed in the Ayuntamiento. The town also features the ruins of an ancient castle and a Roman bridge.

▶ Take the **N432** southeast for 61km (38 miles) to Baena.

4 Baena, Córdoba

The route continues through some of Andalucia's delightful *pueblos blancos*, or white towns. While sharing many common characteristics, each has its own style. Baena is an oil-producing town and is typically Andalucian. A cluster of whitewashed houses climbs up a slope, dominated by the remains of old Moorish battlements. The Iglesia de Santa María la

Mayor dates back to the 16th century. The Convento de la Madre de Dios was built in the Mudejar style and has an interesting carved retable.

▶ *Continue southeast on the* ***N432***. *Close to the River Guadajoz turn south on the* ***A333/N321*** *to Priego de Córdoba.*

5 **Priego de Córdoba,** Córdoba

Priego de Córdoba is one of the region's little gems. Its dazzling white houses, flower-decked windows and tiny, winding streets give it a very Moorish look. Elegant 17th- and 18th-century mansions reflect prosperous times when Priego was the centre of the silk and textile industries. Several churches including La Asunción and La Aurora are masterpieces of fine baroque architecture. An abundance of springs here feed the splendid Fuente del Rey.

Alcalá Zamora, first president of the Second Republic of Spain (1931–6), was born here in 1877. His former home now contains the tourist information office and the museum Casa Natal de D Niceto Alcalá Zamora.

[i] *Calle Río s/n*

▶ *Take the* ***A340/C336*** *west, then right on to the* ***C327*** *for 2km (1 mile) to reach town.*

6 **Cabra,** Córdoba

The pleasant Parque del Fuente del Río (Park of the Source of the River) welcomes you to Cabra, a delightful town with white houses, red-tiled roofs and old narrow streets. The Iglesia de San Juan Bautista dates back to the time of the Visigoths.

▶ *Rejoin* ***A340/C327*** *southwest to Lucena, just off the road.*

7 **Lucena,** Córdoba

At the foot of the Sierra de Arcos is the attractive little town of Lucena renowned for its bronze, furniture-making and copperware. Fine churches are the 15th-century Renaissance Iglesia de San Matéo, the Iglesia de Santiago and the Convento de San Francisco. Lucena was the scene of the capture of the boy-king Boabdil, the last Moorish ruler, by the Count of Cabra in 1483, during an unsuccessful revolt against the Christians.

▶ *Just west of town take* ***A340/C338*** *to Estepa.*

The main square at Lucena and the Iglesia de San Mateo. Inset: detail of the doorway of Iglesia de Santiago

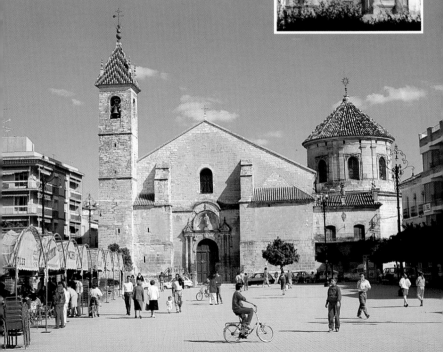

Carriage rides are a restful way of sightseeing in Sevilla, especially through the Parque de Maria Luisa

8 **Estepa,** Córdoba

Estepa, lying among farmlands, is known throughout Spain for its confectionery, especially its Christmas cakes known as *mantecados* and *polvorones*. As well as the churches of Santa María la Mayor, La Asunción and Los Remedios, the 18th-century Palacio de los Marqueses de Cerverales is

---

worth a look, along with the Gothic interior of the old castle keep and the splendid Torre de la Victoria (Tower of Victory), all that remains of a former convent. There are good views from a nearby lookout point called El Balcón de Andalucía.

▶ *Take **A92/N334** west to Osuna.*

9 **Osuna,** Córdoba

The history of Osuna dates back to the time of the Iberians. Like so many towns in southern Spain, Osuna was taken by the Romans and then ruled by the Moors until 1239, when it was captured by Ferdinand III. Of the many fine monuments note the Colegiata, a Renaissance church that houses valuable works of art. La Universidad (University) is another important building, with its minaret-like towers. The Casa de los Cepeda, Palacio del Cabildo Colegial and Palacio de la Antigua Audiencia have elegant façades. The Museo Arqueológico is in the old Torre de Agua (Water Tower).

▶ *Return to Sevilla on the **A92/N334**.*

BACK TO NATURE

The Lagunas de Córdoba, a series of salt-water lakes around Aguilar de la Frontera northwest of Cabra, are inhabited by many different species of waterfowl in the winter. An attractive and rare visitor is the white-headed duck, with its lovely blue bill. Some of the lakes shrink or dry up during summer, but fill again after the rains. Flamingos and shelduck inhabit the Laguna del Salobral, the largest of the lakes.

SPECIAL TO...

A turn to the right just before Cabra leads to El Picacho and the Ermita Virgen de la Sierra (Shrine of the Virgin of the Mountains), which contains the much-venerated image of the patron saint of Cabra.
The province of Córdoba has quite a reputation for wines and enthusiasts can follow the Ruta del Vino (Wine Route) which leaves Córdoba on the NIV and goes southwest to Montemayor and Montilla. You can visit many of the wine cellars, which offer a number of different sherry-type wines.

Exquisitely carved detail defines the little balcony of the church of La Merced at Osuna

Trail of the
New World
Explorers

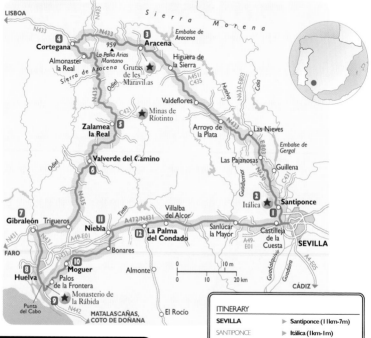

3 DAYS • 353KM • 218 MILES

Sevilla has three major museums: the Museo del Bellas Artes in the old Merced Monastery, with superb Spanish works; the Museo de Arte Contemporáneo, in the old chapel of the Cathedral Chapter; and the Museo Arqueológico in the Palacio del Renacimiento. Among the city's parks and gardens, those of the Alcázar are outstanding, with Moorish to Renaissance sections.

[i] *Avenida de la Constitución, 21B*

From Sevilla take the motorway west over the river. Turn right on to the ***N630*** *to Santiponce.*

1 Santiponce, Sevilla

The chief monument in Santiponce is the former Monasterio de San Isidro del Campo, which was founded in 1298 by Alfonso Guzmán as a Cistercian house. Guzmán, known as 'El Bueno' (The Good One) was renowned for the heroic role he played in defending Tarifa castle against the Moors. The church contains a remarkable 17th-century retable by the artist Martínez Montañés, noted for the figure of St Jerome. Montañés also carved the effigies on the tombs of Guzmán and his wife. A second church marks the first resting place of the body of Cortés, conqueror of Mexico, before it was taken to Mexico.

Take an unclassified road left to Itálica.

2 Itálica, Sevilla

The Roman ruins of Itálica are considered of major significance. Originally founded in 206 BC by Scipio Africanus as a place of retirement for his veteran soldiers, the city flourished and by the 2nd century AD had become one of the most important Roman cities in Spain. Two great Roman emperors – Trajan (AD 52–117) and Hadrian (AD 76–138) – were born here. The most important building is the Amphitheatre, which was one of the largest in the Roman Empire, with a capacity of up to 40,000 spectators. Faintly visible traces can still be seen of a forum, city streets, the foundations of villas and mosaic floors: evidence of the old city. Treasures found here are on display in Sevilla's Museum of Archaeology.

Keep on this unclassified road to rejoin the ***N630****. Turn left to go north on the* ***N630****, then after 25km (15 miles) turn left on to the* ***N433*** *northwest to Aracena.*

Imagine a spectacle in this Roman amphitheatre at Itálica with 40,000 spectactors cramming the terraces

3 Aracena, Huelva

The Convento de Santa Catalina (Convent of St Catalina) has a notable doorway. On top of the Cerro del Castillo (Castle Hill) are the remains of a castle, which was built in the 13th century by the Knights Templar. Of mixed Gothic and Mudejar styles, it features an old tower, originally a minaret

SCENIC ROUTES

This route becomes very scenic after you have joined the N435 from Cortegana through to Zalamea la Real and on to Valverde del Camino. There is also some appealing scenery around Moguer. The route from Huelva to Matalascañas, should you visit the Coto Doñana, offers a beautiful drive along miles of deserted beaches.

and decorated in similar style to the Giralda of Sevilla.

Near Aracena are the Grutas de las Maravillas (Grottos of Marvels). Over 1,000m (1,094 yards) in length, they are noted for the variety of shapes and colours in the stalactites and stalagmites which are reflected in underground pools and rivers.

▶ *Take N433 west to Cortegana, just south of this road.*

RECOMMENDED WALKS
....

Aracena is a good base for walks in the Sierra de Aracena, where you will find orange and lemon groves, great oak forests and tiny isolated villages. There is a superb view of the area from the top of La Peña Arias Montano.

4 Cortegana, Huelva
The small town of Cortegana was originally a Roman settlement known as *Corticata*. Its main assets are its beautiful setting, an interesting little parish church and an old castle.

▶ *Take the regional road southeast. Turn right on the N435 to Zalamea la Real.*

5 Zalamea la Real, Huelva
The town's most notable building is the Iglesia de la Asunción (Assumption), an elegant neoclassical monument from the 17th century. There are several interesting old hermitages.

The impressive Minas de Ríotinto (Rio Tinto Copper Mines) are about 6km (4½ miles) east of town. Already in use during Iberian and Roman times, the mines were abandoned when the Visigoths came, and only regenerated in the 19th century. For a long time they were a British concern, reverting to Spanish ownership in 1954. There are still English-style houses, and a small mining museum in Río Tinto village.

Kite-flying by Aracena's castle ruins
Left: the 13th-century church

▶ Continue on the same road south towards Valverde del Camino. Turn left where signposted into the town.

6 Valverde del Camino, Huelva

The town of Valverde del Camino is noted for its production of wood, metal and leather goods, including leather wine bottles. Buildings of note include the attractive Ermita de la Trinidad and the Iglesia de Nuestra Señora del Reposo (Church of Our Lady of Rest).

▶ Rejoin and take the N435 south. At Trigueros turn right on an unclassified road to Gibraleón.

7 Gibraleón, Huelva

Gibraleón is a town with ancient roots. Some of the people may be descendants of the slaves brought here by the Spaniards in the 15th century. Among the most interesting buildings in the town are the Iglesia de Santiago, the Iglesia de San Juan and the Chapel of El Carmen. The 16th-century Convento del Vado still preserves the remnants of its old walls.

▶ Take the N431 south. Continue straight on to Huelva when the N431 branches off east.

8 Huelva, Huelva

The region played an important role in the events leading to the Voyages of Discovery across the ocean. Christopher Columbus came to Huelva with his son in 1485 and stayed in the nearby Monasterio de la Rábida. The first expedition set sail from the area in 1492, to reach land two months later. At the end of the Paseo del Conquero is the modest white shrine of Nuestra Señora de la Cinta, with a Mudejar roof and a wall painting of the Virgin, patron saint of the city. A tile painting by the artist Zuloaga commemorates a visit made here by Columbus on his return from one of his voyages.

Huelva was severely damaged by an earthquake in 1755 and only a handful of buildings remain from the past. The 17th-century Iglesia de la Merced (now the cathedral) has an elegant doorway of mixed styles and houses an image of the Virgen de la Cinta. The 16th-century Iglesia de San

Pastel-washed houses with graceful balconies beside the Church of Our Lady of Rest at Valverde

Pedro features a tower with attractive tile decorations. The Iglesia de la Concepción, also dating from the 16th century, is noted for its paintings by the Spanish artist Zurbarán.

BACK TO NATURE

The Coto Doñana is one of Spain's largest and most important nature parks. This vast expanse of flat salt marshes (*marismas*), dunes and pine forests lies in the delta of the River Guadalquivir, covering an area of some 50,625 hectares (125,000 acres). Thousands of migratory birds come here, and large colonies of birds nest in the cork-oak trees. It is also the home of a variety of other animals, and has many rare species of flower and plant life. Matalascañas, located down the coast southeast of Huelva, is the usual starting point for visiting the reserve. It can only be visited as part of a guided tour or with special permission.

The Museo Provincial has a collection of antiquities from the region, including an impressive Roman water wheel, some beautiful amphorae (vessels) and a reconstructed Celtic house, in addition to a fine arts section featuring paintings by local artists.

i *Avenida de Alemania, 12*

▶ *Take the N442 and cross over the Río Tinto. Shortly after, take a left turn to the Monasterio de la Rábida.*

9 Monasterio de la Rábida, Huelva

This old Franciscan monastery lies in beautiful surroundings at the mouth of the Río Tinto. It is the place where Columbus received the necessary stimulus to persevere with his plans to sail across the ocean in search of the Indies. Columbus came to the monastery in 1485 with his son. He was well received by the monks, and Father Antonio Marchena, in particular, was instrumental in bring-

---

FOR CHILDREN

Anchored at the Carabelas Quay, Huelva, are replicas of the sailing ships *Santa Maria*, *Niña* and *Pinta* which carried Christopher Columbus and his men on their first expedition across the seas. Children are invited to clamber aboard and get a feel of the past.

---

ing influence to bear with Queen Isabella. After lengthy negotiations, the agreement was finally signed and Columbus was able to fulfil his dreams. The Lecture Cell is where Columbus held many meetings with the monks, the Chapter House displays relics of the explorer, and the Gallery has models of the three caravels that undertook the first voyage. The church

and courtyard date back to the early 15th century and are very attractive. Note the 14th-century statue of the Virgen de los Milagros, to whom Columbus offered his prayers before setting sail. In the beautifully laid-out garden is the Latin-American University, a centre for American studies, and a monument to the Discoverers of America.

▶ *Continue on the same road northeast to Moguer.*

10 Moguer, Huelva

Moguer is renowned as the birthplace and home of the great Spanish poet, Juan Ramón Jiménez (1881–1958), Nobel prize-winner for literature in 1956 and author of the delightful Spanish classic *Platero y Yo*, about a boy and his donkey. His former home is now a museum with relics from the poet.

The 14th-century Gothic-Mudejar Convento de Santa Clara contains the tombs of the convent's founders and has been declared a National Monument. The parish church is noted for its tall, impressive tower.

▶ *Take the A494 north and join the A472 northeast to Niebla.*

FOR HISTORY BUFFS

Palos de la Frontera, 13km (8 miles) southeast of Huelva, is the place from which Christopher Columbus set sail on 3 August, 1492 in the *Santa Maria* on his first voyage of discovery. Columbus sighted land on 12 October and set foot on Cuba and Haiti, where he left some of his men to establish a colony before returning to Palos on 15 March, 1493.
In May 1528, Hernán Cortés landed in the port after he had overthrown the mighty Aztec Empire and conquered Mexico.

The Monasterio de la Rábida, where Columbus prepared for his voyage west, now has a centre for American studies in the garden

11 Niebla, Huelva

The ancient town of Niebla (its name means mist) lies on the bank of the Río Tinto. It was the last town in the Guadalquivir valley to fall to

---

SPECIAL TO...

South of Almonte in the village church of El Rocío is the Shrine of El Rocío, scene of Spain's most famous *romeria* (pilgrimage to a church or shrine). This takes place at Whitsun. People from all over the region process to El Rocío on foot, horseback or in gaily decorated horse-drawn wagons, dressed in traditional costumes. Upon arrival in the village they celebrate with music, dancing and drinking until the climax of the festival, when the statue of the Virgin is brought from the church at dawn and paraded among the crowds by members of the Brotherhoods. Bells peal, fireworks explode and there is much celebration.

the Christians during the Reconquest of Spain, and is noted as being the first place in Spain where gunpowder was used in battle. Its main historical monuments are the Roman bridge over the river and four splendid Moorish entrance gates, known as the Puertas de Sevilla, Socorro, del Buey and del Agua. Of particular charm is the little chuch of Nuestra Señora de Granada (Our Lady of Granada). The Iglesia de San Martín and the 12th-century Castillo de Los Guzmanes also warrant a visit.

▶ Continue on the *A472/N431* to *La Palma del Condado.*

12 La Palma del Condado, Huelva

La Palma del Condado has long been the centre of a wine-producing area and is known for its pleasant white table wine. One of its main attractions is the 16th-century Iglesia de San Juan Bautista, a beautiful white monument with an attractively decorated steeple. The 15th-century Ermita del Valle (Hermitage of the Valley), is a fine example of the Mudejar style.

▶ Return to Sevilla east on the *A472/431.*

The White Towns of Andalucia

3 DAYS • 399 KM • 249 MILES   Sevilla's festivals are world-

famous. During Holy Week there are processions every day

and one at dawn on Good Friday. *Pasos* (platforms), carried by

Penitents, show scenes of the Passion of Christ. The Feria de

Sevilla takes place on six days in April, with horseback parades.

ℹ️ *Avenida de la Constitución, 21B*

▶ *From Sevilla take the **A376** southeast to Utrera.*

① Utrera, Sevilla

The old town of Utrera features an impressive Alcázar with a square tower, some fine Gothic churches and an attractive little main square. The Convento de Nuestra Señora de la Consolación on the edge of the town has a much venerated image of the Virgin, which is believed to work miracles. An annual pilgrimage to the convent takes place in September.

▶ *Take the **A364** southwest. Join the **NIV** and turn left on to the **A475**. Follow this southeastward, then south-west, down to Arcos de la Frontera.*

② Arcos de la Frontera, Cádiz

The first stop in the province of Cádiz is Arcos de la Frontera, one of the most attractive towns in the region. It is perched on top of a high rock, surrounded by steep ravines that descend to the River Guadalete.

The mass of white and stone-coloured houses is dominated by a castle and two churches. Tiny narrow streets and alleys wind their way up the steep slopes, offering splendid views. The Hospital de San Juan de Dios has a white baroque façade and a 16th-century crucifix in the temple. Other outstanding churches are those of Santa María, with a Plateresque west façade, and San Pedro, a massive Gothic structure which has a baroque bell tower, a landmark for miles around.

Arcos de la Frontera, high on a rock above the River Guadalete. Left: church clocks were timepieces for everyone in the town

▶ *Take the **A393** south to Medina Sidonia.*

③ Medina Sidonia, Cádiz

This is an historic little town whose origins can be traced back over 1,000 years. It was once the seat of the dukes of Medina Sidonia – the seventh duke was the Commander-in-Chief of the Armada. The

---

SCENIC ROUTES

Some of the most attractive scenery along this route is to be found around Arcos de la Frontera, which lies amid rugged mountains and green woods. The drive from Vejer de la Frontera through to Cádiz and on to El Puerto de Santa María is also very pleasant, with long stretches of white sandy beaches and pinewoods, indented at times by tall cliffs.

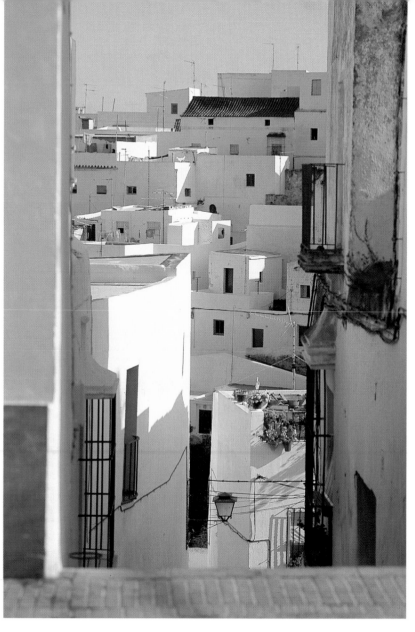

Iglesia de Santa María Coronada was built in the Gothic style at the time of Granada's recapture by the Christians. Some important religious paintings may be seen in the church. The Arch of 'La Pastora' (the Shepherdess) is set in the old Moorish walls in a horseshoe shape. Built in the 18th-century, the Ayuntamiento features an elegant, tiled staircase and the churches of San Agustín and Santiago are also worth a visit.

Some 7km (4½ miles) away are caves known as the Tajo de las Figuras.

▶ *Continue south on the A393 to Vejer de la Frontera.*

❹ Vejer de la Frontera, Cádiz

The medieval town of Vejer de la Frontera is situated on the banks of the River Barbate high above Cabo de Trafalgar (Cape Trafalgar). The place is Moorish

The Moorish look of the White Town of Vejer de la Frontera,

in appearance – in the dazzling white houses and tiny twisting streets, and also in its womenfolk, some of whom dress in black from head to toe, Arab-style, and are known as *Las Cobijadas* (the covered ones). The town features little hidden squares and flower-filled patios, with streets so precipitous that handrails have been added for safety. Its most important building is the 13th-century Iglesia de El Divino Salvador. Built soon after the town was taken from the Moors, it reflects Romanesque, Gothic and Mudejar styles and contains some fine 17th-century paintings.

From here, make a detour to Tarifa southeast on the N340. When you stand on the Punta Marroquí, also called Punta de Tarifa, you are on the southern-most tip of Europe, with the African continent only 14km (8 miles) away. This is where the Mediterranean and the Atlantic meet. Tarifa has a Moorish look and some Roman remains.

▶ Take the **N340** northwest for 29km (18 miles) to Chiclana de la Frontera.

5 Chiclana de la Frontera, Cádiz

Chiclana has neat white houses rising up the hillside and a Mosque-like parish church. A few kilometres away to the west is the splendid sandy beach of La Barrosa, a popular summer resort bordered by pinewoods.

▶ Continue on **N340** northwest, then join the **NIV** for 23km (14 miles) to Cádiz.

6 Cádiz, Cádiz

The old port of Cádiz is noted for its lovely setting. It is built on a rock platform jutting out into the Atlantic Ocean and is connected to the mainland by a bridge. The town's massive ramparts protect it against the force of the waves. It has tall white houses, many of which have *miradors* (lookout towers) and *azoteas* (roof terraces).

Cádiz is thought to be one of the oldest towns on the Iberian peninsula. It was founded by the Phoenicians in 1100 BC under the name of Gadir and was a trading port. It

Cadiz jutts out into the Atlantic and men still fish from the sea front

was later under the control of the Carthaginians, then the Romans.

Cádiz was used as a base for Spanish treasure fleets. In 1587 ships of the Spanish Armada, gathered in Cádiz harbour before setting sail for England. In 1805 the French fleet left from Cádiz before the Battle of Trafalgar. And, here, in 1812, the Spanish Parliament met to establish the first liberal constitution.

One of the town's most pleasing aspects is its lovely parks, among which those of Genovés, Alameda Marqués de Comillas and Alameda de Apodaca are the most attractive. The cathedral features a golden dome and a baroque façade. It was built in the 18th and 19th centuries and hoards of gold and silver treasures and gems may be seen in the museum. Its most precious piece is a processional cross by Enrique de Arfe, which is brought out for the Corpus Christi processions. In the crypt is the tomb of the Spanish composer, Manuel de Falla (1876–1946), who was born in Cádiz and drew inspiration from Andalusian folklore.

The Museo de Cádiz features some great canvases by Zurbarán and works by Murillo. An interesting item in the Museo Históric Municipal is a 19th-century mural of the drawing up of the 1812 constitution.

Its masterpiece, however, is an intricate model of the town as it was in the 18th century, beautifully worked in ivory and mahogany and showing all the streets and houses in minute detail. Spain's first constitution was declared in 1812 in the Oratorio de San Felipe de Neri. Over the altar hangs a painting of the Immaculate Conception by the great Sevillian artist, Murillo.

The old town is a labyrinth of narrow streets opening out on to pleasant squares. Its central point is the attractive Plaza de Miña, shaded by palms and lined by elegant buildings.

[i] *Avenida Ramón de Carranza s/n*

▶ *Take the N443 to join the NIV north to El Puerto de Santa María, 13km (8 miles).*

7 El Puerto de Santa María, Cádiz

The small fishing port of El Puerto de Santa María is noted for its sherry and brandy *bodegas* (cellars) and a tour of one is recommended. The town lies at the mouth of the Guadalete River and features a busy port, lively streets and miles of sandy beaches. The Moorish Castillo de San Marcos (St Mark's Castle) is a watch-tower over the river, where you can enjoy a lovely view of the coast.

[i] *Luna, 22*

▶ *Take the A491 for 27km (17 miles) northwest to Rota.*

8 Rota, Cádiz

The Spanish-American naval base is the major feature of Rota and has brought a cosmopolitan atmosphere to the town, with lively bars, shops and evening entertainment. The town has several pleasant beaches, some old walls and the Luna Castle by the fishermen's quarters. Rota is also an agricultural centre, noted for its tomatoes and watermelons.

▶ *Continue north on a minor road, then join the A491 to Chipiona.*

9 Chipiona, Cádiz

The lighthouse of Chipiona, visible from a great distance, is a famous landmark for navigators. This is a popular holiday resort with beaches of fine white sand and good fishing in some areas. The little town has white-washed houses, quaint streets and a profusion of flowers. The Iglesia de Santa María de la Regla contains a shrine to the Virgin, venerated by seamen.

▶ *Take the A480/C441 east for 9km (6 miles) to Sanlúcar de Barrameda.*

10 Sanlúcar de Barrameda, Cádiz

Lying at the mouth of the River Guadalquivir, the little port of Sanlúcar de Barrameda was the departure point for Columbus's third voyage to the New World in 1498, and the Portuguese Magellan also sailed from here in 1519 on his first voyage around the world.

There is a lively fish auction in the afternoons and this is the home of Manzanilla wine, a fine accompaniment to seafood.

▶ *Take the A480/440 southeast to Jerez de la Frontera.*

A palm tree avenue leads up to the cathedral in Jerez de la Frontera

11 Jerez de la Frontera,
Cádiz

Set among vineyards, the town of Jerez is the home of sherry, to which it has given its name. The *bodegas*, some of which are very grand, are the great attraction and tours can be made.

The town has a somewhat aristocratic air, with broad avenues and large squares. The Colegiata, built in the 17th and 18th centuries in Gothic style, contains paintings by Zurbarán. The Alcázar is an impressive 11th-century building with a Gothic church and Arab baths.

_i_ _Calle Larga, 39_

▶ _Return to Sevilla on the **A4/E5**._

ARAGON, NAVARRA & LA RIOJA

Aragon, Navarra and La Rioja lie to the north and south of the basin of the River Ebro, which runs from the Cantabrian Mountains in the northwest through the Catalonian Mountains and down to the Mediterranean. Along the banks of the Ebro are the green irrigated lands known in Spain as *huertas*. The capital of Aragon, Zaragoza (Saragossa), lies in the Ebro depression on the right bank of the river and is a major agricultural centre. Southern Aragon is an area of arid plains and the bleak windswept plateaux that form part of the Montes Universales mountain range. Temperatures here are extreme.

To the northwest is the small province of La Rioja, one of Spain's most important wine-growing regions, known particularly for its red wines, which have an unmistakable flavour. The Upper Rioja is mountainous and humid, while the Lower Rioja consists of irrigated flatlands and enjoys a mild climate.

Upper Aragon and the northern part of Navarra lie within the great Pyrenees chain. Mountain peaks, lush green valleys and waterfalls, and rough stone houses with steep slate roofs are typical. To the west, the countryside changes and is divided into small fields.

Navarra has links with the Basque country and was once the home of the 'Vascons', the Basque ancestors. Late in the 8th century Charlemagne wrested it from the Moors. During the 11th century Navarra was annexed for some time by the kingdom of Aragon. It was ruled by the kings of France between 1234 and 1512, when it was gained for King Ferdinand by the Duke of Alba and integrated with Castile. The pilgrim route to the shrine at Santiago de Compostela went through Navarra and as a result there was a great flowering of Romanesque art all along the 'Way of St James'.

The little village of Aguero set amongst lush fields under the harsh rocks of the Pyrenees

Many traditions in Navarra are rooted in Basque culture. The lively *jota* is danced in Navarra and Aragon, and one of Spain's most famous celebrations is Pamplona's riotous festival of 'Sanfermines'.

Tour 13

Southern Aragon is an area of arid plains, windswept plateaux and wild rugged mountains. While it may not appear to be the most hospitable of regions at first glance, there is some magnificent scenery. A visit to an oasis surrounding an old monastery, however, does provide a change. Stops are included at several interesting little towns and villages, built from the stone of the region and barely distinguishable from the surrounding landscape. The area is rich in Mudejar art (work of the Moorish people under Christian rule), and many fine examples of this intricate style of decoration can be seen along the route. South of Zaragoza is the most important wine-growing region of the province, labelled the 'wine route'.

Tour 14

Leaving the plains of Huesca, the route turns north and follows the course of the rivers to one of the important staging points of the Pilgrim's Way to Santiago. The landscapes change continuously with great panoramas of mountain peaks, eroded gorges and wooded valleys, fresh green forests and clear sparkling streams. All along the route are delightful Pyrenean villages, walled towns and castles, which bear traces of their medieval past. Many consist of a cluster of semi-detached houses rising up a steep hill to form a protective enclave. Here you will find evidence of the Mozarabic-Romanesque style that is characteristic of the region. A visit to an old fortress – ancient stronghold of King Sancho Ramirez of Aragon – is also included. Another attraction is a visit to one of Spain's most impressive national parks.

Tour 15

On this tour you will see a variety of landscapes, from the plains of the south, characterised by the rich reddish-brown colour of the terrain, to the fertile regions and mountains of La Rioja. This little piece of land lying on the western side of the Ebro Valley is one of Spain's important wine regions. The route passes through medieval walled towns and castles, a number of which were built in strategic positions on hilltops overlooking the neighbouring provinces of Aragon and Castile, separate kingdoms at the time.

You will find fine examples of Moorish, Romanesque and Gothic art in the churches and buildings, with some special historic interest provided by one of the staging points along the 'Way to Santiago'.

Steep winding streets and alleys crowd the centre of Albarracín, a typical village of southern Aragon

The Ancient
Kingdom of Aragon

2/3 DAYS • 642KM • 398 MILES

Zaragoza is a busy commercial town, midway between Madrid and Barcelona. The Old Cathedral with Gothic and Mudejar influences, the Renaissance-inspired La Lonja and the 11th-century Aljafería, built by the Moors, are important buildings.

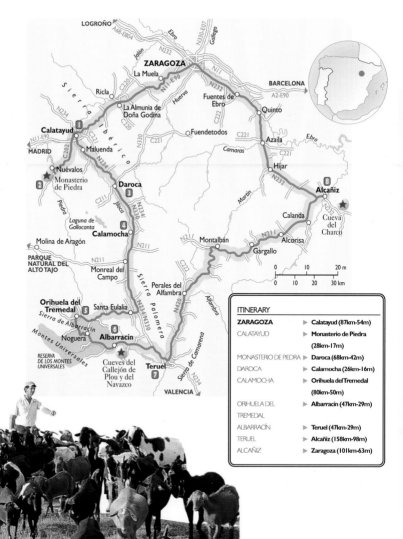

ⓘ *Plaza del Pilar s/n*

▶ *Take the **NII** southwest for 87km (54 miles) to Calatayud.*

❶ Calatayud, Zaragoza

The history of Calatayud goes back to the time of the Moors and its name is derived from Kalat-Ayub, who founded the old castle, now in ruins, in the 8th century.

The town is on a hillside, merging with its surroundings. The Iglesia de Santa María la Mayor has an elegant Renaissance doorway and the Iglesia de San Sepulcro (12th to 17th century) was once the centre of the Knights Templars of Spain. A number of other churches in the town show attractive examples of the Mudéjar style of art.

ⓘ *Plaza del Fuerte*

▶ *Take the **C202** southwest for 28km (17 miles) to the Monasterio de Piedra (Monastery of Stone).*

❷ Monasterio de Piedra, Zaragoza

The beautiful oasis that surrounds the Monasterio de Piedra makes a welcome change from the surrounding arid land, and a tour of the gardens will probably be as much of an attraction as a visit to the monastery itself. They have been turned into a lovely parkland of grottoes, pools and cascades sloping down to the banks of the River Piedra. Look out for the Cola de Caballo waterfall, which tumbles down from a considerable height and is most impressive. You can look

SCENIC ROUTES

The route runs through areas of rugged mountains, barren land and forests, and some spectacular scenery, especially around La Muela between Zaragoza and Calatayud (NII); and past La Almunia de Doña Godina to Calatayud (NII). The area around the Monastery of Piedra is lush with forests and waterfalls. The N234 from Calatayud to Daroca offers dramatic scenery. The road from Calamocha to Orihuela del Tremedal and on to Albarracín through the mountains of the Montes Universales is very attractive.

One of the waterfalls near the Monasterio de Piedra

FOR HISTORY BUFFS

The village of Fuendetodos is the birthplace of the great Spanish painter, Francisco Goya. It lies about 24km (15 miles) east of Cariñena, which is on the N330 between Zaragoza and Daroca. You can see the modest house where he was born in 1746 and visit the small museum which contains relics and a collection of transparencies of his works.

down on it from a lookout point, while a splendid view can be had from the Iris Grotto. On the way to the monastery you will see two beautiful little lakes known as the Baño de Diana and the Lago del Espejo lying between two tall rocks.

The monastery was founded as a Cistercian house in 1194 and the oldest parts are the keep, chapter house and refectory. The attractive cloister was built in the 13th-century, and the elegant staircase with an impressive vault dates from the 14th and 15th centuries.

▶ *Take the **C202** back to Calatayud and join the **N234** (direction Teruel) to Daroca.*

8 Daroca, Zaragoza
Daroca is a medieval delight. It lies tucked away in a gorge on the River Jiloca, surrounded by hills. The walls date back to the 13th century and extend for some 3km (2 miles), with over 100 towers still remaining from the past. The Colegiata de Santa María was built between the 13th and 15th centuries and in the Chapel of the Holy Relics a shrine holds holy altar-cloths said to have been used to wrap the consecrated hosts during an attack by the Moors in the course of morning mass in 1239. The cloths were later found stained with blood and proclaimed sacred relics.

▶ *Take the **N330** to Calamocha.*

4 Calamocha, Zaragoza
Calamocha is a pretty little village with narrow streets and some fine, well-preserved mansions. It has an old Moorish bridge and tower, and a baroque-style parish church.

▶ *Continue south on the **N234/N330** Turn right to Santa Eulalia then continue west to Orihuela del Tremedal.*

5 Orihuela del Tremedal, Teruel
The tour goes through some lovely mountain scenery to Orihuela del Tremedal, set among the pine-clad slopes of the Sierra de Albarracín. The parish church is an impressive baroque building and there is a fine 16th-century Ayuntamiento.

▶ *Take a winding regional road southeast to Albarracín.*

BACK TO NATURE

Bird-watchers will be in their element at the Laguna de Gallocanta, southwest of Daroca, Spain's largest inland lake. Among its inhabitants are red-crested pochards, larks and harriers. Little and great bustards can be found in the surrounding countryside and cranes are winter visitors.

The castle walls of Albarracín stand in contrast with the narrow streets and arches of the village below, left.

⑥ Albarracín, Teruel
Designated a National Monument, the town is very picturesque, with steep winding streets, old archways and timbered houses. Many have overhanging storeys, with wooden balconies and lovely wrought-iron grilles. The cathedral, rebuilt in the 16th century, features a large square belfry topped by a lantern. The chapter house contains a collection of valuable 16th-century tapestries from Brussels.

Important prehistoric rock paintings can be seen in the

RECOMMENDED WALKS

The Montes Universales to the south of Albarracín has a National Game Reserve and offers splendid walks among its wild landscapes of barren rocks and mountains with strange rock formations.

BACK TO NATURE

Northwest of Albarracín is the Sierra de Albarracín. If you are lucky you might spot a red deer, while birds of prey such as griffon vultures, goshawks and red kites soar overhead. Botanists will be intrigued by the plant life, with birthwort, dense-flowered orchids and gromwells being among the species to look for. Butterflies include the Camberwell Beauty.

caves of El Callejón de Plou and El Navazco, located a short distance to the south.

i *Plaza Mayor*

▶ *Take the regional road south-east to join the N330. Turn right to Teruel.*

7 **Teruel,** Teruel

Teruel, capital of its own province, stands high on a plateau surrounded by a deep moat, through which the River Turia flows. The original town of Turba was Iberian. In 218 BC it was sacked by the Romans. It was then under Moorish domination for several centuries before being retaken by the Christians. A large number of Moors, known as Moriscos, remained here, however, and were renowned for their skills in masonry and ceramics.

The town has five Torres Mudejares (Mudejar towers) built between the 12th and 16th centuries. These have square belfries on top adorned with ceramic tiles. The base of each structure has an arched opening, which gives access to the street, and the façade is richly decorated with brick-work and tiles. The ornate towers of the churches of San Martín and El Salvador are considered among the finest examples of their kind. Built in the 12th century, almost side by side, the 'twin towers' are a handsome landmark of Teruel.

The original stucture of the cathedral dates back to the 12th century and was recog-nised as a cathedral only in the 16th century. It is noted for its tall, slender tower and cupola, which was built in 1538 and is covered with colourful tile decorations. The 13th-century Iglesia de San Pedro shows Mudejar influence.

Remains of the fortifications include the solid tower, Torre Lombardara, and the gates of La Traición and La Andaquilla also

SPECIAL TO...

The legend of the Lovers of Teruel dates back to the early 13th century and tells of a love affair between Diego de Marcilla and Isabel de Segura, two young people from Teruel. An enforced separation ended tragically in Romeo-and-Juliet style. The bodies of the couple lie in a mausoleum adjoining the church of San Pedro. This romantic story is popular all over Spain, and has been told in many poems and dramas.

belonged to the old battlements. A prominent feature of Teruel is the Acueducto de los Arcos (Aqueduct of the Arches), which was constructed in 1558 by the French architect Pierre Vedel along Roman lines.

i *Tomás Nogués, 1*

▶ *Take the N420 north, then turn onto the N211 east to Alcañiz, 158km (98 miles).*

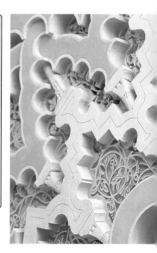

The Old Cathedral at Zaragoza with its 17th-century belfry. Above: detail from the Moorish Aljafera.

8 **Alcañiz,** Teruel

The ancient town of Alcañiz is built up a hillside, surrounded by orchards and olive groves. This fertile area is noted for the production of high-quality olive oil, and for *almendrados*, a sweet paste made from almonds.

The town is crowned by the 12th-century Castillo de los Calatravos, once the seat of the military Order of Calatrava in Aragon. Parts are Romanesque in style, from the 12th century, others are in Gothic style. The castle is now a parador.

One of Alcañiz's most impressive buildings is the Colegiata de Santa María la Mayor. Built in 1736, it is very tall with a magnificent portico. Among the town's most delight-ful features is the Plaza de España, a large square with the attractive La Lonja, whose tall, elegant portals were once the meeting place of the market. Adjoining is the handsome Renaissance Ayuntamiento.

At Valdealgorfa, 12km (7½ miles) away, is the Cueva del Charco del Agua, where there are prehistoric rock paintings.

i *Calle Mayor, 1*

▶ *Return to Zaragoza on N232.*

Pyrenean
Landscapes
of Upper Aragon

Huesca is a typical Pyrenean town, built above the River Isuela.

A Gothic cathedral, a Renaissance Ayuntamiento, and a

Romanesque former monastery, San Pedro el Viejo, are the

most important places to see.   **2/3 DAYS • 408KM • 253 MILES**

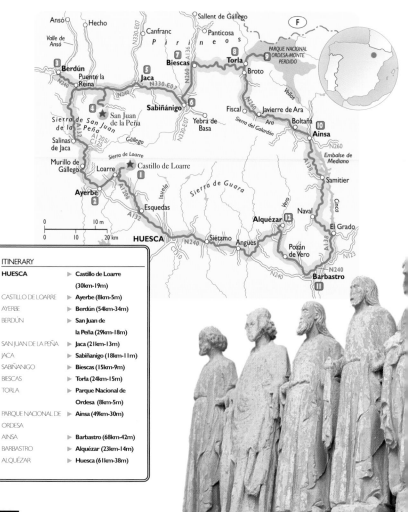

i *Plaza de la Catedral, 1*

▶ *Take the A132 northwest. At Esquedas turn right and take the A1206 to Castillo de Loarre.*

1 Castillo de Loarre, Huesca
The last part of this journey takes you through some stunning scenery to the impressive Castillo de Loarre, which towers majestically over the Ebro Valley beneath the Sierra de Loarre.

Originally built as a fortress, it was actually in use as a monastery in the 12th century, even though the area was under Moorish domination at that time. The church building is encircled by massive walls with cylindrical towers and two entrance gates, from which there are magnificent views of the surrounding landscape. The church was completed in the 12th century and features a tall nave and a cupola in Romanesque style.

▶ *Return to the A1026 and turn right through the village of Loarre to Ayerbe, 8km (5 miles).*

The fortress-monastery looking out from the hilltop at Loarre

2 Ayerbe, Huesca
Stop here briefly to visit two buildings. The Ayuntamiento, housed in the Palacio del Marqués de Ayerbe is a fine old building from the 15th century. The Torre de San Pedro dates back to the 12th century.

▶ *Take the A132 north to join the N240 to Berdún.*

3 Berdún, Huesca
Berdún is a cluster of houses huddled together up the hillside. This village forms an excellent base for excursions north into the Valle de Ansó, which offers some spectacular scenery of deep gorges and green valleys, together with some charming little villages.

▶ *Return to and continue along the N240. Turn right on to a regional road to San Juan de la Peña.*

4 San Juan de la Peña, Huesca
Tucked away under a great rock is the ancient Monasterio de San Juan de la Peña (St John of the Crag). It has a magnificent setting overlooking a Pyrenean valley with a

FOR HISTORY BUFFS

From Berdún a road leads north through some magnificent scenery to the small town of Ansó. Inscribed on a wall in the Museum of Costume is a list of names of those who were killed in the Spanish Civil War (1936–9). Heading the list is José Antonio Primo de Rivera. Son of General Primo de Rivera, who had served as prime minister under the former monarch, and founder of the Falangists, he was shot in prison in Alicante in 1936.

SPECIAL TO...

Aragon has a traditional dance called the *jota*, which dates back to the 18th century. It is a lively affair involving great bounding steps and is accompanied by guitars or a small version of the guitar known as the *bandurrias*. The dance is performed at festival times, when the men wear the traditional costume of black velvet jacket over a blouse with slashed sleeves, black knee breeches, a colourful cummerbund and a bright handkerchief on the head.

beautiful view of snow-capped mountains to the north.

The original monastery was founded in the 9th century by a monk called Juan, who is said to have decided to end his wanderings on this spot. Additions were made later to the original structure, which was built from the rock, and the Benedictine monastery of San Juan de la Peña was then formally founded by Sancho Ramírez, son of King Ramiro I. The monastery is associated with the legend of the elusive Holy Grail, claimed to have been passed on to the monks here for safekeeping by

King Ramiro. The cloister was built in the 12th century and is a superb example of Romanesque art, with beautiful carved capitals showing scenes from the Bible. Tombs of noblemen can be found in the Pantheon of Nobility and the Pantheon of the Kings. Don't miss the delightful Gothic-style Capilla de San Vicente.

▶ Rejoin **N240** and go east to Jaca, 21km (13 miles).

A Spanish version of bowls/boules under the trees at Jaca

8 Jaca, Huesca

Jaca is one of the major stages on the Way to Santiago, the pilgrimage route to Santiago de Compostela in Galicia that was established after the supposed tomb of the Apostle James the Great was discovered there in the 9th century. The great days of the pilgrimages were in the 11th and 12th centuries and pilgrims came from all over Europe.

The cathedral of Jaca is an outstanding example of what is known as the Romanesque style of the Pilgrim's Way, developed between the Pyrenees and Galicia. Notable are the chapels of San Miguel, the 16th-century Trinidad (Trinity), with a Romanesque grille, and the Capillo de San Jerónimo, a fine example of baroque art.

Housed in the cathedral's cloisters is the Museo Diocesano, which contains a fine collection of 12th to 15th century Romanesque and Gothic frescoes, collected from churches in the region.

BACK TO NATURE

The solitude of San Juan de la Peña and its surroundings provides ideal conditions for bird-watching. Look out for such species as griffon vultures who come to roost in the high cliffs that surround the monastery. Kestrels, golden eagles and rock thrushes may also be spotted here.

FOR CHILDREN

There are a number of festivals that would appeal to children. On the first Friday in May a pilgrimage takes place in Jaca to commemorate the Christian victory over the Moors. This is a colourful festival, with mock fights between the warring forces, music and dancing. On 25 June is the feast of Santa Oroisa, which is celebrated with processions and traditional dances performed by dancers from Yebra de Basa.

Below the 16th-century Ciudadela (Citadel) is the impressive medieval bridge, Puente San Miguel, which was much used in former times by pilgrims on the Way to Santiago. In contrast, take a look at the modern style of architecture of the Palacio de Congresos (Congress Palace) and the Palacio de Hielo (Ice Palace).

i *Avenida Regimiento de Galicia, 2–local 1*

▶ *Continue southeast on the N330 to Sabiñanigo.*

6 Sabiñanigo, Huesca
This small mountain town in beautiful surroundings has an interesting Museo Etnológico de Artes Populares, featuring regional art. Near by are several

At Jaca, the Ciudadela's moat must have been a formidable defence

SCENIC ROUTES

An interesting detour can be made by taking the N330 north through a beautiful mountainous route to Canfranc, a frontier town with France. Built high up on a hill overlooked by a castle, this old town has changed little with the passage of time. The international railway station is a fascinating relic of the past.

churches of Moorish-Romanesque style, such as those in Larrede, Oros Bajo, Satue and San Juan de Busa.

▶ *Take N260 north to Biescas.*

7 Biescas, Huesca
Biescas is a pretty little summer resort with neat white houses and red-tiled roofs. The parish

church was erected by the Knights Templar. Look out for the Ermita de Santa Elena on the outskirts of town, perched on top of a steep rock.

If you have time, visit the picturesque little villages of Panticosa (with a spa and lake) and Sallent de Gallego, a good fishing and mountaineering centre (north on the C136).

▶ *Take N260 east to Torla.*

8 Torla, Huesca
The drive continues through typical Pyrenean scenery to the little mountain village of Torla, with its narrow, winding streets and hidden corners. Torla serves as the entrance to the Parque Nacional de Ordesa.

▶ *Take the road for a short distance into the Parque Nacional de Ordesa y Monte Perdido.*

9 Parque Nacional de Ordesa, Huesca
This is an area of exceptional beauty and great geological interest, covering a vast expanse of mountains, valleys and forests. It was designated a National Park in 1918 to protect the rich flora and fauna and the natural surroundings and has been increased in size over the years. A deep canyon through ridges of limestone has created gigantic rock formations in magnificent shades of grey, red and ochre. Weather conditions normally allow access by car between May and September. The park has marked pathways, which take you to caves, pools

RECOMMENDED WALKS

There are endless possibilities for walking in the mountains and valleys of the Aragonese Pyrenees. Torla is a good base for walks into the Ordesa National Park, where there are marked trails offering superb scenery.

Torla, a typical mountain village, overpowered by the dramatic cliffs of the Pyrenees

and waterfalls, and a number of lookout points offering magnificent views. Among the numerous beauty spots don't miss the Tamborrotera Waterfall, which can be viewed from a lookout point near the park's entrance.

▶ *Return to Torla and take the* ***N260*** *south to Ainsa.*

BACK TO NATURE

The Ordesa National Park is home to mammals such as ibex, chamois, mountain goat, polecat, badger and wild boar and a great number of different species of birds, including some rare ones such as the golden eagle and bearded vulture.

---

⑩ Ainsa, Huesca

The old walled town of Ainsa is built on a promontory overlooking the junction of the rivers Cinca and Ara. In the 11th century it was the capital of a small kingdom formed by García Jiménez after his victories against the Moors. The town has old stone houses and a pretty main square, the Plaza Mayor, bordered by attractive arcades. The Romanesque church features an interesting bell-tower and elegant cloister.

▶ *Take the* ***A138*** *south and join the* ***N240*** *west to Barbastro.*

⑪ Barbastro, Huesca

Barbastro is a city with ancient roots. The original town was devastated by Pompey and received the name of *Brutina*, after Decius Brutus. Occupied by the Moors, it was retaken by the Christians in 1064. The cathedral is a fine building in the late Gothic style. It has an elegant interior, with lovely stellar vaults and altarpieces by Damian Forment and his pupils. The Palacio de los Argensolas, built in the late 15th century, is now the Ayuntamiento.

▶ *Take the regional road northeast for 23km (14 miles) to Alquézar.*

⑫ Alquézar, Huesca

A drive through rugged terrain takes you to this fascinating little village straggling up the slopes of a rock, overshadowed by a large castle. The town has a Moorish appearance, with reddish-brown buildings that merge in with the natural colours of the surroundings. Leave your car in a parking area at the entrance to the village and proceed on foot, through narrow streets lined with large arcades and galleries. Up the hill is the castle, built in the 12th century. The Colegiata inside the castle has the remains of an elegant Romanesque cloister and a small museum, which contains a beautiful Gothic statue of Christ.

▶ *Rejoin the* ***N240*** *and return to Huesca, 61km (38 miles).*

RECOMMENDED WALKS

From Alquézar there is an interesting walk to the Grotto of Villacantal which is believed to date back to prehistoric times. Near by is another cave where animal paintings, thought to be some 4,000 years old, can be seen from the outside.

Navarra & Wine Country

ITINERARY	
PAMPLONA	▶ **Artajona (32km-19m)**
ARTAJONA	▶ **Tafalla (11km-7m)**
TAFALLA	▶ **Ujué (19km-12m)**
UJUÉ	▶ **Olite (19km-12m)**
OLITE	▶ **Tudela (53km-33m)**
TUDELA	▶ **Tarazona (23km-14m)**
TARAZONA	▶ **Agreda (20km-12m)**
AGREDA	▶ **Soria (50km-31m)**
SORIA	▶ **Logroño (107km-66m)**
LOGROÑO	▶ **Estella (48km-30m)**
ESTELLA	▶ **Pamplona (43km-27m)**

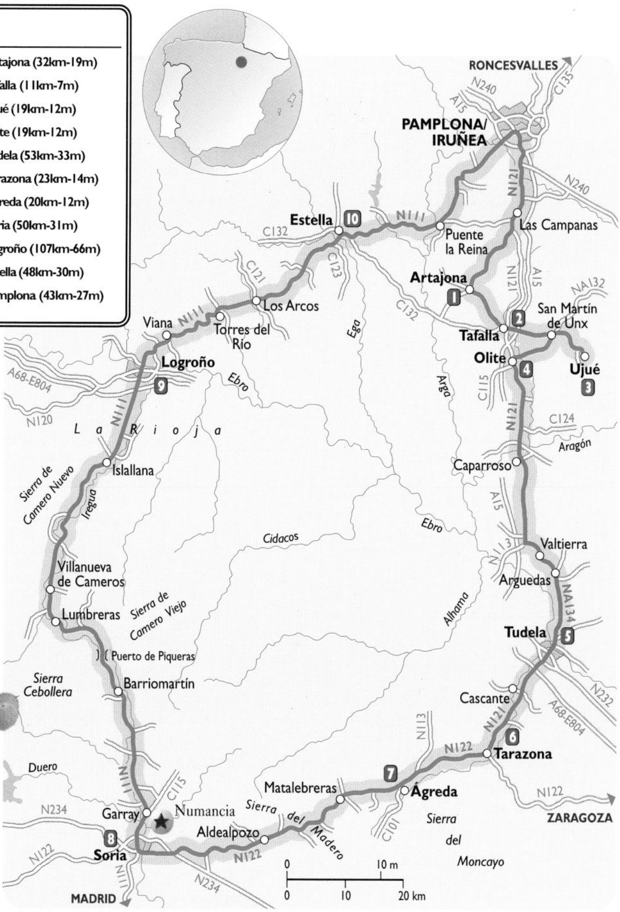

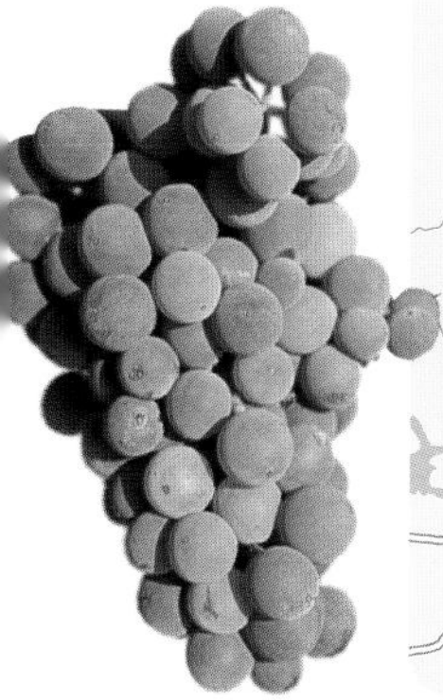

2 DAYS • 425KM • 263 MILES Pamplona (Iruñea), the Roman city of Pompey, is famous for the festival of *Sanfermines*, the running of the bulls, held in July. Once capital of the kingdom of Navarra, today it has to be content with a province. A maze of narrow streets surrounds the massive cathedral with its 14th-century cloister, an architectural gem. The town's focal point is the Plaza del Castillo, partly encircled by old ramparts.

The glassed-in balcony, offering protection from inclement weather, is found in many parts of Northern Spain; here in Pamplona.

ℹ️ *Eslaba 1*

SPECIAL TO...

The *Sanfermines*, described in Hemingway's novel *The Sun also Rises*, is one long round of music, dancing and drinking. Early each morning the bulls selected to fight later in the day are let loose to run through the streets, and the men of the town show their courage by racing in front.

▶ *Take the **N121** south. Branch off right and take the regional road southwest to Artajona.*

❽ Artajona, Navarra
From quite a distance you can spot the fortifications that surround the medieval town of Artajona. Known as El Cerco de Artajona, this conclave of solid ramparts and square towers is a very impressive sight. On the summit stands the fortified Iglesia de San Saturnino. Dating back to the 13th century, it is noted for its finely sculpted façade and 15th-century retable.

▶ *Take the regional road south-east for 11km (7 miles) to Tafalla.*

FOR HISTORY BUFFS

A drive north of Pamplona for some 48km (30 miles) brings you to the mountain pass of Roncesvalles. This was the scene of a battle in 778 between the forces of Charlemagne, trying to withdraw to France, and the Basques of Navarre. The hero Roland, a commander of Charlemagne's army, was killed during the fighting, and a monument commemorates the event. Near by is the town of Roncesvalles, which contains an impressive 12th-century Augustinian abbey.

RECOMMENDED WALKS

One of the most pleasant areas for walking on this tour is around Roncesvalles, which offers beautiful surroundings of meadows, woods and valleys, with little villages dotted about the countryside. If you enjoy walking in woods, try the forest of Garralda, which is in the vicinity and famous for its magnificent oaks.

SCENIC ROUTES

On the N121 Olite to Tudela road, there is a scenic stretch between Caparroso and Arguedas. Sections of the drive after Tarazona to Agreda on the N122 also offer some impressive scenery. The desolate red-brown landscapes around Soria gradually give way to twisting mountain roads around Puerto de Piqueres and enter the wine-growing region of La Rioja, where the fertile plains of the southern part lead to the mountainous areas of the north.

▶ *Take the NA132 east and branch off southeast to Ujué, just after San Martín de Unx.*

3 Ujué, Navarra

The last bend in the road reveals the sight of this quaint hilltop village, dominated by a huge fortified church. A walk through its tiny winding streets and alleys and up narrow steps is a journey back into the Middle Ages. The Iglesia de Santa María dates back mostly to the late 11th century, with 14th-century additions. In the central chapel is a statue of Santa María la Blanca. The church is surrounded by the massive towers of the old fortifications with fine views of the Pyrenees.

▶ *Return to San Martín de Unx and take the regional road southwest to Olite, 19km (12 miles).*

4 Olite, Navarra

The medieval castle of Olite gives the appearance of a whole city in itself. It was once the seat of the Court of Navarra and has been excellently preserved. The castle was built in the 13th and 15th centuries and restored in 1940. It is an imposing structure of massive walls and tall square towers, part of which has now been turned into a parador. Below lies the little town of

The tower and turret, with arrow-slit window, add a fortress-like element to this church at Olite

Olite. The Iglesia de Santa María la Real is noted for its 14th-century Gothic portal. The Iglesia de San Pedro and the convents of San Francisco and Santa Clara all date from the Middle Ages.

[i] *Plaza de Carlos III el Noble, s/n*

▶ *Take the N121 south towards Tudel; then turn left for the NA134 to Tudela.*

5 Tudela, Navarra

Tudela is an old episcopal town as well as the second city of Navarra. It lies on the banks of the River Ebro, and is the centre

2 Tafalla, Navarra

The ancient town of Tafalla lies on the banks of the River Cidacos, overlooked by the 14th-century fortress of Santa Lucia. The old part of town is around the main church and here you will find the attractive Plaza de los Fueros, together with a network of little streets and handsome mansions with elegant façades. The Romanesque Iglesia de Santa María is noted for the large 16th-century Renaissance altarpiece by the Basque sculptor, Juan de Ancheta. Of interest, too, is the 16th-century retable from La Oliva by the Flemish artist, Roland de Moys, in the Convento de la Concepción.

of a rich agricultural area. It was taken from the Moors in 1119, but retained Moorish influences for centuries. This is clear in the old Moorish quarter and the Mudejar-style architecture of many of the brick-built houses.

The cathedral is an imposing monument, built between the 12th and 13th centuries. An outstanding feature is the Gothic entrance, known as the Puerta del Judicio (Doorway of the Last Judgement). A wide archway over the door is decorated with sculpted figures portraying the *Last Judgement*. Inside, the church has many notable works of art from the Gothic period. The 18th-century Capilla de Santa Ana is noted for its rich interior and fine baroque altarpiece. The Romanesque cloister, with finely carved capitals, contains the tomb of Don Fernando, son of King Sancho El Fuerte (The Strong One) whose tomb is in the nearby Iglesia de San Nicolás. He died in 1234 and lay here in Tudela until he was reburied in Roncesvalles.

Other buildings of interest include the Ayuntamiento, with notable archives, the Renaissance Casa del Almirante (House of the Admiral) and the Iglesia de la Magdalena, which has a Romanesque tower and finely sculpted door. The Plaza Nueva was 'New' in the 18th century.

[i] *Plaza Vieja s/n*

▶ *Continue on the N121 southwest to Tarazona.*

6 Tarazona, Zaragoza
The present town of Tarazona was built on the site of the Celtiberian city of Turiaso. It was occupied first by the Romans, then by the Moors, and was recaptured in 1118 by the Christian King Alfonso I of Aragon. It continued as a royal residence until the 15th century. The town is noted for

the number of Mudejar-style buildings and is often referred to as the 'Aragonese Toledo'.

The cathedral, begun in the 12th century, shows a combination of styles, mainly Mudejar and Gothic, with influences of baroque and Plateresque art. The Iglesia de la Magdalena has an impressive Mudejar tower, and the Guildhall façade has reliefs of the legends of Hercules. The 14th- and 15th-century Palacio Episcopal was once the residence of the Kings of Aragon. The 16th-century Ayuntamiento has a frieze around the building depicting the capture of Granada.

[i] *Iglesias, 5*

▶ *Take the N122 southwest for 20km (12 miles) to Agreda.*

7 Agreda, Soria
Perched high on a rock is Agreda, once an important frontier town overlooking the kingdoms of Aragon and Castile. Dominating the town is the Castillo de la Muela, which still shows traces of old Moorish ramparts. Buildings of interest

include the Iglesia de San Miguel; the Iglesia de Nuestra Señora de la Peña, with panel paintings from the Gothic period; and the Convento de la Concepción, which contains the tomb of Sister María de Agreda (1602–65), mystic and religious advisor to Philip IV of Spain.

Agreda is a good base for trips into the Sierra del Moncayo, which can be explored by car or on horseback.

▶ *Continue southwest on the N122 to Soria.*

8 Soria, Soria
Soria has inspired many Spanish poets. One of the most famous was the Sevillian poet, Antonio Machado (1875–1939), who lived here for a time. Outstanding among its many fine edifices is San Juan de Duero, a 12th-century monastery just outside the centre. At one time it belonged to the Knights Templars and features a beautiful cloister. The Palacio de los Condes de Gómara is a majestic building, built in the 16th century and dominated by an impressive

Terraced gardens at Agreda, once a stronghold on the frontier between Castile and Aragon

tower. The Catedral de San Pedro (12th–16th centuries) is noted for its elegant doorway and Romanesque cloister. The 12th-century Iglesia de Santo Domingo has a richly decorated Romanesque façade, and the colonnades of the Iglesia de San Juan de Rabanera, preserved from the original cloister, have an unusual Romanesque-Oriental design.

About 8km (5 miles) north of the town are the remains of Numancia, an old Celtiberian fort renowned for its resistance to a siege by the Romans, until it fell in 133 BC. The Romans built over the old city and many objects of significance were discovered during 20th-century excavations; some are in the Museo Numantino in Soria.

ℹ️ *Plaza Ramón y Cajal s/n*

▶ *Take **NIII** north to Logroño.*

9 Logroño, La Rioja
Logroño, capital of the region of La Rioja, stands on the banks of the Ebro. Its tower and the town's outline form a graceful silhouette, centred around the Iglesia de Santa María de la Redonda with its impressive baroque towers. The Imperial Church of Santa María de Palacio was founded in the 11th century and has a lofty pyramid-shaped tower built in the 13th century. The 15th-century cathedral has a baroque façade from the 18th century, and the 13th-century Iglesia de San Bartolmé is noted for its

Watching the world go by in the quiet town of Soria

Romanesque-Gothic doorway. An historic stone bridge used by the pilgrims on their journey to Santiago de Compostela spans the River Ebre.

ℹ️ *Paseo del Espolón s/n*

▶ *Take the **NIII** north to Estella.*

10 Estella, Navarra
The old town of Estella lies on the banks of the River Ega. During the Middle Ages it was the residence of the Kings of Navarra and a staging point for pilgrims. The Iglesia de Santo Sepulcro stands on the pilgrim route and has three palaces among its old mansions. The 12th-century Iglesia de San Pedro de la Rua has a fine façade and Romanesque cloister.

ℹ️ *San Nicolás, 1*

▶ *Return to Pamplona on **NIII**.*

SPECIAL TO...

La Rioja is famous for its wines. The best-known is the full-bodied *tinto*, a high-quality red wine. It also produces the *claretes*, which are light red wines and the golden *blancos* which are dry and aromatic. In late September there is a Wine Festival in Logroño, with bullfights, parades and poetry competitions.

FOR CHILDREN

Children should enjoy a festival that takes place in Anguiano (southwest of Logroño) on 21 and 22 July in honour of Mary Magdalene. The celebrations centre around the Danza de los Zancos, or Stilt Dance, when a troupe of dancers, wearing colourful traditional costumes, descend the steps of the church on stilts and then proceed down the hill at great speed.
A detour of some 49km (30 miles) southeast of Logroño, on the N232, will take you to Calahorra where there is a zoo, at Término del Vadillo.

CENTRAL SPAIN & THE WEST

A vast part of Spain is the great central plain known as the Meseta, or tableland, ringed by hills and bordering Portugal. In the centre lies Madrid, capital of Spain and the highest capital in Europe, at an altitude of 646m (2,120 feet). To the north is Castile-Leon, while the south contains Castilla-La Mancha. In the southwestern section is Extremadura, which is also part of the Meseta.

The main central Cordillera sweeps down the Castilian plain from northeast to southwest, and is divided into the Sierra de Guadarrama, Sierra de Gredos and the Peña de Francia. The dry, barren Toledo mountains dominate the landscape south of Madrid, while to the east is the wild Serranía de Cuenca. The Duero, Tajo, Guadiana and Guadalimar are four important rivers that rise in the heartlands of the region and flow down to the Atlantic. Dramatic changes of scenery and climatic differences are contained within the region, where wild eroded landscapes contrast with green forests and the dry flatlands of the south.

A profusion of pinnacles decorates Segovia's late-Gothic cathedral

Castile is derived from the word *castillo*, meaning castle. This was a land of castles built to defend its borders during the conflicts between the Moors and Christians. Later, further fortifications were erected between the kingdoms of Castile and Aragón. The marriage of Isabella of Castile and Ferdinand II of Aragón in 1469 joined these two kingdoms and unified Spain.

La Mancha is a vast plain, where windmills and castles serve as a reminder that this is Don Quixote land. Extremadura has played an important role in history as the birthplace of many of the great explorers. It presents a panorama of dry, rocky moorlands, with irrigated areas around the Alagón and Tajo.

Among the crafts still practised in Castile are the traditional blue-and-yellow ceramics from Talavera and pottery in La Mancha.

Tour 16

Art is the essence of this tour. Admirers of El Greco can see his greatest masterpieces in the best possible setting – Toledo. This jewel of a town is one of Spain's major attractions, renowned for its spectacular setting as well as for the treasures to be seen here. Another highlight is a visit to one of the famous Royal Palaces, with their lavishly decorated rooms and elegant gardens. A drive south through the plains of south Meseta is rewarded by a glimpse of La Mancha country.

Tour 17

This eastern section of Castilla-La Mancha offers an unusual itinerary with terrific scenery. The route takes in some of the splendid old fortified towns that once protected the borders between warring kingdoms. A total contrast is provided by a visit to the fascinating 'hanging houses', and a drive through some spectacular scenery to an

Plaza Mayor, the centre of old Madrid, is a great place to relax

area of extraordinary rock formations. The journey picks up the trail of Don Quixote, which leads down to the great plains and windmills of La Mancha.

Tour 18

The first part of this tour travels west through the Central Cordillera, with the magnificent scenery of the Guadarrama Mountains to the north and the southern peaks of the Sierra de Gredos. In the mountains are two special monuments: a great monastery and a memorial to the fallen of the Civil War, close in geography but centuries apart. A walled city in a dramatic setting and an ancient monastery are combined with visits to some fine churches and a crafts centre.

Tour 19

Royal palaces and ancient castles form the basis of this tour, with the focus on a beautiful golden city, where the famous Alcázar and Aqueduct rate high among Spain's many attractions. A number of palaces in this area were originally built

as Royal hunting lodges. The circular tour to the northwest of Madrid passes through the magnificent forests and lush green valleys found around the Guadarrama Mountains.

Tour 20

This tour explores a lesser known area of Spain. Extremadura is a sparsely populated region in the extreme west of the country, sharing an extensive border with Portugal. The fascination of the area lies in its very remoteness and the desolation of its landscapes, some of which are magnificent. Cortés and Pizarro were born here, as were many other great explorers.

Tour 21

This tour covers an area northwest of Madrid. The region has close associations with Spain's great hero, El Cid, the valiant conqueror of the Moors. A dominant feature of the tour is one of the country's most famous cathedrals, which is known for its impressive interior, where you can see the tomb of El Cid.

Art Treasures of
Castilla-La Mancha

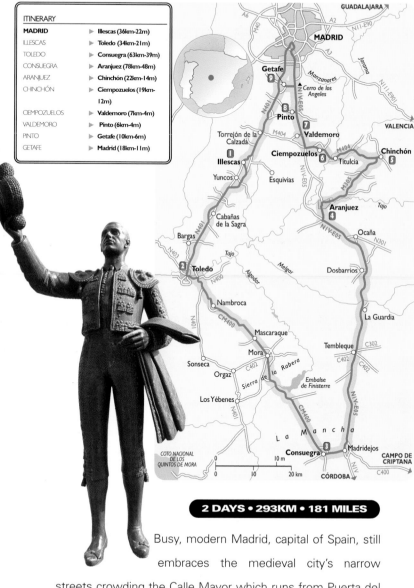

2 DAYS • 293KM • 181 MILES

Busy, modern Madrid, capital of Spain, still embraces the medieval city's narrow streets crowding the Calle Mayor which runs from Puerta del Sol, Madrid's focal point.

ⓘ *Plaza Mayor, 3*

FOR CHILDREN

From April to October children can enjoy a ride on the 'Tren de la Fresa' (Strawberry Train), which runs from Madrid to Aranjuez at weekends. Wooden carriages are drawn by a steam engine and the name stems from when the service was used to transport strawberries during the last century. Today, strawberries are distributed among the passengers by hostesses in period costumes. The journey takes about an hour.

▶ *From Madrid take the N401 southwest to Illescas.*

❶ Illescas, Toledo

Those with a special interest in art will want to stop here to look at paintings by El Greco. A collection of five works by the great master himself are to be seen in the church of the Hospital de la Caridad, among them paintings from 1600 to 1604. While here, take a look at the 13th-century parish church of Santa María, which dates back to the 16th century and has a fine Mudejar tower.

▶ *Continue on the N401 to Toledo.*

❷ Toledo, Toledo

Toledo is indisputedly one of Spain's finest jewels. It is rich in art and treasures, combined with a great deal of historical interest. Once the capital of an Iberian tribe, it was taken over by the Romans in 192 BC and called *Toletum*. In 1085 the city was captured from the occupying Moors by King Alfonso VI of Castile and it became the residence of the kings of Castile, continuing to flourish as a centre of art and learning. It reached the height of its splendour at the end of the 15th and first half of the 16th centuries. When King Philip II transferred the capital to Madrid in 1561, however, Toledo lost its status.

The cathedral stands majestically on the Plaza Mayor (main

The richly carved alterpiece in Toledo Cathedral, one of the finest Gothic cathedrals in Spain

square). Built between 1227 and 1493 on the site of the Great Mosque, it is widely regarded as the finest Gothic cathedral in Spain, with influences of the Mudejar style to be seen in some parts. Its elegant tower looks over the city. The sanctuary is the most richly decorated area of the interior. Expanded in the 16th century, it is noted for the retable depicting the *Life of*

FOR HISTORY BUFFS

Eight kilometres (5 miles) east of Illescas is the small town of Esquivias, where Cervantes set up house after his marriage in 1548 to Catalina de Salazar y Palacios, said to have been the inspiration behind his poem *Galatea*. The records of his marriage can be seen in the registry of the church of Santa María.

The spectacular setting of Toledo, overlooking the River Tajo

Christ. The Chapter House is distinguished by its fine Mudejar ceiling and stucco doorways.

The Sacristy has an excellent collection of paintings by El Greco, Goya, Van Dyck and other famous artists. The Treasury Room boasts an elegant Plateresque door by Covarrubias and a fine Mudejar ceiling. Of particular interest, however, is the splendid 16th-century gold- and silver-gilt monstrance by Enrique de Arfe. It stands 3m (10 feet) high and weighs about 200kg (440 pounds) and is carried through the streets during the Corpus Christi processions.

Toledo has been an inspira-tion for many writers and poets, but mention Toledo and most people think of El Greco, the name Domenikos Theotoko-poulos is usually known by, who came from Crete to Toledo around 1577. Here he remained and painted, producing many masterpieces. The Iglesia de Santo Tomé contains *The Burial of the Count of Orgaz*, one of his most famous paintings. The museum in the former hospital of La Santa Cruz has a collec-tion of his work, including the notable *Assumption of Our Lady*. Other valuable works of art may also be seen in the Hospital de Tavera, a private collection which contains several paintings by El Greco. Enthusiasts will want to visit the Casa y Museo de El Greco, which stands very close to the place where he lived from 1585 until his death in 1614. The famous *View of Toledo* features among the superb collection of his work to be seen in the museum.

The Alcázar (Citadel) stands in a prominent position on the highest point of the town. It was destroyed and rebuilt many

---

SPECIAL TO...

There is a long tradition of Arab-originated craftwork in Toledo, which is known for its damascene articles, metalwork and steel ornaments inlaid with gold or silver. Knives, jewellery and all sorts of adornments for the home make attractive, if somewhat overdone, souvenirs.

BACK TO NATURE

Situated in the wooded Montes de Toledo (Toledo mountains), in the southern part of the region, is the Coto Nacional de los Quintos de Mora (Quintos de Mora game reserve), which is the natural habitat of a wide variety of wildlife. Here you may spot any number of different animals, such as red deer, roe deer, boars, rabbits and hares. Birdlife includes partridges, wood pigeons, turtle doves, bee-eaters and quail. Also look for eyed and wall lizards among the rocks.

3 Consuegra, Toledo

This part of the itinerary takes you south to the flat desolate heartlands of La Mancha, immortalised by the pen of Miguel Cervantes in his classic tale of the adventures of Don Quixote and his faithful servant Sancho Panza. The very essence of La Mancha is conjured up here by the silhouette of an old ruined castle and 12 white windmills, many of which have been rebuilt and some of which are museums for pottery and wine. The village of Consuegra has a charming main square overlooked by a large tower. It was here that Don Diego died, the only son of Spain's great hero, El Cid.

SCENIC ROUTES

This route travels south to La Mancha through vast flat expanses of fields that stretch away to invisible horizons. Occasional trees, hills and hamlets relieve the landscape. Its very remoteness and the subtle colours have a definite appeal, a sentiment shared by Cervantes, who chose this setting for the travels of Don Quixote. No visit to La Mancha is complete without a glimpse of the famous windmills in the southern part of the region. You will see them around Consuegra, but for a good 'windmill run' take the C400 southeast from Consuegra to Campo de Criptana (southeast on the C400, then left on to the N420).

At Consuegra, one of the famous windmills on the La Mancha plain immortalised by Cervantes

times during the course of its history. In the 16th century Charles V had the fortress converted into a royal residence. It was damaged during the wars of the 18th and 19th centuries, and devastated by the siege in 1936 during the Civil War. The garrison, then a cadet school, was besieged by Republican forces. The inmates of the garrison, which included many women and children, held out heroically for some eight weeks until relief came. The reconstructed building is now a national monument.

☐ *Puerta de Bisagra s/n*

▶ *Leave by the N401/N400, turn right on to the N401, then left on to the CM400 to Consuegra.*

▶ *Take the **CM400** east to Madridejos and join the **NIV** north. Continue for 78km (48 miles) to Aranjuez, which lies 5km (3 miles) off this road.*

4 Aranjuez, Madrid

The town is dominated by the famous Palacio Real (Royal Palace). Grand entrance gates lead to a large courtyard where you can admire the palace's lovely façade. It was built in the classical style, showing harmony and symmetry in its proportions. The central staircase is Italian in design, and the walls on either side are hung with tapestries from Belgium. The elegant salons include the Sala de la China, the Salon del Trono and el Arabe, which was built for Queen Isabella II and whose sumptuous decorations bear a resemblance to those of the Alhambra at Granada.

Close by is the Casa del Principe (Prince's House). This small palace was built in the neo-classical style by Charles IV for his son and is noted for the Pompeiian Gallery, which is filled with magnificent marbles and statues. Another important building is the Casa del Labrador (Labourer's House), which resembles the Petit Trianon at Versailles. Also neo-classical in style, it has an ornate interior decorated with silk hangings. Its collection of treasures includes Roman mosaics, porcelain clocks and a magnificent gallery of Greek statues.

Several gardens surround the palace and are beautifully

Fountains refresh the gardens of the Palacio Real, Aranjuez

laid out with waterfalls and pools, graceful statues and attractive little pavilions. The gardens bear different names, including the Jardín del Rey (King's Garden), Jardín de la Reina (Queen's Garden), Jardín de la Isla (Island Garden), situated on a tiny man-made island between two sections of the river, with its avenue of plane trees, and the Jardín del Príncipe (Prince's Garden), which contains many exotic species of trees.

[i] *Plaza San Antonio, 9*

▶ *Take the regional road (M305) northeast to Chinchón.*

5 Chinchón, Madrid
One of the most attractive features of this charming little village is the Plaza Mayor. The square is surrounded by three- and four-storey houses with wooden balconies, from which spectators used to watch the famous bullfights here in the old days. The parish church overlooking the square contains a painting of the Assumption, which has been attributed to Goya (whose brother was once the town's parish priest).

▶ *Take the M404/C404 west to Ciempozuelos.*

6 Ciempozuelos, Madrid
A brief stop here is suggested for those with a special interest in art and architecture. Two monuments are of note. The Sanatorium is a magnificent example of the neo-Mudejar style of architecture, and the

Houses in Chinchón's Playa Mayor have balconies, once grandstands for bullfights in the square below

small parish church contains the fine painting, *The Head of Mary Magdalena*, by Claudio Coello.

▶ *Carry on along this road, then turn right on meeting the NIV. Drive for a short distance north and turn left to Valdemoro.*

7 Valdemoro, Madrid
More works by the artist Claudio Coello can be seen in the little 16th-century parish church, along with paintings by Goya and by his brother-in-law, Francisco Bayeu.

▶ *Rejoin the NIV and continue north. Turn left to Pinto after a short distance.*

8 Pinto, Madrid
The major attraction of Pinto is the Castillo de los Duques de Frías, an imposing structure dating back to the 15th century, where the Princess of Eboli, notorious for her intrigues at the court of Philip II, was confined from 1578 to 1581. The parish church was built in the Gothic-Plateresque style and has some finely carved decorations.

▶ *Take the NIV north again and turn left on to the M406 to Getafe, 10km (6 miles).*

9 Getafe, Madrid
Getafe's most notable building is the Renaissance-style Iglesia de la Magdalena, with huge columns and a splendid retable. Inside there are paintings by two baroque artists, Claudio Coello and Alonso Cano.

Just beyond the junction of the M406 and the NIV, a turning to the right takes you to the Cerro de los Angeles (Hill of Angels). This conical hill is considered the geographical centre of Spain and is marked by the 'Corazón de Jesús' (Heart of Jesus) monument, which is topped by a figure of Christ and a church. There are superb views from here over the plains of Castile, the Guadarrama mountains and Madrid.

▶ *Take the road east to the NIV and return to Madrid.*

FOR HISTORY BUFFS

In the Valley of Jarama, north of Chinchón where the C300 joins the NIII, a tough battle was fought during the Spanish Civil War (1936–9). Americans were among the volunteers on the Republican side. You can still trace the old trenches.

RECOMMENDED WALKS

The hot, dry plains of La Mancha may not be conducive to much walking, but the fresh green gardens of the Palace of Aranjuez are most agreeable for a quiet stroll. Among the several gardens in the palace grounds, the Jardín del Príncipe has inspired many artists with its shady trees and graceful monuments.

TOUR

17

Traces of
Don Quixote

3 DAYS • 668KM • 416 MILES

BURGOS Atienza ZARAGOZA
Sigüenza
Almadrones
Masegoso de Tajuña
Cifuentes
Armallones
Torija La Alcarria
Guadalajara
Tajo
Embalse de Entrepeñas
MADRID Sacedón Cuervo Nacimiento del Cuervo
Alcalá de Henares Serranía de Cuenca
Arganda Embalse de Bolarque Embalse de Buendía Cañaveras El Ventano del Diablo La Ciudad Encantada
Villarejo de Salvanes
CÓRDOBA Tajo Júcar Huécar Cuenca
Tarancón Uclés
Saelices
Ruinas de Segóbriga Olivares de Júcar Embalse de Alarcón
Villanueva de Alcardete La Almarcha
Quintanar de la Orden Belmonte
El Toboso Mota del Cuervo
La Mancha

ITINERARY

MADRID	▶ **Alcalá de Henares** (33km-21m)
ALCALÁ DE HENARES	▶ **Guadalajara** (23km-14m)
GUADALAJARA	▶ **Sigüenza** (75km-47m)
SIGÜENZA	▶ **Cifuentes** (50km-31m)
CIFUENTES	▶ **Cuenca** (142km-88m)
CUENCA	▶ **La Ciudad Encantada** (35km-22m)
LA CIUDAD ENCANTADA	
BELMONTE	▶ **Belmonte** (123km-76m)
	▶ **Mota del Cuervo** (16k10m)
MOTA DEL CUERVO	▶ **Ruinas de Segóbriga** (60km-37m)
RUINAS DE SEGÓBRIGA	▶ **Uclés** (14km-9m)
UCLÉS	▶ **Tarancón** (16km-10m)
TARANCÓN	▶ **Arganda** (54km-34m)
ARGANDA	▶ **Madrid** (27km-17m)

The Madrid of the Habsburgs is best seen in the magnificent Plaza Mayor, the Casa del Ayuntamiento and the Convento de las Descalzas Reales. The Palacio Real, with superb painted ceilings and many treasures, exemplifies the neo-classical architecture in favour under Spain's Bourbon kings.

ⓘ *Plaza Mayor, 3*

▶ *From Madrid take the **A2**, which becomes the **NII**, northeast to Alcalá de Henares.*

🅞 **Alcalá de Henares,** Madrid
The city has been named a World Heritage site by Unesco, in recognition of the fact that Alcalá was the first planned university town. Founded in 1499 by Cardinal Cisneros, the Complutense University became one of most famous centres of culture and science in western Europe. When it was transferred to Madrid in 1837 the town lost its status and declined. The headquarters of the university were rebuilt between 1543 and 1583 by the great Rodrigo Gil de Hontañón and is the present Colegio Mayor de San Ildefonso. This elegant Renaissance building was damaged during the Spanish Civil War, but has been well restored.

Alcalá de Henares is also known as the birthplace of Miguel de Cervantes, author of *Don Quixote de la Mancha*, and a small museum, the Museo Casa Natal de Cervantes, birthplace of Cervantes, contains items relating to his life. The main square is called Plaza de Cervantes, and the Calle Mayor, where Cervantes was born in 1547, leads off the square.

ⓘ *Callejón de Santa María*

▶ *Continue on the **NII** to Guadalajara.*

SPECIAL TO...

Alcalá de Henares is renowned for its wide variety of sweets and delicious cakes. It is known especially for its *almendras garrapinadas* (caramelised almonds), which are produced by the nuns of the Convento de San Diego and can be bought at the door of the convent. Many different types of cakes, special to Alcalá, can also be found here, such as *rosquillas de Alcalá* (cakes in the form of a ring), *pestiños* (honey cakes) and *canutillos rellenos* (filled cakes in a tubular shape).

The 16th-century buildings of the College of St Ildefonso, originally the University, at Alcalá de Henares

2 Guadalajara, Guadalajara

The finest feature of Guadalajara is the Palacio del Infantado. Built between 1461 and 1492 by Mendoza, second Duke of Infantado, the palace was severely damaged by bombs in 1936 during the Spanish Civil War, but has been restored. The pale façade has diamond stonework decorations and an intricately carved gallery on top. Inside is a lovely two-storey patio with notable Isabelline arching (a type of ornate decoration used in the 15th century during the reign of Queen Isabella the Catholic). Take a look, also, at the Roman bridge over the River Henares.

i   *Plaza de los Caídos, 6*

▶ *Take the **NII** northeast then branch left onto the **N204** to Sigüenza.*

3 Sigüenza, Guadalajara

The castle was founded by the Romans and rebuilt between

Erosion has sculpted the limestone rocks at La Cuidad Encantada

SCENIC ROUTES

The most spectacular part of the journey is between Cuenca and La Ciudad Encantada. The route follows a winding road through firs and pines up to the Serranía de Cuenca, with superb views of the surrounding mountains, gorges and plains. From a lookout point called El Ventano del Diablo (Devil's Window) you can see for miles over the mountains and plains. The route continues through great eroded landscapes to La Ciudad Encantada.

the 12th and 15th centuries, to become the residence of the bishops until the middle of the 19th century. It has a formidable fortress-like appearance, and has now been converted into a *parador* with magnificent views of the surrounding landscapes. The Plaza Mayor is overlooked by the cathedral, a solid structure of great towers and buttresses, built between the 12th and 14th centuries. Across the square is the Museo Diocesano de Arte Sacro which contains a fine collection of religious art.

▶ *Return to the **NII**, turn right for a little way, then left to take the **N204** to Cifuentes.*

4 Cifuentes, Guadalajara

The name of Cifuentes means 'a hundred fountains', and indeed there are springs all over the area. In La Provincia square is the 12th- to 13th-century Iglesia de El Salvador, with a late Romanesque portal and a Gothic rose window, as well as the Convento de Santo Domingo. The ruins of a large 14th-century castle sit on top of the hill.

▶ *Continue south on the **N204** and just east of Sacedon turn left on the **N320**, southeast to Cuenca.*

5 Cuenca, Cuenca

The little main square is dominated by the cathedral, an imposing structure with an attractive pale-coloured façade. Built between the 12th and 13th centuries, it shows a mixture of Gothic and Renaissance styles. Features of special note are the 18th-century high altar and elaborate 16th-century grille before the choir. Around the corner is the Museo Episcopal, which contains two fine El Greco paintings, some beautiful tapestries and a collection of rich gold religious crosses.

A path along the southern wall of the cathedral leads down to the spectacular 'Casas Colgadas', or Hanging Houses, for which Cuenca is famous. The buildings cling to the side of the cliff with balconies that protrude over the precipice. Originally built in the 14th century as a palace, they were

later used as a town hall. By the 19th century they had fallen into decay but were restored in the early part of the 20th century. One of the houses has been converted into the Museum of Abstract Art displaying large, mainly abstract canvases against pure white walls.

i *Glorieta González Palencia, 2–3*

▶ *Take the regional road north. Soon after El Ventana del Diablo lookout point, turn right on to the minor road to La Ciudad Encantada (the Enchanted City).*

6 La Ciudad Encantada,
Cuenca
This is an extraordinary fantasy world of gigantic rock formations, the result of thousands of years of erosion. Nature really has had a go here, and the imagination runs riot with the sheer

---

RECOMMENDED WALKS

Serious walkers will be in their element among the wild rocky landscapes of the Serranía de Cuenca. Northeast of La Ciudad Encantada is a lovely area of rich vegetation and pine forests, offering some gentle walks. A major attraction here is the sight of the source of the River Cuervo (Nacimiento del Cuervo), which emerges partly out of a cave in a series of rippling cascades.

---

size and incredible shapes of the rocks, which resemble a Roman bridge, a giant mushroom, a human profile and even the 'lovers of Teruel' (see page 84, Special To). The route is indicated by arrows marked high up on the stones.

The walls and round towers of the 15th-century castle at Belmonte

▶ *Return to Cuenca by the alternative route, taking the regional road south, through Valdecabras. At Cuenca, take the N420 south to Belmonte (via La Almarcha).*

7 Belmonte, Cuenca
Make a brief stop here to see the old castle on top of the hill. It has circular towers and was built by Juan Fernández Pacheco, Marquis of Villena, in the 15th century as a means of defending his extensive territories. It was later abandoned, but was restored and rebuilt in the 19th century. The old Colegiata church has an impressive collection of altarpieces from the 15th to 17th centuries and some fine choir-stalls.

▶ *Continue on N420 southwest to Mota del Cuervo.*

The dramatic cliffs of Cuenca above the valley gardens

8 Mota del Cuervo, Cuenca

Located right in the heartland of La Mancha country, the small village of Mota del Cuervo represents a typical image of Don Quixote's Mancha – the familiar sight of windmills silhouetted against clear blue skies, with parched plains stretching endlessly away. Take some time to explore the centre of the village, where many of the well preserved old town-houses, adorned with coats of arms, represent a style that you will notice throughout this region.

▶ *Take the N301 to Quintanar de la Orden. Turn right on to the regional road and travel northeast to the Ruinas de Segóbriga, just before the NIII, on the right.*

SPECIAL TO...

Mota del Cuervo produces some interesting pottery and is the only place in the region where 'turntable moulding' is done exclusively by women. It is known for its small polished jugs, called *tinajas*, which have a slim shape and flat handle.

9 Ruinas de Segóbriga, Cuenca

Once part of an important Roman town, the capital of Celtic Iberia, the ruins of Segóbriga include an amphi-theatre, thermal baths and traces of an old wall. The small museum near by contains some local finds.

▶ *Take the regional road to join the NIII. Turn left after 2km (1 mile) then right to Uclés.*

10 Uclés, Cuenca

The massive monastery, whose solemn appearance indicates a certain past importance, once belonged to the knightly Order of Santiago (St James). They were lords of the village from the 12th century, and the castle is sometimes referred to as the 'Escorial of La Mancha'. It has a magnificent Plateresque façade and an elegant 16th-century cloister. The two towers are impressive and parts of the old fortification walls still remain.

▶ *Return to the NIII and head northwest to Tarancón.*

11 Tarancón, Cuenca

The church here has a fine Gothic façade and a notable retable. Another building of interest is the handsome mansion built by Queen María Christina after she married a guardsman, who she made the Duque de Riansares.

▶ *Continue on the NIII north-west to Arganda.*

12 Arganda, Madrid

The splendid Renaissance Iglesia de San Juan Bautista, was built in 1525 and has notable altars in the Churriguer-esque style. The Casa del Rey, a former country house in gardens, once belonged to the Spanish royal family, and there is a castle dating from 1400.

▶ *Return to Madrid on the NIII.*

FOR HISTORY BUFFS

A short distance south of Quintanar de la Orden is the small village of El Toboso, which is claimed as the home of Dulcinea, legendary heroine of Cervantes' *Don Quixote*. The so-called Casa de Dulcinea contains a library relating to Cervantes. The village itself has one windmill and is charming, with little streets and patios, evoking scenes in the book.

Monuments &
Mountains

Madrid's Museo del Prado is a world-class museum, with paintings by El Greco, Velázquez, Goya, Murillo and Zurbarán, among the Spanish greats, and outstanding works from other nationalities. The Museo Nacional Centro de Arte Reina Sofía, home to Picasso's *Guernica,* and the Museo Thyssen–Bornemisza are are also top attractions.

2/3 DAYS • 585KM • 364 MILES

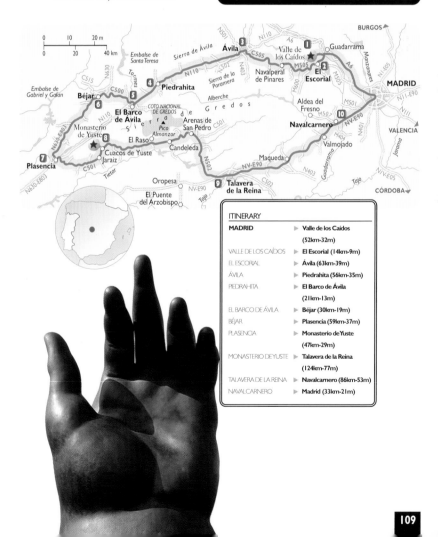

ITINERARY		
MADRID	▶	**Valle de los Caídos**
		(52km-32m)
VALLE DE LOS CAÍDOS	▶	**El Escorial (14km-9m)**
EL ESCORIAL	▶	**Ávila (63km-39m)**
ÁVILA	▶	**Piedrahita (56km-35m)**
PIEDRAHITA	▶	**El Barco de Ávila**
		(21km-13m)
EL BARCO DE ÁVILA	▶	**Béjar (30km-19m)**
BÉJAR	▶	**Plasencia (59km-37m)**
PLASENCIA	▶	**Monasterio de Yuste**
		(47km-29m)
MONASTERIO DE YUSTE	▶	**Talavera de la Reina**
		(124km-77m)
TALAVERA DE LA REINA	▶	**Navalcarnero (86km-53m)**
NAVALCARNERO	▶	**Madrid (33km-21m)**

El Escorial, both monastery and palace, built for King Philip II

whose full title in Spanish is the Monasterio de San Lorenzo de El Escorial, stands as a testimony to King Philip II. He had it built to commemorate his victory over the French at the battle of San Quentin on 10 August (St Lawrence's Day), 1557, and also as a burial place for his father, the great Charles V. It was started in 1567 by Juan Bautista de Toledo, who had trained in Italy, and was completed by his assistant, Juan de Herrera, in 1584.

The building centres around the church, which has two tall towers and a dome. The main entrance is through a large courtyard known as La Lonja. This leads to the vestibule and follows through to the Patio de los Reyes (Courtyard of the Kings). A few steps take you to the entrance to the church, which marks the building's geometric centre.

> *i*   *Plaza Mayor, 3*

> ► *From Madrid take **NVI** then **A6**. At exit 2 turn off to the southwest on **M600**, then almost at once turn right to the Valle de los Caídos.*

0 Valle de los Caídos, Madrid
A tall cross rising in the distance from a rock mass marks the monument of the Valle de los Caídos, dedicated to all those who died in the Civil War (1936–9). At its base is the entrance to the basilica, a vast place of worship, cut out from the granite of the mountain. A flight of steps leads to the church. More steps lead to the crypt, covered by a huge underground dome, made up of several million mosaic pieces depicting saints, personalities and symbols of the Civil War. On opposite sides of the altar are the tombs of General Franco, who died in 1975, and José Antonio Primo de Rivera, founder of the Spanish Falange Party, who was killed in 1936. Behind the altar is the choir, with stalls for the Benedictine monks from the adjoining monastery.

You can also take a funicular up to the Cross from where there is a magnificent view of the surrounding landscape.

> ► *Rejoin the **M600**, turn right and continue to El Escorial.*

2 El Escorial, Madrid
The Monasterio de El Escorial is one of the wonders of Spain. This great granite building,

The Panteón de los Reyes (Royal Pantheon) contains the sarcophagi of most of the Spanish kings since Charles I. A few still remain unoccupied. King Philip and his successors lived in the richly decorated Palacio Real. The Biblioteca de Impresos is sumptuously decorated with tapestries and frescoes by many painters. It contains some 40,000 volumes and hundreds of ancient manuscripts, codices and bibles. Two priceless items are the illuminated *Codex Aureus* made for the German Emperor Conrad II (completed in 1039) and the diary of St Theresa of Ávila.

The Arts Museum has a superb collection of paintings by famous masters. One of these is *The Martyrdom of St Maurice and the Theban Legionary* by El Greco. The Architectural Museum has a fascinating display of documents and plans relating to the construction of the monastery.

Of great interest, too, is the Habitación de Felipe II (Philip II's cell), where he spent the last years of his life in spartan conditions and troubled by pain. He died in an adjoining alcove in 1598. The Casita del Príncipe lies in lovely gardens to the east of the monastery. It was built by Charles IV, and contains elegant furniture and fine paintings.

[i] *Floridablanca, 10*

▶ *Take the **M505** northwest for 63km (39 miles) to Ávila.*

🅱 **Ávila,** Ávila

The medieval walls of Ávila are a familiar landmark in the area and can be seen for miles around. With 88 round towers and nine gates, they extend for 2,526m (2,763 yards), encircling the town. The Catedral de San Salvador forms part of the wall and has a rather fortress-like appearance. It was built between the 11th and 13th centuries and combines Romanesque and baroque styles. Of special note inside are the 16th-century stained-glass windows, the painted altarpiece and the alabaster tomb of Cardinal Alonso de Madrigal, who was Bishop of Ávila and died in 1455. The Basílica de San Vicente is noted for its 14th-century façade and portal.

Ávila within its medieval walls

The Romanesque Iglesia de San Pedro (12th–13th century) has a lovely rose window and fine high altar. The 15th-century Convento de Santo Tomás features beautifully carved choirstalls and a fine retable by Pedro Berruguete. In the mausoleum is the tomb of Prince Juan, only son of the Catholic monarchs Ferdinand and Isabella, who died in 1497 when only 19. When you leave the cathedral by the other door you will find yourself within the walls of the old town. On this square stands the former Convento de Santa Teresa, which contains a chapel built in 1638 on the site of her birthplace. Inside you can see writings of the saint and relics – including her well-preserved ring finger. Facing the convent is the old palace of the former Viceroy of Peru. For more insight into St Theresa's life, look out for the Convento de la Encarnación, where she first took orders and spent some 30 years of her life, latterly as prioress. St Theresa was an exceptional person, remembered for her mystical writing and autobiography. Founder of a number of convents, she was canonised in 1622.

SCENIC ROUTES

West of Madrid the impressive mountain panoramas of the Sierra de Guadarrama give way to the brown windswept plateau and strange boulders to be found around Ávila. Beyond Ávila the route enters the Sierra de Gredos, an area of dramatic mountain ranges and high peaks. The stretch between El Barco de Ávila and Plasencia on the N110 passes through some spectacular scenery of mountains, valleys and pine forests. The drive from Plasencia to the Monasterio de Yuste and beyond Arenas de San Pedro (C501) also offers some outstanding scenery of heavily forested mountains.

BACK TO NATURE

The great mountain range of the Sierra de Gredos, which dominates the region to the west of Madrid, is an important habitat for birds of prey, and among the species that can be seen here are short-toed and booted eagles, red kites and the goshawk, as well as the occasional black stork. Among the many flowers, you can find lupins, peonies and lilies-of-the-valley. The Spanish argus butterfly is special to the area. In the centre of this region is a national park, Coto Nacional de Gredos, where ibex live high up among the crags.

ⓘ *Plaza de la Catedral, 4*

▶ *Take the **N110** southwest to Piedrahita.*

4 Piedrahita, Ávila
The summer resort of Piedrahita was the birthplace of the Grand Duke of Alba, general of the army of King Philip II. Goya spent some time at the duke's palace here and it is said that there was a love affair between the painter and the Duchess of Alba, who was the model for his well known paintings of *La Maja*.

▶ *Continue on the **N110** to El Barco de Ávila.*

5 El Barco de Ávila, Ávila
A drive through magnificent mountain scenery brings you to the town of El Barco de Ávila, where a brief stop will enable you to visit the 14th-century Castillo de Valdecorneja and the Gothic parish church, which contains some fine paintings. Spare a glance, too, for the old bridge over the River Tormes.

▶ *Take the **C500** west to Béjar.*

6 Béjar, Salamanca
The Palacio Ducal, an elegant 16th-century palace with a Renaissance courtyard, houses the Museo Municipal. The Ayuntamiento is noted for its attractive arcades. In the Iglesia de San Gil is a museum housing the works of the great sculptor Mateo Hernández, renowned for his animal figures sculpted from hard stone.

ⓘ *Paseo de Cervantes, 6*

▶ *Take the **N630** to Plasencia.*

7 Plasencia, Cáceres
The cathedral, started in the 13th century and never completely finished, is a splendid structure with an attractive Plateresque north doorway. Inside, notice the finely sculpted statues by Gregorio Hernández (17th century) on the altarpiece, a 15th-century retable by Hernández in the Capilla Mayor and a graceful 15th-century cloister. The old quarters around the cathedral contain narrow streets, fine façades and houses with attractive wrought-iron balconies. Stepped streets lead up to the old ramparts, where you can walk and enjoy the fine views.

▶ *Take the **C501** east for some 45km (27 miles). Turn off north to the Monasterio de Yuste.*

8 Monasterio de Yuste, Cáceres
Set deep in the woods is the old Monasterio de Yuste. It was founded by Hieronymite monks in 1404 and severely damaged by the French in 1809 during the Peninsular War. The monastery fell into decay for a long period until its recent restoration. This was where Emperor Charles V retired to in 1556 after his abdication, leaving the throne to his son Philip II. You can see the royal chambers where Charles lived until his death in 1558, including his bedroom from where he could hear mass. A path leads to a terrace from which there are good views of the surrounding plains.

Madrid's 18th-century Cibeles fountain shows the Greek goddess of fertility riding her chariot

RECOMMENDED
WALKS

The region of Gredos offers countless walks, and there are a few marked paths. There is a very pleasant walk from the Club Alpino to the lake (Laguna de Gredos) at the foot of the Almanzor peak. Other walks include a route along the Gargantas de Gredos del Pinar and the Garganta de Chilla, from El Raso.

▶ *Return to and continue east on the C501. Join the N502 after Arenas de San Pedro and continue south to Talavera de la Reina.*

9 Talavera de la Reina,
Toledo

Talavera de la Reina is famous for its attractive blue-and-yellow tiles, or *azulejos*, which have been produced since the 15th century. The tiles have been used over the centuries to adorn palaces, mansions, churches and other buildings. Craftsmen took their skills to Mexico after the Conquest in 1521 and the traditional craft continued. The Museo Ruiz de Luna displays potteryware from the 15th to 19th centuries. Places of interest in the town include the 13th-century Romanesque Iglesia de San Salvador, the Gothic Colegiata de Santa María la Mayor (13th–15th centuries), the Mudejar-style parish church of Santiago and the Capilla de Nuestra Señora del Prado, which is adorned with beautiful glazed tiles dating back to the 16th and 18th centuries.

ⓘ *Ronda del Cañillo*

SPECIAL TO...

El Puente del Arzobispo, southwest of Talavera de la Reina, is an important pottery centre and produces a variety of attractively decorated ceramics. Embroidery is also a popular craft in Spain and is often undertaken by families in rural areas.

▶ *Join and take the NV east-wards. Branch off left for a short distance to Navalcarnero.*

10 Navalcarnero, Madrid
Make a brief stop here to take a look at the delightful little porticoed square and the parish church, which houses a notable retable and a fine work depicting the Apostles. Here, in 1649, Philip IV was married to Anne of Austria.

FOR CHILDREN

A few miles northwest of Navalcarnero is the town of Aldea del Fresno, where you will find Safari Madrid, an excellent safari park. A swimming pool, fairground, mini golf and horse riding are among the attractions on offer.

▶ *Rejoin the NV and return to Madrid, 33km (21 miles).*

The Route of
the Royal Palaces

The Puerta del Sol is the nerve centre of Madrid, an area for shopping enthusiasts with two large department stores, while the elegant part of town is to the north, around Serrano, Goya and Conde of Peñalver. On Sunday, visit El Rastro (the flea market), south of Calle Mayor, with its colourful stalls, stirring gypsy music and lively crowds.

2/3 DAYS • 364KM • 226 MILES

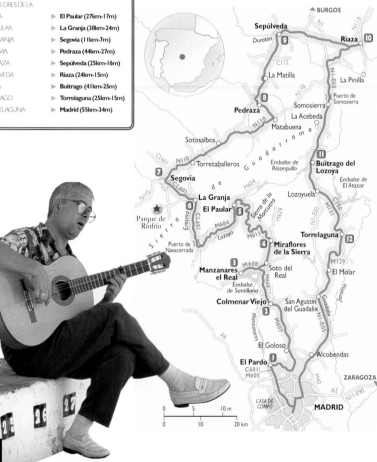

ℹ️ *Plaza Mayor, 3*

▶ *From Madrid take the **NVI** northwest. At Puerte de Hierro take the **M605/C601** north to El Pardo.*

0 El Pardo, Madrid

The way to El Pardo is through the Bosque del Pardo, delightful wooded parkland where you might glimpse deer, wild boar or an eagle soaring above. These were old royal hunting grounds dating back to the 14th century. In the middle of this lush greenery lies the little town of El Pardo and the Palacio Real El Pardo. The palace was built by Philip III over an earlier palace (built by Philip II and subsequently destroyed by fire), and was enlarged in the 18th century. General Franco resided here for 35 years until his death in 1975.

Elegant reception rooms and private apartments are lavishly furnished with ornate clocks, mirrors, lamps and candelabra, as well as Sèvres' porcelain and a collection of 360 tapestries. Also on show are General Franco's Great Dining Room, where cabinet meetings took place, and his private office, which contains a notable portrait of Queen Isabella.

In the town across the river is the Convento de Capuchinos (Capuchin Convent), which contains a remarkable sculpture, the *Christ of El Pardo*, by Gregorio Fernández.

▶ *Head east to join the **M607/C607**. Turn left and go north to Colmenar Viejo.*

SCENIC ROUTES

The most scenic parts of this route are to be found in the Sierra de Guadarrama, with its forested mountains and valleys. The road continues through hills and pine forest, and the land becomes lush and green near La Granja. From La Granja to Segovia it passes through rolling hills and plains, which become an ochre colour around Segovia. On the way back there are winding roads and sweeping views of the Sierras as you travel from Pedraza through Sepúlveda and Riaza to Buitrago.

King Phillip IV rides out in front of Madrid's neo-classical Royal Palace

2 Colmenar Viejo, Madrid

A drive past the old royal deer park takes you to the pleasant little town of Colmenar Viejo, where the main attraction is the Gothic parish church. It was built in the 14th century and has an impressive entrance door. Inside is a fine 16th-century Plateresque retable.

▶ *Continue north to rejoin the M607/C607. Go straight across this road, however, and continue north on the M609. Take a left turn, then left again on to the M608 to Manzanares el Real.*

3 Manzanares el Real, Madrid

The 15th-century castle was once the property of the Marquis of Santillana, a famous poet at the court of King Juan II in the Middle Ages. It now belongs to the Dukes of El Infantada and has been passed to the state for restoration.

▶ *Turn northeast on the M608. Turn left at Soto de Real on to the M611 and continue north to Miraflores de la Sierra.*

RECOMMENDED
WALKS

South of the castle at Manzanares el Real is the man-made lake, Embalse de Santillana, where you can stroll along the shores.

An 18th-century sphinx in the gardens at La Granja

FOR CHILDREN

Children will enjoy a visit to the Parque del Ríofrío. Situated in the foothills of the Sierra de Guadarrama, 11km (7 miles) southwest of La Granja, these were old hunting grounds surrounding the Riofrío Palace, which stands in the middle of the park. Fallow deer and stags roam freely in this beautiful expanse of grasslands and oak woods.

---

4 Miraflores de la Sierra, Madrid

A lookout point on the outskirts of this picturesque town offers a magnificent view of the mighty mountains of the Sierra de Guadarrama. You can also see the source of the River Manzanares.

▶ *Continue northwest on the same road. Turn left on joining the M604 to El Paular.*

5 El Paular, Madrid

The old Carthusian Monasterio de Santa Maria de El Paular lies in the valley of the River Lozoya. It dates back to 1390 and was the first Carthusian monastery in Castile. It was abandoned in the 19th century and fell into decay. It is now under restoration and inhabited by Benedictine monks. An impressive Gothic door leads to the interior of the church. Its main features are a fine screen and a retable, an outstanding work, with rich sculptures and exquisite filigree work. Do not miss the splendid Gothic cloister with its four sets of vaults.

▶ *Take the M604 southwest and join the CL601 north to La Granja.*

6 La Granja, Segovia

La Granja de San Ildefonso, to give it its full name, is famous for its magnificent French-style palace. The present palace was commissioned by Philip V (grandson of Louis XIV) and was completed in 1723. A few years later it was remodelled and turned into a miniature of Versailles. The main façade of the palace faces the gardens. Inside are a series of elegant rooms and galleries decorated in the rococo style. On the first floor are the sumptuous Throne Room and the Royal Bedroom. Outstanding is the magnificent collection of Spanish and Flemish tapestries.

The gardens cover an area of 145 hectares (358 acres). The lower part is famed for its beautiful fountains. The upper gardens have not been tended and are inhabited by deer.

▶ *Continue on the CL601 to Segovia.*

7 Segovia, Segovia

The aqueduct was built by the Romans in the 1st century AD, and is still used for conveying water from the neighbouring sierras to the town. It is considered one of the most impressive monuments of its kind and is a prominent landmark of Segovia. It consists of huge granite blocks held together by butterfly ties

formed by molten lead, and features 118 arches, 43 of which are double-tiered.

Segovia is also famous for the view of its magnificent Alcázar. This was first built in the 12th century and remodelled later. A pathway leading down to the aqueduct offers wonderful views of the Alcázar silhouetted against the sky, and further views over the countryside. Within the Roman walls are the old quarters, with a small main square, picturesque streets and elegant façades.

On the highest point of the town is the cathedral, an elegant structure built in the same mellow-coloured stone, with a tall square tower and pinnacles. It was built between 1525 and 1593 and is a fine example of late-Gothic art. Its large interior is noted for its brilliant stained-glass windows, impressive

Like something from a fairy-tale, the Alcázar at Segovia stands silhouetted above the town

sculptures and finely decorated altars. The 15th-century cloister was part of the original cathedral, which was destroyed in the 16th century but was reconstructed at a later date. A collection of 17th-century Flemish tapestries is housed in the chapter house. Other places to visit

Ordinary life continues beneath the Roman aqueduct at Segovia

are the Capilla de Vera Cruz,
the Monasterio El Parral and
the 12th-century Iglesia de San
Martín, in the charming Plaza
San Martín.

i *Plaza Mayor, 10*

▶ *Take the N110 northeast. At
Matabuena take the unclassified road left to Pedraza.*

8 Pedraza, Segovia

Entry to this old walled village
is through the Puerta de la Villa
(town gate), which leads straight
to the delightful Plaza Major. A
stroll through its quaint narrow
streets and hidden corners will
take you past many fine build-

9 Sepúlveda, Segovia

This attractive old town still has the remains of Roman fortifications. The focal point is the pleasant Plaza Major, which is overlooked by the old Ayuntamiento. Behind are the ruins of a castle. A walk around town reveals a number of interesting buildings in what is known as the Sepúlveda-Romanesque style. Up the hill is the ancient Iglesia del Salvador. Dating back to the 11th century, it features a galleried portico and separate belfry.

▶ Take the regional road east across the **NI** to join the **N110**. Turn left on this road to Riaza, 24km (15 miles).

10 Riaza, Segovia

Riaza is a picturesque little summer resort with ancient walls, old streets, arcades and elegant mansions, which centre around its attractive main square. In the parish church is a notable pietà.

▶ Take the **N110** southwest to join the **NI**. Turn left and continue south to Buitrago.

11 Buitrago del Lozoya, Madrid

The small medieval town of Buitrago was once the domain of the noble Mendoza family, who wielded much power in Spain in former times. Access to the old town of narrow streets is through a gate in the ancient walls that surround it. To one side of the town is the castle.

▶ Continue south on the **NI**. At Lozoyuela take a left turn on to the **M131** to Torrelaguna.

12 Torrelaguna, Madrid

Torrelaguna was the birthplace of the wife of San Isidro Labrador, patron saint of Madrid, and of Cardinal Cisneros, founder of the University of Alcalá de Henares, which was later moved to Madrid. Around the arcaded Plaza Mayor are the elegant Ayuntamiento and some fine palaces and mansions. An outstanding monument is the beautiful Gothic Iglesia de Santa María Magdalena.

▶ Continue south on the **M131**. Turn right on to the **M129**, then rejoin the **NI** and return south to Madrid, 55km (34 miles).

ings bearing coats of arms from bygone days. In the 16th century François I, King of France, and his son were imprisoned in the huge castle standing atop a massive rock.

▶ Leave Pedraza to the north-west. At La Velilla turn right and take the regional road northeast to Sepúlveda.

Remote Lands
of the West

Cáceres is one of Spain's hidden secrets, yet it has much to offer. The Celts, Romans and Visigoths have all been here and left their mark. The Plaza Santa María is a lovely square, lined with the golden façades of fine buildings, and the old quarters hold a wealth of treasures.

2/3 DAYS • 516KM • 321 MILES

ITINERARY		
CÁCERES	▶	**Trujillo (47km-29m)**
TRUJILLO	▶	**Guadalupe (83km-52m)**
GUADALUPE	▶	**Mérida (132km-82m)**
MÉRIDA	▶	**Badajoz (62km-39m)**
BADAJOZ	▶	**Alburquerque (45km-28m)**
ALBURQUERQUE	▶	**Valencia de Alcántara (35km-22m)**
VALENCIA DE ALCÁNTARA	▶	**Arroyo de la Luz (92km-57m)**
ARROYO DE LA LUZ	▶	**Cáceres (20km-12m)**

ℹ️ Plaza Mayor, 10

▶ Take the **N521** east to Trujillo.

⓪ Trujillo, Cáceres

The old town of Trujillo is of great historical interest and has strong associations with the discoveries and conquests of the New World. It is sometimes referred to as the 'Cradle of the Conquistadores', as a number of leading explorers and conquistadores were born here. The most famous was Francisco Pizarro (1475–1541), who overthrew the mighty empire of the Incas and conquered Peru (1531–4), bringing untold wealth to Spain. He married an Inca princess, but was in the end killed in his own palace by compatriots.

Other natives of Trujillo who have their place in history include Alonso de Monroy, known for his exploits in Chile; Francisco de Orellana (who departed in 1542 to explore the jungles of the Amazon); Diego de Paredes (nicknamed the 'Samson of Extremadura' for his physique), whose involvement was with Venezuela; and Hernando de Alarcón, who explored California. The discovery of the Americas in 1492 and subsequent explorations put Trujillo on the map, and the town flourished during the Golden Age of Spain.

The main square, Plaza Mayor, is one of Trujillo's most attractive features. A splendid equestrian statue pays tribute to Pizarro. The monument in bronze (erected in 1927) is the work of the American sculptors Charles Runse and Mary

Southwestern Spain's hot climate makes eating at an outdoor café part of every holiday

Harriman. The square is built on different levels, connected by broad steps and lined with beautiful portals and façades. Of special interest is the Palacio de los Marqueses de la Conquista. This was built by Hernando Pizarro, brother of the Conquistador, who also went to seek his fortune in Peru, but later returned to his native lands. It is a magnificent palace built in the Plateresque style and noted for its elaborate window grilles and beautiful corner balcony.

Other buildings of special interest include the Palacio de los Duques de San Carlos, another palace built by the Pizarro family, and the Palacio de Orellan-Pizarro, which features an attractive courtyard adorned with the coats of arms of the Pizarros and the Orellanas.

The old part of town is a fascinating jumble of streets and alleyways, lined with many elegant mansions bearing coats of arms. A walk up narrow cobblestoned streets leads to the lovely 15th-century Gothic Iglesia de Santa María la Mayor. It features a Romanesque bell tower and has an attractive interior, which contains the tomb of Diego García de Paredes, born here in 1466. A Romanesque figure of the Virgin of La Coronada may be seen in the 13th-century Iglesia de

Santiago. At the top of the town is the old castle, which was built by the Moors on Roman foundations. A wall shrine with the figure of the patron saint, Nuestra Señora de las Victorias, lies above the main gate, known as El Triunfo (The Triumph). There are wonderful panoramic views from the castle of the surrounding landscapes of the Extremadura.

ℹ️ Plaza Mayor s/n

BACK TO NATURE

The Parque Natural de Monfragüe lies to the northeast of Cáceres, and is a vast area of great rugged peaks, deep gorges and forests, watered by the River Tagus, which cuts right through it. The area is rich in flora and fauna and is a breeding ground for a great variety of birds. Among the many birds of prey that make their home here are the imperial eagle, black vulture, peregrine and several species of owl. Many animals, including deer, wild boar, moufflon and even the elusive Spanish lynx, live in the area.

FOR CHILDREN

Children can enjoy boating on the lakes in the region. A good choice would be the Embalse de Alcántara, which is northeast of Cáceres and provides facilities for various watersports.

RECOMMENDED WALKS

The country north of Cáceres and Trujillo, a somewhat isolated area, offers interesting scenery. There are pleasant spots for walking along the shores of the reservoirs here, and also by the banks of the River Tagus.

▶ Take the *C524 southeast. At Zorita take the C401 east, then turn left to Guadalupe.*

2 **Guadalupe,** Cáceres

The main attraction of Guadalupe is the monastery, a fortress-like structure of battlements and turrets in mellow stone lying high up above the little village of Guadalupe. The monastery was originally built by Alfonso XI for the Hieronymites, who lived here between the 14th and 19th centuries. Since 1928 it has been occupied by monks of the Franciscan order. The church contains the much-venerated statue of the Black Virgin, known as La Virgen Morena, whose headdress is richly encrusted with gems. The sanctuary has long been an important pilgrimage centre, and religious festivals take place here on 8 and 30 September and 12 October, the day of La Hispanidad (Day of the Discovery of the Americas).

ⓘ *Plaza Mayor s/n*

▶ *Rejoin the C401 and take the NV from Miajadas southwest to Mérida.*

3 **Mérida,** Badajoz

Important Roman remains are the major attraction of Mérida. The original town of *Augusta Emerita* dates back to the 2nd century AD and was named after its founder, the governor Augustus. It flourished under

The Roman theatre at Mérida is still used for performances

the Romans and was then ruled by the Moors between 713 and 1229, when it was taken by the Catholic King Alfonso IX.

The Teatro Romano is most impressive. The original theatre was built by Agrippa, son-in-law of Augustus, and rebuilt in the 2nd century BC, after it had been destroyed by fire, with a seating capacity for some 6,000 spectators. The theatre provides a magnificent setting, and plays are staged here in the summer. The arena dates back to the 1st century BC and it is believed the chariot races that took place here were watched by up to 14,000 people. Below the arena are traces of the Casa Romana del Anfiteatro (Patrician Villa), with faintly visible signs of the old pavements and parts of the walls, showing mosaic decorations. The Museum of Roman Art houses a fine collection of Roman, Gothic and Moorish objects, Roman sculptures, mosaics, coins and pottery.

The Alcazaba was built by the Moors in the 9th century on an original Visigoth building. Later it was converted into a monastery.

Spanning the River Guadiana, the Puente Romano

FOR HISTORY BUFFS

A drive along the N430 east of Mérida, followed by a right turn on to the C520, leads to Medellín, where Hernán Cortés, conqueror of Mexico, was born in 1485. Cortés landed in Mexico in 1519 with a small band of men and advanced to Tenochtitlan, capital of the Aztec Empire, where he was received by the Emperor Montezuma. By 1521 he had overthrown the Aztec Empire, and he built a new capital. Later Cortés fell from favour and returned to Spain, where he died in 1547, disillusioned and forgotten. A statue of the conqueror stands on the 17th-century bridge over the River Guadiana.

The Plaza de la Soledad in Badajoz, a frontier town which has endured battles and sieges in many wars

is an impressive structure extending for 792m (866 yards) with 64 arches. The bridge is an important feature of Mérida, along with the Acueducto Romano, which is another outstanding structure. The bridge over the small River Albarregas is also Roman.

Mérida has a pretty main square, the Plaza de España, which is lined with arcades and overlooked by the Iglesia de Santa María (13th–15th century). To the northwest is the Arco de Trajano, a Roman triumphal arch, which stands 13m (43 feet) high and was once the town's north gate.

i Avenida J Alvarez Saenz de Buruaga s/n

▶ Continue on the **NV** west for 62km (39 miles) to Badajoz.

4 Badajoz, Badajoz
Badajoz is set on the banks of the River Guadiana, not far from the Portuguese border. It is the capital of the province of Badajoz and a bishopric. The town was called *Colonia Pacensis* by the Romans and received its present name from the Moors. A small Moorish kingdom was established here, until it fell to the Catholic King Alfonso IX of Leon in 1229.

FOR CHILDREN

One particular attraction for children is the zoo in Almendralejo, some 26km (16 miles) south of Mérida on the N630.

Over the years its strategic position, so close to Portugal, caused the town to be involved in many bitter battles during the various European wars.

The town's focal point is the Plaza de España, which is overlooked by the 13th-century Gothic Catedral de San Juan (St John). It has a fortress-like tower and a 17th-century Renaissance façade and doorway. There are fine old tapestries in the sacristy and a splendid gold and silver monstrance on display in one of the chapels.

The town is overlooked by the old Moorish Alcazaba, from which there are good views. The 16th-century Palacio de la Diputacion contained within the Alcazaba, now houses the Museo Arqueológico Provincial, which has an extensive collection of archaeological finds from the region. The Puente de Palmas is a 16th-century granite bridge with 32 arches over the River Guadiana.

i Plaza de la Libertad, 3

▶ Take the **N523** north. Branch off on the **C530** and travel north to Alburquerque.

5 Alburquerque, Badajoz
A drive over the mountain pass of Los Conejeros will bring you to the village of Alburquerque, which is dominated by the remains of a massive 13th-century castle, once the scene of fierce fighting between the Portuguese and the Moors. A climb up to the castle ruins offers, as you would expect, fine

views of the surrounding countryside. The village down below is surrounded by ancient walls and well worth strolling around. It has two interesting churches: the 13th-century Gothic Iglesia de Santa María del Mercado and the parish church of San Mateo, in the Gothic-Renaissance style.

▶ *Continue on the **C530** and take a left turn to Valencia de Alcántara.*

6 Valencia de Alcántara,
Cáceres

This little frontier town serves as a customs post for travellers to and from Portugal, 14km (8½ miles) away. It is a very pleasant town, with old walls and the ruins of a 13th-century Moorish castle. Two churches of special interest are the 13th-century Iglesia de la Encarnación, which has a very fine Gothic façade,

and the 16th-century Iglesia de Nuestra Señora del Rocamador, whose Christ figure has been ascribed to the artist, Berruguete.

A number of dolmens have been discovered in the area, signifying the presence of prehistoric man.

▶ *Take the **N521** east and turn left on the **C523** to Arroyo de la Luz.*

7 Arroyo de la Luz, Cáceres

On the way here you might like to make a detour to Alcántara, which features a famous Roman bridge over the gorge of the River Tajo. The bridge dates back to AD 106 and is an impressive structure of huge dimensions.

The charming little town of Arroyo de la Luz is an important pottery centre for the region. Its

The Plaza San Jorge, Cáceres, a town full of beautiful unspoilt Gothic and Renaissance buildings

main building of interest is the Iglesia de la Asunción, which has a splendid Gothic portal and contains a notable carved retable, a work of the artist Luis Morales, a native of Badajoz.

▶ *Rejoin the **N521** and return to Cáceres.*

SCENIC ROUTES

This region is an area of arid, brown-coloured lands, with bare rugged mountains and dry valleys, combined with fertile lands. One of the most scenically attractive areas is along the C530 from Alburquerque to Valencia de Alcántara.

Historical Cities
& Cathedrals

Salamanca has the oldest university in Spain and many lovely buildings of which those in the Plaza Mayor are perhaps the most attractive, topped by the Ayuntamiento. From the left bank of the River Tormes there is a splendid view of the town across the Roman bridge.

2/3 DAYS • 579KM • 361 MILES

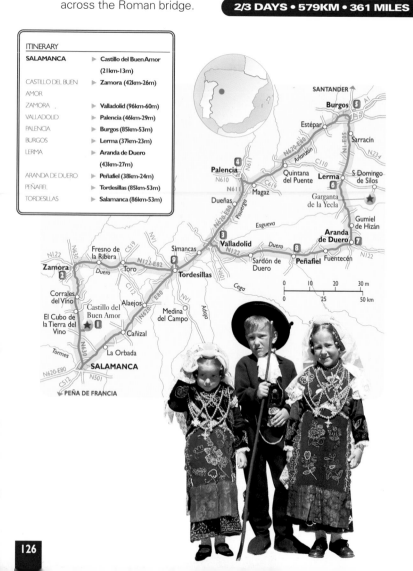

ITINERARY		
SALAMANCA	►	**Castillo del Buen Amor** (21km-13m)
CASTILLO DEL BUEN AMOR	►	**Zamora** (42km-26m)
ZAMORA	►	**Valladolid** (96km-60m)
VALLADOLID	►	**Palencia** (46km-29m)
PALENCIA	►	**Burgos** (85km-53m)
BURGOS	►	**Lerma** (37km-23m)
LERMA	►	**Aranda de Duero** (43km-27m)
ARANDA DE DUERO	►	**Peñafiel** (38km-24m)
PEÑAFIEL	►	**Tordesillas** (85km-53m)
TORDESILLAS	►	**Salamanca** (86km-53m)

1 Castillo del Buen Amor,
Salamanca
Make a short detour to visit the 13th-century Castillo del Buen Amor, an old fortified palace with large circular towers. It has an impressive interior with a fine Mudéjar coffered ceiling and an inner patio.

▶ *Rejoin the **N630** and continue north to Zamora.*

2 Zamora, Zamora
Zamora was long under Moorish domination, and was the scene of many battles between the Moors and the Christians, during which 'El Cid', conqueror of the Moors, played an important role. The cathedral stands near the right bank of the River Duero. It was built between 1151 and 1174 and is largely Romanesque, with a square tower and an impressive Byzantine-style cupola. Some splendid sculptures adorn the Puerta del Obispo (Bishop's Door). Inside, the aisles are Romanesque-Gothic. In the Capilla Mayor (Main Chapel) is a notable

RECOMMENDED WALKS

There are some beautiful areas for walking in the Sierra Peña de Francia, to the south of Salamanca. It offers superb mountain scenery, together with woods, lush green valleys and picturesque little villages dotted about the countryside. Much of the route follows the course of the River Duero, where you can take some time off and stroll along its banks. Around Tordesillas there are pleasant pathways along the river shaded by trees.

[i] *Casa de las Conchas, Rua Mayor*

▶ *From Salamanca take the **N630** north for 21km (13 miles) and branch right on to a private road, following signs for Castillo del Buen Amor.*

Top: the Ayuntamiento at Salamanca looks out over the famous Plaza Mayor. Right: the tower of the new cathedral

15th-century altarpiece and several impressive tombs. The cloister houses a museum that among other exhibits has a collection of 15th- to 17th-century Flemish tapestries.

The little 12th-century Iglesia de Santa Magdalena is a fine example of the Romanesque style of architecture that was most evident in Zamora in the 12th century. Sculpted *pasos* (or floats) which are paraded during Zamora's impressive Holy Week processions can be seen in the Museo de la Semana Santa. The 12th-century Iglesia de San Cipriano is noted for its finely decorated façade.

Standing on the Plaza Mayor are the 17th-century Ayuntamiento and the Gothic Iglesia de San Juan, which has attractive paintings around the altar. There is a good view of the town from the Puente Viejo (old bridge).

SCENIC ROUTES

Much of this itinerary offers interesting rather than spectacular scenery. One of the most attractive sections of the drive is between Zamora and Toro on the N122, which follows the course of the River Duero, offering pleasant views.

ⓘ *Calle Santa Clara, 20*

▶ *Take the N122 east. Join the N620 at Tordesillas and continue northeast to Valladolid.*

❸ Valladolid, Valladolid
The busy industrial town of Valladolid lies in the heart of the 'Meseta Central' plateau, in an area of flat landscapes. In the centre, near the Plaza Mayor, is the cathedral. This was started in 1580 on a grand scale by the renowned architect Juan de Herrera. Building continued in the 18th century under Alberto Churriguera, but the cathedral was never completed. Of special note is an impressive

16th-century high altar by the sculptor Juan de Juni.

Adjoining the cathedral is the Museo Episcopal, which contains religious relics, jewellery and a magnificent silver monstrance in the shape of a temple, made by the great Toledo craftsman, Juan de Arfe.

The former Colegio de San Gregorio (St Gregory's College) was built between 1488 and 1496. It has an Isabelline-Gothic façade carved with elaborate decorations including coats of arms. The Museo Nacional de Escultura on the first floor has an impressive collection of Spanish sculptures, including works by several of Spain's prominent artists of the 16th and 17th centuries.

Also worth a visit is the small Museo Oriental, which houses an attractive collection of art brought to Spain by missionaries from China and the Phillippines. The 12th- to 14th-century Iglesia de Santa María la Antigua is the oldest church in Valladolid and features a fine Romanesque tower. The 13th-century Iglesia de San Pablo has a superbly decorated façade, flanked by two quite simple towers. Valladolid university, a venerable institution founded in the 14th century, has a fine building which delights in a magnificent 18th-century baroque façade.

FOR HISTORY BUFFS

Literary experts might be interested in making a special visit to the Casa de Cervantes in Valladolid, away from the centre of town, where the famous author of *Don Quixote* lived between 1603 and 1606. The house has been well preserved, and contains a small museum where you can visit the room thought to have been the writer's study and look at one of his manuscripts on display.

SPECIAL TO...

The town of Valladolid is surrounded by an important wine-growing region, which stretches south towards Salamanca and takes in part of the province of León to the north. The best-known wines are those of La Nava, Roa and Peñafiel, which can be either red or white and tend to be fairly strong, and the heavy red wines of Toro which are grown further west. During the month of October you can make a little tour of the area, following the traditional 'Routes of the Wine'.

ⓘ *Santiago 19, bajo*

▶ *Continue on the N620. Branch off left on to the N611 to Palencia.*

❹ Palencia, Palencia
The Gothic cathedral stands on the small square called Plaza Santa, just off the Plaza Mayor. It was built between 1321 and 1516 on the ruins of a Romanesque chapel erected by Sancho the Great. The interior is decorated in a mixture of Gothic, Isabelline, Plateresque and Renaissance styles. Some fine sculptures include works by Gil de Siloé and Simon of Cologne. The Capilla Mayor (main chapel) contains a magnificent main altarpiece with paintings by Juan of Flanders. The Chapel of the Holy Sacrament, behind the main chapel, features a notable retable by Valmaseda. Among many valuable objects in the Treasury is a beautiful 16th-century silver custodia by Juan de Benavente. A museum in the cloister contains an El Greco painting, together with other fine works of art and some 15th-century sculptures.

The 13th-century Iglesia de San Francisco has a sacristy with fine Mudejar vaulting. The parish church of San Miguel (13th–14th century) is noted for

The 14th-century Santa Mariá Arch, gateway to Burgos, with the spire of the cathedral beyond

its Romanesque portal and impressive tower. In the 16th-century Convento de Santa Clara (Convent of St Clare) is a reclining figure of Christ. Of special interest is the Capilla de San Bernardo (Chapel of St Bernard), where El Cid's marriage took place.

i Calle Mayor, 105

▶ Leave southeast by the N610. Rejoin the N620 and continue northeast to Burgos.

5 Burgos, Burgos

Burgos is famed for its cathedral which is one of the largest and most impressive in Spain. The city was closely associated with the great Rodrigo Díaz de Vivar, better known as 'El Cid

Campeador' (El Cid the champion). His body found a final resting place in the cathedral here in 1929.

The cathedral was founded by Ferdinand III in 1221, with a second phase of building in the 15th century, when its two tall pinnacles were added by John of Cologne. This imposing limestone structure has a richly decorated Gothic façade. In the transept is the tomb of

Historical Cities & Cathedrals

El Cid. His wife Ximena lies beside him. There is a fine 16th-century altarpiece in the Capilla Mayor and the finely carved choirstalls also date from the same century. The Capilla del Condestable (Constable Chapel) was designed by Simon de Cologne in 1482 in the Isabelline style. In the centre is an elaborately carved tomb of the Constable and his wife.

A number of beautifully designed chapels are placed around the interior of the cathedral. Of particular note are those of Santa Ana, whose magnificent retable includes the impressive Tree of Jesse, and the Capilla del Santo Christo, which contains a much venerated image of Christ. The 14th-century cloister contains an impressive figure of Christ at the Column by Diego de Siloé (16th-century). In the chapter house are some beautiful 15th- and 16th-century Flemish tapestries. Of special interest is the Capilla de Santa Caterina, which has some interesting historical documents, including the marriage contract of El Cid.

There are numerous monuments to visit in the city. The Santa María Arch, built in the 14th century, is a masssive entrance gate originally part of the city walls. The 14th-century Iglesia de San Gil is noted for its pietà sculpture and magnificent 13th- to 14th-century altarpiece. The Gothic Iglesia de San Estéban has an impressive doorway and the 15th-century Iglesia de San Nicolás features a notable high altar and lovely vaulting. In the Plaza del General de Primo de Rivera stands an equestrian statue of the hero El Cid, brandishing a sword.

The 15th-century Casa del Cordón is the place where Christopher Columbus was received in 1496 by the Catholic monarchs Ferdinand and Isabella after returning from his second voyage across the Atlantic. King Philip I died here in 1506.

On the outskirts of town are two buildings of religious significance: the Real Monasterio de las Huelgas, (see the textile museum, Gothic cloister and figure of St James), and the Cartuja de Miraflores. Here you can see

Flowers along a little street in the village of Lerma

the resplendent tombs of King John and Isabella of Portugal and the Infante Alfonso, whose early death in 1468

FOR CHILDREN

Children will enjoy taking a safari into the Valwo safari park in Matapozuelos, near Valladolid. The great variety of animals to be seen here represent the five continents of the world, including elephants, pumas, tigers, rhinoceros, giraffes, monkeys and hippopotamus. This extensive park has been designed so that the animals can roam around in semi-liberty, in enclosures that are as similar as possible to their natural habitats.

Pottery is one of the local crafts in Salamanca; this market offers shoppers a tremendous selection of different shapes and sizes

8 Peñafiel, Valladolid
The splendid silhouette of the Castillo de Peñafiel rises high above the little village of the same name. Built in the 14th century, the castle has 12 round towers and an impressive keep. Other attractions in the village are the Plaza del Coso, where spectators at the bullfights used to watch from the balconies of the surrounding houses, and the 14th-century Iglesia de San Pablo (Church of St Paul), which features some fine Mudejar architecture as well as Renaissance vaulting over the Capilla Infante (16th-century).

▶ *Continue west on the N122. At Valladolid take the N620 southwest to Tordesillas.*

9 Tordesillas, Valladolid
In the monastery here, Juana la Loca (the Mad One), daughter of Ferdinand and Isabella and mother of Emperor Charles V, locked herself away after the death in 1506 of her husband Philip the Fair. She died here in 1555. The monastery, built between the 14th and 18th centuries, has some patios with Mudejar decorations and a Gothic church with a 15th-century altar.

▶ *Return to Salamanca on the N620.*

BACK TO NATURE

A regional road just after Lerma leads southeast to the ancient Monasterio de Santo Domingo de Silos, which offers an interesting visit. The monks here have made some highly successful recordings. A few miles further on is the Garganta de la Yecla (Yecla Gorges), a fascinating wonder of nature, consisting of a deep gash in the rocks, very narrow in places, with a little stream flowing between. You can follow the course of the gorge.

---

resulted in the succession to the throne of his sister, Queen Isabella the Catholic. Above the tombs of King John and Isabella rises a magnificent altarpiece by Gil de Siloé and Diego de la Cruz.

ℹ *Plaza Alonso Martínez, 7*

▶ *Take the N1 south to Lerma.*

6 Lerma, Burgos
The 17th-century Palacio del Duque de Lerma (Ducal Palace) is one of several elegant mansions built during this period. Of interest is the tomb of Archbishop Cristóbal de Rojas de Sevilla which lies in the 17th-century Colegiata.

▶ *Continue on the N1 south to Aranda de Duero.*

7 Aranda de Duero, Burgos
The main attraction in Aranda de Duero is the late-Gothic Iglesia de Santa María la Real. Founded in the 15th century by Ferdinand and Isabella, its chief splendour is the magnificent Isabelline doorway with rich gilded decorations. Take a look, too, at the attractive little 13th-century Iglesia de San Juan and the Capilla de le Virgin de las Vinas, which is a popular pilgrimage centre.

ℹ *La Sal*

▶ *Take the N122 west to Peñafiel.*

GREEN SPAIN

This region in the north of Spain consists of the Basque country (Euskadi), Cantabria, Asturias and Galicia. Although there are historical, cultural and administrative divisions, the area shares some common geographical factors. Spain's Atlantic seaboard is wetter than any other part of Spain, resulting in fresh green landscapes. To the north the Bay of Biscay, or 'Mar Cantábrico', has a magnificent coastline of rugged cliffs, inlets and sandy beaches. The Basque mountains start where the western Pyrenees end and give way to the Cordillera Cantábrica, which sweeps across the north. The Cordillera includes the Picos de Europa, and rises to more than 2,500m (8,000 feet). Galicia to the west has a distinctive coastline of rugged cliffs and fiord-like inlets known as the 'Rías Altas' in the north and the 'Rías Bajas' down the west.

The four areas have very different histories. The Basques were a strong, independent race, with a long history of seeking self-determination. Cantábria, further west, has a number of caves containing wall paintings that prove the presence of palaeolithic man. Asturias was once a separate kingdom, and played an essential part at the very beginning of the Reconquest. Galicia was occupied by the Celts as early as the 6th century BC. Santiago de Compostela, where the tomb of St James the Apostle (Santiago) was the goal of pilgrimages, led the development of the area from the 9th century. Galicians have their own language, Gallego, which bears some resemblance to Portuguese.

The Basque country has green pastures, maize-growing areas and fruit and walnut trees. Further south are vast plains with vineyards and cornfields. Cantábria is known for its dairy products, and Asturias is a cider-producing area. Fishing plays an important role in Galicia, and the region is famous for its seafood. In the Basque country many names are written first in Basque and then in Castilian. Galicia has a similar situation with its own language.

North and west Spain is green, the light is softer and old red-roofed houses line the village streets

Tour 22

Tucked away in the far north-western corner of Spain is Galicia, a little world of its own. Its jagged coastline of high cliffs and estuaries is reminiscent of the Norwegian fiords, and its countryside, climate and culture are far removed from the popular images of Spain. This tour is full of surprises, combining green hills, rivers and valleys, Roman towns and a spectacular coast interrupted by many picturesque fishing villages. The highlight is a visit to Spain's most important shrine, which has been the centre of pilgrimages for centuries. The town and its cathedral are among the most important and attractive monuments in the country.

Tour 23

This tour will delight anyone who enjoys spectacular mountain scenery. The route travels south from Oviedo into the Picos de Europa, making a stop in one of the major towns in the area, whose cathedral is known for its stained-glass windows. Following this are a number of visits to charming mountain towns. One of the most attractive parts of the tour is a trip to an important sanctuary in a secluded setting, surrounded by a magnificent panorama of green forested mountains. This is thought of as the birthplace of Christian Spain, as the first steps towards resistance to the Moorish occupation took root here. The tour rounds off with a drive along the northern coast and takes a look at the region's most important port.

Tour 24

Hills, valleys and remote rural villages form the background of this tour, which will appeal to those who love peace and quiet in beautiful surroundings. Exploration of the hinterland will take you through some isolated countryside. Delightfully unspoilt mountain villages dotted about the slopes will give you an insight into a way of life that has seen little change with the passage of time. The coastline here is softer than that of the neighbouring regions, and some of the seaside resorts are very picturesque, with attractive harbours, promenades and splendid sandy beaches. The famous prehistoric caves in the area are of great historical and cultural interest.

Tour 25

The Basque country is characterised in the north by the green landscapes of wooded hills and lush valleys. It has a rugged coastline with magnificent sandy beaches tucked in between spectacular cliffs. This itinerary includes some beautiful drives along the coast and stops in picturesque little resorts. A visit to Spain's busiest northern port provides a contrast to some of the typical small Basque mountain villages you will encounter in the interior of the country. The people and distinctive customs of the Basque country give the region an unmistakable character.

World of
Galicia

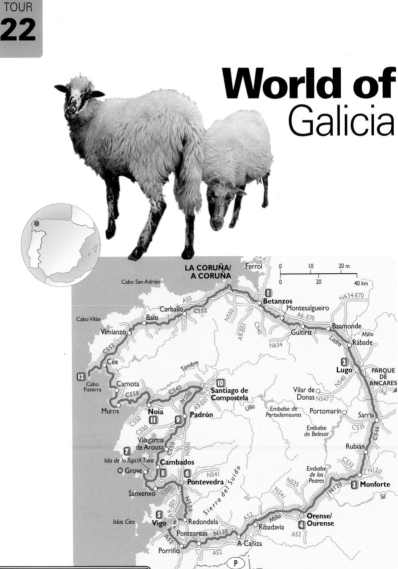

**LA CORUÑA/
A CORUÑA**

3 DAYS • 702KM • 435 MILES

The capital of Galicia, La Coruña was the starting point for King Philip II's 'invincible' Armada sent against England in 1588. The old town is an area of narrow cobbled streets and little squares with notable churches. The Torre de Hércules, a Celtic/Roman lighthouse, offers splendid views.

ℹ️ *Dársena de la Marina s/n*

▶ *From La Coruña take the
NVI for 23km (14 miles)
to Betanzos.*

La Coruña's harbour where up-to-date offices, traditional buildings and fishing boats rub shoulders

FOR HISTORY BUFFS

Northeast of La Coruña is the town of Ferrol, birthplace of General Francisco Franco, who was born here in 1892 and ruled Spain for 37 years until his death in 1975. The town is one of Spain's major naval bases and is built around a beautiful bay, overlooked by the castles of San Felipe and La Palma.

🄾 Betanzos, La Coruña

Betanzos is a small town of great charm, with medieval walls and steep narrow streets, lined with attractive houses and balconies. It has several notable churches. The 14th to 15th-century Iglesia de Santa María del Azogue has an elegant façade and a fine Flemish altarpiece. The Monasterio de San Francisco was built in the 14th century, in the shape of a cross, by the Conde de Andrade, lord of Betanzos. In the church is his tomb, a vast sepulchre resting on a boar and a bear. Another notable church is the parish church of Santiago, rebuilt in the 15th century by the tailors' guild. Note the fine carving of St James, known as the Slayer of the Moors, over the doorway. Inside are several chapels, one of which contains an impressive retable in Isabelline style.

ⓘ *Rúa de Emilio Romay*

▶ *Continue on the **NVI** to Lugo.*

2 Lugo, Lugo
Massive great slate walls surround the old Roman city of Lugo. Originally a Celtic settlement, it became a city of some importance under the Romans, who called it *Lucus Augusti*. Much of the old town was destroyed by fire, first under the Moors and then the Visigoths, and it was the scene of fierce battles during the Napoleonic Wars. The *murallas* (town walls) have a perimeter of over 2km (1¼ miles). They date back to the 2nd century AD and were reinforced during the 14th century.

The Plaza de España is the town's attractive main square. It is lined with elegant buildings and is enhanced by a fountain in the centre, complete with a statue of *Hispana*. The Ayuntamiento on the east side of the square has an impressive rococo façade.

On the western side is the cathedral. It was first erected in the 12th century, with alterations and additions continuing during the 15th and 18th centuries. Parts of the building show the Romanesque style, with traces of French influences related to the fact that Lugo was on the route of the French pilgrims going to Santiago. Much of the cathedral is Gothic. It has twin towers and an impressive 18th-century façade. Notable features inside are the rococo altarpiece in the Capilla Mayor, decorated choir-stalls and a lovely 18th-century Gothic cloister. In the south ambulatory is the wooden statue of the 'English' Virgin, which was transported here from St Paul's Cathedral, London, during the 16th century. The museum has a collection of paintings and religious relics. Worth a visit is the 13th-century Iglesia de Santo Domingo, which features some fine Romanesque doorways and an impressive retable. The Museo Provincial displays some interesting ceramics, coins and regional handicrafts.

ⓘ *Plaza de España Galería, 27–29*

Maize stored in a *hórreo*

▶ Take the **NVI** *southeast and after about 6km (4 miles) turn right on to the* **C546** *and go south to Monforte, 65km (40 miles).*

❸ Monforte, Lugo

The picturesque little village of Monforte is partly encircled by old ramparts and overlooked by a castle with a huge tower, which once belonged to the Counts of Lemos, hence the village's full name of Monforte de Lemos. Of major interest in the village is the Colegio de la Compañía (Jesuit College), whose church contains a beautiful 17th-century retable by Francisco Moure and three paintings by El Greco. Note, too, the fine 16th-century Renaissance doorways of the former Benedictine Monasterio de San Vicente del Pino.

▶ Take the **N120** *southwest to Orense (Ourense).*

❹ Orense/Ourense, Orense

Orense was founded by the Romans because of its thermal springs, around which the ancient town developed and

---

RECOMMENDED WALKS

Imagine yourself as a Roman sentry when you follow their route along the path round the top of the 3rd-century walls of Lugo. A walk along the ramparts also offers magnificent views of the surrounding countryside.

SPECIAL TO...

In Galicia you will see many stone buildings constructed on tall granite supports, with a saddle roof and a cross on top. These *hórreos* are mainly used to store maize and were built to protect the crops from humidity and vermin. Between May and July the wild horses are rounded up in the mountains and brought to special corrals (*curros*) to be branded and have their manes and tails cut. This forms part of a rodeo-type festival known as La Rapa das Bestas (the marking of wild horses), held in towns throughout the region.

from which it got its name, *Aquae Urentes*. In the 6th and 7th centuries it was the seat of Suevian kings. The town suffered damage during the Moorish

invasion in 716, but was built up again in the 10th century. Modern Orense is a busy commercial centre, but the old section of the town is delightful. The Palacio del Obispo (Bishop's Palace) stands on the corner of the Plaza Mayor and is noted for its attractive courtyard. This is now the Museo Arqueológico y de Bellas Artes, where you can view items

from prehistoric and Roman times, religious relics and a fine arts section.

The Catedral de San Martín was first built between the 12th and 13th centuries and renovated in the 16th and 17th centuries after damage caused by wars and earthquakes. It is noted for its triple-arched portal, Pórtico del Paraíso (Paradise), which is richly decorated and preserves some of its original colouring. Note the large 16th-century Gothic retable and the carved choirstalls. An interesting item is the crucifix in the Capilla del Crucificado (Chapel of the Crucified Christ), said to have been found on the coast of western Galicia and brought here in 1330.

Take a look at the fine Gothic arches of the nearby Claustro de San Francisco.

The 13th-century Romanesque Iglesia de la Trinidad, located in the southern section of the town, features two large round towers and a fine Gothic doorway. The Puente Viejo (old bridge), which spans the River Miño, is quite an impressive struc-

ture, dating back to the 13th century. The little chapel in the nearby Campo de los Remedios contains a statue of the Virgen de los Remedios, to which pilgrimages are made.

ⓘ *Curros Enríquez, 1*

▶ *Take the N120, then the A52 west to Vigo.*

❺ Vigo, Pontevedra
Vigo is a major naval and fishing port, and one of Galicia's largest towns. Although it has Roman origins, its real growth began in the 16th century when trading links were established with America. During the 15th and 16th centuries it was constantly under threat of attack by English ships seeking to divest the Spanish fleets of their precious cargoes. In 1702 a returning Spanish fleet was virtually destroyed by English and Dutch seamen. Treasures of immense value were seized and the Spanish fleet never recovered from the attack.

Vigo is a pleasant town with old and new sections. The old part, the fishermen's quarters, called the Berbes, can be fun and there is plenty of lively action in the Pescadería (fish market) when business is on. A stroll along the Paseo de Alfonso XIII promenade offers a good view of the harbour. In the new town there are some attractive buildings around the Plaza de Compostela. There is a sweeping view of the town and bay from the Castro (castle) on top of the hill.

ⓘ *Estación Marítima de Trasatlánticos s/n*

Vigo's statue celebrating the wild horses of Galicia

15th-century Spanish *primiteves*, in addition to an interesting display of maritime exhibits.

> ℹ️ *General Gutierrez Mellado 1*

> ▶ *Take the **C550** west for 35km (22 miles) to Isla de la Toja/A Toxa.*

7 Isla de la Toja/A Toxa, Pontevedra

This island has long had a reputation as the most exclusive summer resort in Galicia. It is linked to the mainland by a bridge. The neighbouring village of O Grove, back on the mainland, has an attractive little fishing harbour, known for its excellent shellfish.

> ▶ *Retrace the route for 5km (3 miles) from O Grove, then continue on the **C550** east then north to Cambados.*

8 Cambados, Pontevedra

Cambados is a pleasant little village by the sea. The manor house of El Pazo de Fefinanes, which stands on the grandiose square of the Plaza de Fefinanes, is a typical example of the Pazo style of architecture, a style unique to Galicia and popular with the nobility of the region in the 17th and 18th centuries. The 17th-century church in the square is built in a similar style to the manor.

> ▶ *Continue on the **C550** toward Padrón. Turn left on to the **N550** just south of the town.*

9 Padrón, La Coruña

Padrón is the place where the legendary vessel carrying the Apostle St James landed. He is said to have preached Christianity in Spain for seven years before returning to Judaea. In the parish church by the bridge is the mooring stone of the boat. The 11th-century Colegiata de Santa María contains impressive tombs.

> ▶ *Take the **N550** north to Santiago de Compostela.*

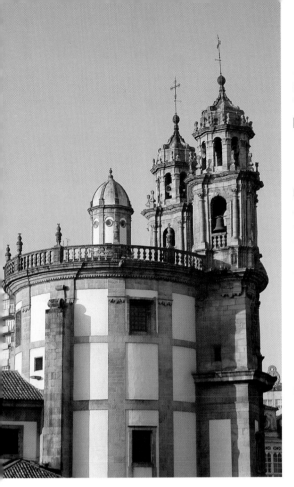

Granite is the building stone of the rocky west of Spain: here, elaborate granite turrets top a circular tower in Pontevedra

> ▶ *Head northeast towards Redondela. Turn left at the **N550** and travel north to Pontevedra.*

BACK TO NATURE

The archipelago called the Islas Cies is a paradise for birdwatchers. The islands are reached by ferry from Vigo and have been declared a nature reserve. They are important breeding grounds for many marine birds, and here you can see colonies of herring gulls and guillemots. Great numbers of ducks also converge here in winter.

---

6 Pontevedra, Pontevedra

This small provincial capital lies on the wide curve of the banks of the River Pontevedra. It has a bustling new town, and an old section that has changed little with time. The old port was known as *Pontis Veteris* (the old bridge) and parts of the old encirclement walls can still be seen.

The 18th-century Iglesia de la Peregrina (Pilgrimage), in the old quarter, is built in an unusual Italian-inspired baroque style. The Gothic Iglesia de Santa María la Mayor, built by the mariners' guild, has a lovely garden setting and is noted for its impressive baroque façade. The Museo Provincial, which is housed in two 18th-century mansions, has a varied collection of items which includes treasures from the Celtic Bronze Age and works by

⑩ Santiago de Compostela,
La Coruña

This is Spain's most famous pilgrimage centre, and the cathedral is the town's crowning glory. According to legend, the remains of the Apostle St James were found in 813 on the site of the present cathedral by the bishop of Iria Flavia, who was guided by a star. The name of Compostela is derived from Campus Stellae (Field of the Star). St James was made patron saint of Spain and by the mid-10th century masses of pilgrims were travelling from all over Europe, through France and along the north of Spain, to visit his shrine. The route they took became known as the Camino de Santiago (The Way to Santiago).

The cathedral, which stands on the Plaza del Obradoiro (or Plaza de España), dominates the whole town. It was built between 1060 and 1211, and is considered to be one of the finest achievements of Romanesque architecture. It is combined with a magnificent baroque façade from the 16th and 17th centuries. The richly carved decorations that adorn the west entrance are the work of the sculptor Fernando Casas y Novoa. A statue of St James stands high on the front gable between two imposing towers. Within the west front entrance is the magnificent Pórtico de la Gloria (Door of Glory), a masterpiece of 12th-century Romanesque work by Mateo. The interior is simple, the main focus being the Capilla Mayor. Above the high altar is a silver shrine with a richly decorated statue of St James, and below is the crypt, which contains the tombs of the Apostle and his two disciples, St Theodore and St Athanasius.

Other notable features are the beautiful wrought-iron grilles, the large Plateresque cloister and the finely carved Puerta de las Platerías (Goldsmith's Door). The museum and treasury contain some interesting religious items.

When in the cathedral ask about the Botafumeiro. This is a gigantic incense-burner that is normally kept in the library and brought out on feast days and special occasions. It is hung from the transept dome and is swung from side to side, higher and higher, by eight priests with ropes. This ceremony goes back to the time when large numbers of unwashed pilgrims descended on the cathedral to worship at the shrine of St James and some form of fumigation was necessary.

On the cathedral square are the elegant Renaissance Hostal de los Reyes Católicos, now a *parador* but originally founded by Fernando and Isabella as a hostel for poor pilgims; the handsome Palacio del Obispo (Bishop's Palace); and the 18th-century Ayuntamiento. Other places of interest in Santiago include the seminary of San Martín Pinario, which features an elegant doorway, and the twin-towered Convento de San Francisco. The 18th-century university is noted for its handsome classical façade.

ℹ️ *Rua del Villar, 43*

▶ *Take the* **C543** *west to Noia.*

FOR CHILDREN

The Parque Infantil 'La Selva' in Santiago de Compostela is a small park with ramps to climb, a labyrinth to get lost in, chute rides and various amusements to keep the youngsters happy.

---

⑪ Noia, La Coruña

Noia (Noya) is a pleasant little village situated in a large bay, with a few churches and handsome mansions. A notable building is the Casa de los Churrachaos, formerly the home of the local feudal lords.

▶ *Take the* **C550** *northwest to Cée. Turn left on to the road to Cabo Fisterra.*

The stupendous Cathedral at Santiago de Compostela dominates the old quarter of the city

⑫ Cabo Fisterra, La Coruña

A most fitting end to this tour is a stop at Cabo Fisterra – 'end of the world' – to enjoy the dramatic setting of the lighthouse, poised on top of a great rock jutting out to sea. This is the most westerly point of Spain and was once the 'edge of the unknown'.

▶ *Return to La Coruña on the* **C552**, *115km (71 miles).*

SCENIC ROUTES

Galicia offers very attractive landscapes of green hills and valleys, with striking coastal scenery. One of the most beautiful parts of the tour is the drive from Santiago to Cabo Fisterra on the C550, where the coast of the Rías Bajas offers magnificent views of cliffs and inlets, wooded hills and sandy beaches.

The Green Belt
of Asturias

Oviedo, the major industrial centre of Asturias, developed in the 8th century as the capital city of the kingdom. In the old part of the town, visit the Gothic Basílica del Salvador (Cathedral) north of the Plaza Mayor. Its south tower rises 82m (270 feet) and offers a splendid view and the Capilla del Rey Casto is the pantheon of the Asturian kings. On Mount Naranco see the two Romanesque churches, successors to King Ramiro's 9th-century summer palace.

2 DAYS • 470KM • 292 MILES

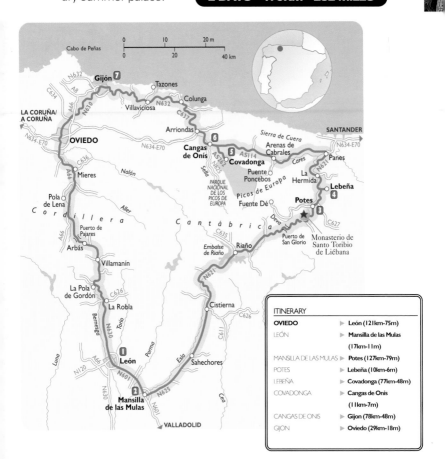

ITINERARY		
OVIEDO	►	León (121km-75m)
LEÓN	►	Mansilla de las Mulas
		(17km-11m)
MANSILLA DE LAS MULAS	►	Potes (127km-79m)
POTES	►	Lebeña (10km-6m)
LEBEÑA	►	Covadonga (77km-48m)
COVADONGA	►	Cangas de Onis
		(11km-7m)
CANGAS DE ONIS	►	Gijon (78km-48m)
GIJON	►	Oviedo (29km-18m)

the old. It was the capital of the kingdom of León for a period between the 10th and 13th centuries, and fortification walls were built around the city by the Asturian kings. The year 1230 saw the unification of the kingdoms of León and Castile and a loss of status for León. In the Middle Ages it was one of the main staging points for pilgrims travelling to Santiago de Compostela.

The old quarters lead off from the Plaza Mayor, which is surrounded by attractive portals. The cathedral lies to the north of the square. It was built between the 13th and 14th centuries and is a remarkable work of Gothic architecture. The west façade is outstanding, with two great steeples and a central turreted gable, with a large rose window and three ornately carved doorways. The cathedral is renowned for its superb stained-glass windows, the earliest of which date back to the 13th century and are to be seen in the central choir chapel and the rose windows in the west and north fronts. The Capilla Mayor has an impressive 15th-century Gothic altarpiece with a magnificent painting of the Entombment. The cloister is in the Plateresque style and has notable frescoes.

The Colegiata de San Isidoro dates back to the 12th century and forms part of the ancient ramparts. It features a huge Romanesque tower and

Left: maize drying. Below: a granary worker wearing the traditional special clogs

---

[i] *Plaza de Alfonso 11, El Casto, 6*

▶ *From Oviedo take the A66 then the N630 to León.*

❶ León, León
León lies at the confluence of two rivers, the Torío and Bernesga, and is known for its beautiful cathedral of Santa María de la Regla. As the centre of a thriving mineral industry, the town presents a sharp contrast between the new and

SCENIC ROUTES

This itinerary takes in the famous Picos de Europa, and most of the route passes through magnificent scenery. Between Oviedo and León (N630) the route becomes very attractive after Mieres, with superb views over the beautiful Cordillera Cantábrica (Cantábrian Mountains). The drive from Cistierna to Riaño on the N621 offers magnificent views and continues to Gijón through some of the most spectacular scenery of Asturias, with an outstanding stretch, known as the Cares Route, between Panes and Cangas de Onís.

The Green Belt of Asturias

From the little village of Potes you can explore the Picos de Europa

Stork's nest on the tower of the Colegiata de San Isidoro in León

two impressive doorways. In the Capilla Mayor is a fine 16th-century altarpiece and the remains of St Isidore, to whom the church was dedicated.

A number of handsome buildings are located around the central Plazuela de San Marcelo, including the Ayuntamiento, a splendid building with twin towers.

i *Plaza de la Regla, 4*

▶ *Take the **N601** southeast to Mansilla de las Mulas, 17km (11 miles).*

2 Mansilla de las Mulas, León
Make a brief stop to look around this little village, which is surrounded by walls and has an attractive main square lined with arcades.

▶ *Take the **N625**, then the **N621**, northeast through Riaño to Potes.*

3 Potes, Asturias
Potes lies in a valley below the sharp peaks of the Picos de Europa. This little mountain village has great charm, with old wooden houses and a large 15th-century tower, which is now the town hall. It is an excellent centre for excursions into the mountains.

The Monasterio de Santo Toribio de Liébana, 3km (2 miles) west was founded by Franciscans, and became important in the following century when a piece of the True Cross was brought here from Jerusalem. This can be seen in a small chamber beyond the cloister. There is a fine view of Potes and the surrounding mountains from the end of the road.

From Potes make sure you visit Fuente Dé, situated 21km (13 miles) to the west. A road along the River Deva leads through forests and mountains to the Fuente Dé *parador*. Near by is the terminal of a cable-car that takes you up some 800m

(2,625 feet) through magnificent scenery to the top of the rock. There are superb panoramic views from the lookout point here, called the Mirador del Cable, extending over the valley of the River Deva, the village of Potes and the central range of the Picos de Europa.

▶ *Continue on the **N621** north to Lebeña, which is reached by bearing right off this road.*

RECOMMENDED WALKS

The Picos de Europa provides countless hikes and walks in beautiful surroundings. A drive south of Arenas de Cabrales brings you to Puente Poncebos, from which you can take a magnificent walk along the Cares Gorge. A pathway cut out from the rock takes you along the gorge, offering fantastic scenery and dizzy views of the swirling waters of the River Cares far below. You need a good head for heights. There are also some fine areas for walking in the beautiful oak forest, Bosque de Muniellos, or around the Lagos de Somiedo.

4 Lebeña, Asturias

The small Mozarab Iglesia de Santa María de Lebeña lies at the foot of steep cliffs, among elegant poplars. It was built in the 10th century and has been well preserved. Note the fine vaulting and horseshoe-shaped arches, which bear finely carved Corinthian capitals.

▶ *Rejoin and continue north on the N621. At Panes take the AS114 west and at Soto de Cangas branch left on the AS262 to Covadonga.*

5 Covadonga, Asturias

The sanctuary of Covadonga is tucked away in a remote valley. The setting is superb and the place exudes an aura of mysticism. The kingdom of Asturias was founded in this region after the defeat of Muslim forces in 722 by a Gothic nobleman called Pelayo, who led the Asturians to a resounding victory against the Moors.

The sanctuary is dedicated to the patron saint of Asturias, la Virgen de las Batallas (Virgin of the Battles). Pilgrimages are made here on 8 September to venerate her image, which stands over the altar in the Santa Cueva (Holy Cave). Behind are the tombs of Pelayo, who died in 737, his wife Gaudiosa and King Alfonso I.

BACK TO NATURE

The Parque Nacional de 'Los Picos de Europa' is a vast region of great natural beauty, known for its magnificent forests. It is watered by the rivers Cares and Deje and contains the two glacier lakes, Enol and Ercina. It is home to wild cats, pole-cats, foxes, wolves, badgers and chamois, which inhabit the higher slopes. Among the many different types of birds, you can see various species of eagles, owls and magpies, while the rivers are full of a variety of fish, which are preyed upon by secretive otters.

The Basílica was erected at the end of the 19th century in neo-Romanesque style and features two tall spires. The Tesoro de la Virgen (Virgin's Treasury) contains some fine treasures, including a brilliant diamond-studded crown.

ⓘ *Plaza la Basílica*

▶ *Rejoin the AS114 and turn west to Cangas de Onís.*

6 Cangas de Onís, Asturias

Once the Reconquest of Spain had been started by the Christians at the Battle of Covadonga in 722, the court was established at Cangas de Onís and Asturias became known as a symbol of the Christian resistance against the Moors. Some elegant old mansions can still be seen from those glorious times. Of major interest is the 8th-century Capilla de Santa Cruz, which stands on a Celtic burial mound. Look out for the old Puente Romano (Roman bridge) which spans the gorge of the River Sella.

ⓘ *Jardines del Ayuntamiento, 2*

▶ *Take the 637 northwest. On reaching the N632 turn left to Gijón.*

An ancient bridge across the River Sella at Cangas de Onís

7 Gijón, Asturias

Before arriving at Gijón you might like to branch off at Villaviciosa and take a short detour along a lovely route to the charming little fishing harbour of Tazones.

Gijón is one of the most important towns in Asturias, with a busy port. It is situated between two wide bays with the old town built on an isthmus, while the harbour stretches away to the west.

First Roman and then Visigoth, the town was known as *Gigia*. It was under Moorish domination for a period in the 8th century, after which it was for a time residence of the kings of Asturias. Charles V built the harbour in 1522, and it provided shelter for the ships of the Spanish Armada. The harbour was rebuilt in 1766 and has since been enlarged several times. The town was severely damaged during fighting in the Spanish Civil War. Much of it was then rebuilt and has been enlarged more recently, with the result that Gijón is essentially a modern town.

Gijón was the birthplace of Gaspar Melchor de Jovellanos

(1744–1811), renowned in Spain as a writer, statesman and economist. In 1794 he founded the Instituto Jovellanos as an institute for education in the natural sciences. This is located to the northeast of the town and now serves as the Provincial College of Industry and Nautical Science. His birthplace, Casa de Jovellanos (in the old part of town), has been restored and is now a museum with paintings by Asturian artists. Other places of interest in Gijón are the baroque Palacio del Conde de Tevillagigedo (15th- to 16th-century), with two imposing towers, and the 16th-century Colegiata de San Juan.

The port is very busy and has large docks that handle commercial business and

passenger lines. The harbour has been considerably enlarged and extends to the west for several kilometres. Gijón is also a popular seaside resort. Its long sandy beach, Playa de San Lorenzo, is usually packed in summer.

The old fishermen's quarter, known as the Cimadevilla, is built up the slopes of the Santa Catalina hill. Here you will find an area of tiny, narrow streets, old houses, bars and lots of activity. There are fine views of the harbour and the mountains of the Picos de Europa from the top of the hill.

ℹ️ *Marqués de San Estéban 1*

▶ *Return to Oviedo southwest on the N630.*

SPECIAL TO...

Those who like strong cheese will enjoy *picón*, a blue cheese produced in Arenas de Cabrales by a slow ripening process which takes place in caves. This cheese goes down well with a glass of cider, which is a speciality of Asturias. The area to the east of Gijón is an apple-growing region that produces cider (*sidra* in Spanish). In the middle of July there is a cider festival in Nava. Traditionally, the cider is poured into the glass from a pitcher held above the head.

Scenes from the life of Christ on the altar of Oviedo cathedral

Landscapes of
Cantabria

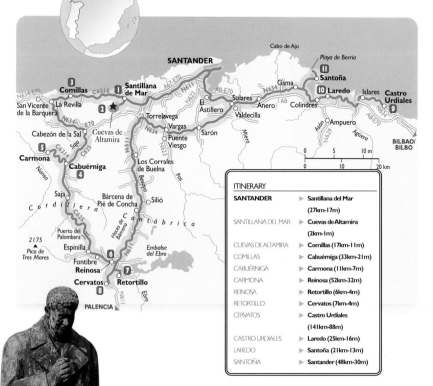

ITINERARY

SANTANDER	▶	**Santillana del Mar** (27km–17m)
SANTILLANA DEL MAR	▶	**Cuevas de Altamira** (2km–1m)
CUEVAS DE ALTAMIRA	▶	**Comillas** (17km–11m)
COMILLAS	▶	**Cabuérniga** (33km–21m)
CABUÉRNIGA	▶	**Carmona** (11km–7m)
CARMONA	▶	**Reinosa** (52km–32m)
REINOSA	▶	**Retortillo** (6km–4m)
RETORTILLO	▶	**Cervatos** (7km–4m)
CERVATOS	▶	**Castro Urdiales** (141km–88m)
CASTRO URDIALES	▶	**Laredo** (25km–16m)
LAREDO	▶	**Santoña** (21km–13m)
SANTOÑA	▶	**Santander** (48km–30m)

2/3 DAYS • 390KM • 244 MILES

While Santander's history goes back to the Romans, much of it was rebuilt after being devastated by a tornado in 1941. The 13th-century Gothic cathedral, just off the Avenida de Alfonso XIII, has been rebuilt three times. The royal palace of La Magdalena was presented to Alfonso XII at the beginning of the 20th century, when Santander was a favourite summer resort of the Spanish kings. The Palace is now the International University.

ℹ️ *Plaza Porticada, 5*

▶ *From Santander take the N611 southwest. Turn right on to the C6316 to Santillana del Mar.*

❶ Santillana del Mar,
Santander

Santillana del Mar is an architectural delight, with beautiful mansions and churches, together with picturesque balconied houses and typical red-tiled roofs. Its little squares and old façades appear like stage settings from the past. Coats of arms on many façades relate to seamen of former times who returned from important voyages of discovery.

A focal point is the Plaza de Ramón Pelayo, which is lined with elegant buildings of the 14th to 16th centuries. The Romanesque Colegiata, one of the loveliest buildings, dates back to the 12th century with fine sculptures in the nave and aisle. The cloister contains a Renaissance altarpiece.

ℹ️ *Bajo Casas Aguila y Parra*

▶ *From Santillana take the road for 2km (1 mile) to the car-park of the Cuevas de Altamira (Caves of Altamira).*

SPECIAL TO...

The festival of La Folia at San Vicente de la Barquera (west of Comillas) on the Sunday after Easter involves decorated boats, music and celebrations.

Evening sunlight gilds the church and houses of Santillana del Mar

❷ Cuevas de Altamira,
Santander

The prehistoric wall paintings that were discovered in the Altamira Caves in the latter part of the 19th century are among the most significant in the world. For conservation reasons, however, the caves are now closed to the public. Anyone who has a serious interest must apply for a permit to visit, from at least 14 months to two years in advance (see Practical Information for details). Alternatively, you can visit the Neocueva, which is an exact reproduction of the original cave, and is open to the general public.

149

Landscapes of Cantabria

The Altamira caves have a depth of 270m (885 feet) and are most impressive, containing paintings of animals that were hunted by palaeolithic man some 11,000 to 16,000 years ago. The paintings still retain their colours and reveal the unmistakable shapes of bison, deer and wild boars.

More prehistoric animal paintings can be seen in the caves of El Castillo and La Pasiega in Puente Viesgo, south of Torrelavega on the N623.

▶ *Rejoin the C6316 and continue west to Comillas, 17km (11 miles).*

3 Comillas, Santander
The little town of Comillas rises up a hill overlooking the sea. The resort has some elegant buildings and a pleasant beach. Of special note is the neo-classical Palacio del Marqués de Comillas, which stands in attractive gardens. In these is also a building known as 'El Capricho' (meaning 'the whim') designed by Antonio Gaudí, architect of the Templo de la Sagrada Familia and other buildings in Barcelona.

▶ *Take C6316 west to join the N634 and head southeast. Turn south at Cabezón de la Sal on C625 to Cabuérniga, 33km (21 miles).*

4 Cabuérniga, Santander
Take a look round this little mountain town, capital of the valley, with its quaint old houses and large wooden balconies.

▶ *Take the C6314 northwest for 11km (7 miles) to Carmona.*

5 Carmona, Santander
Carmona is another small village, typical of the area, where the pattern of life has seen little change from the old days. The detour is worthwhile, not only for a glimpse of this picturesque little place, but also for its beautiful surroundings.

SCENIC ROUTES

The road from Cabuérniga to Reinosa travels through the beautiful Cordillera Cantábrica mountains on the C625, over the passes of Puerto de Tajahierro and Palombera with magnificent views to Reinosa. The N611 from Cervatos up to Torrelavega follows a winding mountain road with many bends before passing through the dramatic Hoces de Bárcena gorge. The drive from Torrelavega on the N634 becomes very attractive again after Solares.

▶ *Return to Cabuérniga and continue south to Reinosa.*

6 Reinosa, Santander
Set high up in the valley of the River Ebro is the little mountain town of Reinosa which has some charming streets and is a popular summer resort.

▶ *Continue south on the N611. Shortly, turn left to Bolmir, East of Bolmir turn right to Retortillo, 6km (4 miles).*

7 Retortillo, Santander
Stop here to see the Roman ruins of *Juliobriga*, just outside the village. You can get a good idea of the layout of this fortified village from the bell tower of the ruined church.

RECOMMENDED WALKS

There are plenty of places for walking in the Cordillera Cantábrica. The village of Fontibre (northwest of Reinosa) is a good base for a number of walks, with marked trails you can take in various directions. The Valle de Campo is a beautiful area of poplar trees and lush vegetation, where you will find the source of the Ebro, one of Spain's most important rivers.

▶ *Return by the same route to the N611. Turn left and drive south to Cervatos, just off the road.*

8 Cervatos, Santander
The major feature of interest in this small village is the 12th-century Romanesque Colegiata, notable for the carvings that adorn the frieze above the door. Look for the figures of the three monkeys shown covering their ears, eyes and mouth, signifying prudence and wisdom in the beliefs of eastern cultures.

▶ *Take the N611 north. At Torrelavega take the N634 east to Castro Urdiales.*

9 Castro Urdiales, Santander
This attractive little fishing port has been a popular summer resort for a long time,

and dates back to Roman times.

The Gothic Iglesia de Nuestra Señora de la Asunción features an impressive Puerta del Perdón. Visit also the Castillo of Santa Ana (now a lighthouse), the medieval fortress and the Roman bridge.

▷ *Take the coastal road* **N634** *west to Laredo.*

🔟 Laredo, Santander

The little town of Laredo lies to the east of the wide bay of Santoña. With its pleasant villas and splendid beach it is a popular seaside resort. The old part of the town is picturesque, with some handsome old buildings and cobbled streets. There are ruins of two former monasteries in Laredo, as well as a 13th-century church.

▷ *Continue west on the coastal road and turn right at Cicero for the 5km (3 miles) to Santoña.*

⓫ Santoña, Santander

To the west of the bay is the port of Santoña on a peninsula beneath a steep rock. The town was fortified in earlier times – Napoleon is said to have had plans to conquer it. The Romanesque Colegiata was built between the 12th and 13th centuries. About 2km (1¼ miles) away is the splendid beach of Berria.

▷ *Take the* **C629** *southwest to Gama and rejoin the* **N634** *back to Santander.*

Journey's end for these old fishing boats. Left: the Virgin del Mar ocean beach close to Santander

Exploring the
Basque Country

2 DAYS • 358KM • 222 MILES San Sebastián (Donostia in Basque) is the provincial capital of Guipúzcoa. The elegant buildings along the promenade are a reminder of the 19th century, when San Sebastián was Spain's most fashionable resort. The Alameda del Boulevard is a lively area of restaurants and shops, while to the west is the busy fishing harbour.

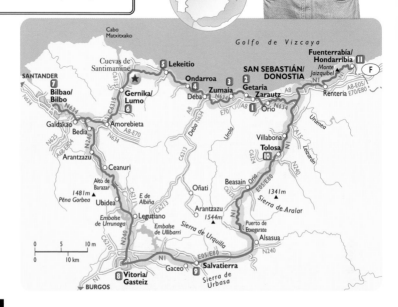

i *Paseo de los Fueros, 1-bajo*

▶ *From San Sebastián take the N1 south. Turn right on to the N634 to Zarautz, 26km (16 miles).*

❶ Zarautz, Guipúzcoa

You may like to make a quick stop en route in the picturesque little fishing port of Orio, which lies along the bank of an estuary.

The old harbour at Zarautz (Zarauz in Basque) is backed by the tall Monte de Santa Barbara. It has a splendid beach and is a popular summer resort. Places of major interest are the Gothic/baroque Iglesia de Santa María, the Iglesia de San

The lovely horseshoe-shaped beach at fashionable San Sebastián is popular with the Spanish

Francisco and the hermitages of San Pelayo and San Pedro. The Torre Lucea and the 15th-century Palacio del Marqués de Narros are also impressive. Zarautz was once an important shipyard. It was here that the *Victoria* was built, between 1519 and 1522, to carry Juan Sebastián Elcano, companion of Magellan, around the world.

i *Nafarroa, 26*

▶ *Continue on the N634 for 4km (2 miles) to Getaria.*

2 Getaria, Guipúzocoa
There is some magnificent scenery as you approach Getaria and a fine view down over the pretty little fishing village which stands on a promontory. The Gothic parish church of San Salvador overlooks the harbour, and has underground tunnels linking the two. Over the breakwater is the little fortified Isla San Anton (known as the 'Ratón de Getaria', mouse of Getaria, for reasons unknown), which rises up steeply to a lighthouse. It offers a rewarding view of the area. The Ayuntamiento contains frescoes describing the voyage around the world of the navigator, Juan Sebastián Elcano, who was born here.

▶ *Continue west for 6km (4 miles) to Zumaia (Zumaya).*

3 Zumaia, Guipúzcoa
Nestling at the foot of the Monte Santa Clara hill is Zumaia, another delightful little resort with a charming harbour and attractive houses. The Villa Zuloaga, formerly a monastery, is now a museum founded by the great painter Ignacio Zuloaga, and has a superb collection of paintings by Spain's most famous painters including Zuloaga, El Greco and Goya.

▶ *Follow the N634 and continue along the coastal road to Ondarroa.*

4 Ondarroa, Vizcaya
You are now in the neighbouring province of Vizcaya. The resort of Ondarroa is set in a bay that is protected by low hills. The town encompasses a combination of attractive old cottages and more modern blocks. It has a sandy beach and a pleasant harbour with lively fishermen's quarters. A Roman bridge, the Puente Romano, spans the river.

▶ *Continue on the coast road northwest for 12km (7 miles) to Lekeitio (Lequeitio).*

5 Lekeitio, Vizcaya
Lekeitio is another popular seaside resort of attractive houses and a good beach, which separates the resort area from the fishing port. The 16th-century Iglesia de Santa María is a fine example of Vizcayan Gothic architecture. Narrow cobbled streets lead down to the old part of town. The palaces of Abaróa and Uribarren are particularly elegant buildings.

▶ *Take the 6212 west for 23km (14 miles) to Gernika-Lumo.*

6 Gernika-Lumo, Vizcaya
The famous painting, *Guernica*, by Pablo Picasso is a reminder of the terrible event that took place here in 1937 during the Spanish Civil War, when German aircraft bombed the town, killing a large number of people. The town was devastated, but has been rebuilt in the traditional style. Originally displayed in the Museum of Modern Art in New York, Picasso's painting was returned to Spain and now hangs in the Centro de Arte Reina Sofía, in Madrid, together with all the preliminary sketches.

The Casa de Juntas (Assembly Hall) contains an interesting library and archives. The Sala de Juntas (Council Chamber) is the venue of the

General Assembly of officials of the provinces of Biscay. It also serves as a chapel, which is known by the rather grand title of 'la Iglesia Juradera de Santa María de la Antigua'. Near by is a monument commemorating the 1937 attack on the town.

Some 5km (3 miles) north the Cueva de Santimamine wall paintings, believed to date back some 13,000 years, were discovered in 1917.

ℹ *Artekale, 8*

▶ *Take the 6315 south and join the N634 west to Bilbao (Bilbo).*

FOR CHILDREN

Children might enjoy a trip on the funicular railway Finicular de Artxanda. This departs from Plaza Finicular and ascends to the village of La Reinata, Monte Archanda, which offers a sweeping view of Bilbao's old dockyards. Many horse-riding excursions into the countryside are available, catering for adults and children. Contact the tourist office in Bilbao for information on the various riding centres to be found in the region.

The rivers of the Basque country end in picturesque harbours like this one at Ondarroa

Two other museums are also worth a visit; the Museo Arqueológico Etnográfico e Histórico Vasco, for its collection of tombs, arms and carvings, and, over in the new town, the Museo de Bellas Artes, which features works by famous Dutch and Spanish painters of the 15th and 16th centuries.

You can also enjoy a stroll through Bilbao's lively old quarter (Casco Viejo) where the attractively arcaded square (Plaza Nueva) and the Gothic Catedral de Santiago feature among its attractions.

> ⓘ *Paseo del Arenal, 1*

> ▶ *Return east along the N634 and take the N240 southeast for 66km (41 miles) to Vitoria.*

8 **Vitoria-Gasteiz,** Alava
Vitoria is the capital of Alava, and of the Basque Country, as well as being the seat of a bishop. A focal point of the old town is the Plaza de la Virgen Blanca, which is surrounded by houses and balconies typical of Vitoria. In the centre is an

7 **Bilbao (Bilbo),** Vizcaya
Bilbao is the capital of the Basque province of Vizcaya and its largest port. Although essentially an industrial town, Bilbao is now home to an outstanding attraction, the Guggenheim Museum. The museum houses an important collection of 20th-century European and American art, including works by Matisse, Brancusi, Modigliani, Picasso, Ernst, Miró and Dalí. Attention is also drawn to the spectacular design of the complex itself, a brilliant creation of gleaming shapes and forms by the American architect Frank Gehry.

RECOMMENDED WALKS

Many areas all over the region offer splendid walks, and information is available from the local tourist offices.
In Bilbao a short walk is a climb up the hill from behind the church of San Nicolás de Bari, which brings you to the Gothic-style Begoña Basilica. It was built in 1588 and is the place of worship of Begoña, the patron saint of Bilbao. A colourful *romería* is held here on 15 August.

SPECIAL TO...

The national sport of the Basque country is *pelota* (also known as jai-alai). There are variations, but basically it is a type of ballgame played between four men in a court called a *frontón*, using scoop rackets and a small, hard ball which travels at tremendous speed. The sport is supposed to be the fastest in the world. Each town and village has a court and a team.
The Basque country has its own folklore, including the unusual *aurresku*, a war-like dance, and the *ezpata dantza*, a sword dance, accompanied by flutes and a drum.

imposing monument commemorating Wellington's victory over the French at the battle of Vitoria in 1813. Overlooking the square is the 14th-century Iglesia de San Miguel. A stone image of the Virgen Blanca (White Virgin), patron saint of the city, can be seen in a niche on the outside portal. Inside is a fine 17th-century altarpiece by Juan de Velázquez and Gregorio Hernández. The Catedral de Santa María was built between the 14th and 15th centuries in the shape of a Latin cross and is noted for its richly decorated triple-arched tympanums. An impressive *Assumption* can be seen in one of the side chapels. Look out also for a bullfighting scene carved on one of the pillar's capitals.

In the Plaza Santo Domingo near by is the Museo de Arqueología (Archaeological Museum), which displays objects from the Celtiberian and Roman times, among other items. The 14th-century parish church of San Pedro features a fine doorway and impressive sculpted tombs of the Alava family. From the middle of the 15th century, Vitoria was a centre for craftsmen who worked predominantly in the wool and iron trades. The Portalon, built in wood and

BACK TO NATURE

There is an area of great natural beauty in the province of Alava, north of Vitoria, around three artificial lakes. Embalse de Urrunaga (Lake Santa Engracia) is situated along the road from Bilbao to Vitoria. On the slopes of the mountain are the Cuevas de Mairelegorreta, which are well worth a visit. Embalse de Albiña (Lake Albina), east of the N240, lies at the entrance to the Aramayona valley. Further south is Embalse de Ullívari (Lake Ullívari), which stores water in the Gamboa canyon. The lake offers watersports and fishing.

brick, is a remaining example of one of the many trading houses of the medieval and Renaissance times. Other attractive areas are the Plaza del Machete and the Cuchillería (street of cutlery), where you will find the 16th-century Casa del Cordón, noted for its fine Gothic ceiling, and the Bedaña Palace, a 16th-century mansion with a magnificent façade. The new cathedral of María Immaculada, which was consecrated in 1969, has been built in a rather unusual neo-Gothic style.

The industrial town of Tolosa is set amongst the Basque hills

ℹ️ *Parque de la Florida s/n*

▶ *Take the NI to Salvatierra.*

9 **Salvatierra,** Alava
The little town of Salvatierra was founded by Alfonso X in 1256. It still preserves its medieval streets and parts of the old defensive walls. Its two main churches, those of San Juan and Santa María, have a somewhat fortress-like appearance.

▶ *Follow the **N1** east and then north to Tolosa.*

🔟 Tolosa, Guipúzcoa
Tolosa was capital of the province of Guipúzcoa for a period in the middle of the 19th century and is now a thriving industrial town (known for the *boinas*, or Basque beret). There are Roman antiquities and ancient buildings of the Templars.

▶ *Continue on the **N1** north, bypassing the centre of San Sebastián, and then east. Turn off north for Fuenterrabía.*

⓫ Fuenterrabía/Hondarribia, Guipúzcoa
This little town was a stronghold over a long period of time and consequently the scene of many battles. It is now a popular seaside resort. The remains of its ancient walls are preserved as a national monument and the 12th-century Palacio del Rey Carlos V (now a *parador*) was built as a defence against pirate raids.

There are some lovely views from these ancient walls. Other buildings worth taking a look at are the 16th-century Iglesia de Santa María (mainly Gothic with Renaissance influences), and the 17th-century Ayuntamiento.

A short drive up to the ridge of Monte Jaizquíbel leads to the Santuario de Nuestra Señora de Guadalupe which offers fine views.

▶ *Rejoin the **N1** back to San Sebastián, 25km (16 miles).*

ACCIDENTS
Road users involved in an accident should mark the presence of their vehicle and try to move it to the hard shoulder or lay-by. The police should be contacted if the accident has resulted in serious casualties. SOS telephone posts are normally available on motorways only. Other roads are patrolled by traffic police. You are advised to obtain a Bail Bond from your insurer (see below). See also **warning triangles**.

BAIL BONDS
An accident in Spain can result in the impounding of car and property, and a Bail Bond is advisable. It provides a written guarantee that a cash deposit, usually of up to £1,500 will be paid to the Spanish court as surety for bail and for any fine which may be imposed. However, the Bail Bond is not insurance cover as such, insofar as the insurers must be reimbursed. Bail Bonds are usually available from vehicle insurers.

BREAKDOWNS
If your car breaks down try to move it to the side of the road, or to a position where it will obstruct the traffic flow as little as possible.

Switch on your hazard warning lights and place a warning triangle at the appropriate distance on the road behind. Bear in mind the prevailing road conditions and, if near or on a bend, the triangle should be placed where it is clearly visible to following traffic.

See also **warning triangles**.

CAR HIRE
If you are not taking your own car, you can make arrangements to hire before departure. Many package holidays include car hire as an option. The main car hire companies are represented in Spain.

MOTORING IN SPAIN

CHILDREN
Children under the age of 12 are not permitted to travel as front-seat passengers unless using a suitable restraint system. *Note* under no circumstances should a rear-facing restraint be used in a seat with an airbag.

CRASH (SAFETY) HELMETS
Crash helmets are compulsory for motorcyclists.

DIMENSIONS AND WEIGHT RESTRICTIONS
Private cars and towed trailers or caravans are restricted to the following dimensions: height – 4m; width to 2.5m; length – 12m. The maximum permitted overall length of private vehicle/trailer or caravan combination is 12m. Trailers with an unladen weight in excess of 750kg must have an independent braking system.

DOCUMENTS
Licences issued by European Union countries are acceptable (for UK and Republic of Ireland driver's licences should be of the pink EU-type). Visitors from other countries should have an international driving licence, which should be obtainable from the motoring organisations in their home countries.

The minimum age at which visitors from the UK or Republic of Ireland may use a temporarily imported motorcycle (over 75cc) or car is 18. The holder of an older all green UK licence (in Northern Ireland any licence issued before 1 April, 1991) should consider exchanging it for a new style licence if time allows to avoid any local difficulties. Alternatively these older

licences may be accompanied by an International Driving Permit (IDP).

Note The licence of a Spanish driver who needs glasses to drive is endorsed accordingly. Such drivers must carry a spare pair of glasses in their vehicle. It is strongly recommended that visiting motorists should do the same to avoid any misunderstanding with the local authorities.

You also require the vehicle's registration document, plus a letter of authorisation from the owner, if not accompanying the vehicle, and the current insurance certificate (a green card, obtainable from your insurance company, is recommended). You are required to display a nationality plate or sticker on the vehicle.

DRINKING AND DRIVING
The laws in Europe regarding drinking and driving are strict and the penalties are severe. The best advice is, as at home, if you drink don't drive.

DRIVING CONDITIONS
Driving is on the right. Tolls are charged on some of the motorways. The surfaces of the main roads vary, but are generally good. Secondary roads are often rough, winding and may be encumbered by slow horse-drawn traffic.

In the Basque area, local versions of place-names appear on signposts together with the national version. In winter snowfalls frequently close many of the roads across the Pyrenees.

FUEL
You will find comparable grades of petrol in Spain, with familiar brand names along the main routes. It is wise to keep the tank topped up, particularly in remote areas.

Remember when calculating mileage per litre (gallon)

that the extra weight of a caravan or roof rack increases the petrol consumption. It is best to use a locking filler cap.

INSURANCE

Comprehensive insurance, which covers you for some of the expenses incurred after a breakdown or an accident, is advisable. See also **Bail Bonds**.

LIGHTS

Full headlights are prohibited in built-up areas. Motorcyclists must use dipped headlights during the day. A replacement set of bulbs is required.

MOTORING CLUB

The Real Automóvil Club de España (RACE), which has its headquarters at Calle José Abascal 10, 28003 Madrid tel: 915 94 74 00, fax: 915 94 72 49, is associated with local clubs in a number of provincial towns. The office hours of the RACE in Madrid are 8.30–5.30 Monday–Thursday and 8.30–2.30 Friday during the summer (15 June–15 September) and for the rest of the year 8.30–5.30 Monday–Friday.

POLICE

There are three different police organisations in Spain dealing with different aspects of public order.

Policía Municipal whose main responsibility is urban traffic, are the local police. They are identifiable by their blue uniforms and white checked bands on their vehicles. Policía Nacional, who wear grey uniforms and berets, deal with law and order and national security. Crimes should be reported to the police station (*comisaría*). Guardia Civil, who are responsible for border posts, policing country areas and the coast and highway patrols, wear olive green uniforms.

There are also special Basque police in the Basque country, recognisable by their red berets.

ROADS

The surfaces of the main roads vary, but on the whole are good. The roads are winding in many places, and at times it is not advisable to exceed 30–35mph. Secondary roads are often rough and you can come across some unexpected bad patches. Look out for the sign '*carretera en mal estado*' ('road in poor condition'). In the Basque and Catalan areas some place-names appear on signposts in both the local and the national versions.

Spain has a good network of motorways and dual carriageways. About half of these are toll roads (*autopistas*) and the rest are free (*autovías*).

Emergency telephones are located every 2km on all Spanish motorways and dual carriageways.

Unfamiliar Road Signs

Aduana Customs
Alto! Pare Stop
Calzada Deteriorada Bad road
Ceda el Paso Give way
Cuidado Caution
Curva Peligrosa Dangerous bend
Despacio Slow
Desviacion/Desvío Diversion
Direccion Unica One way
Entrada Entry
Estacionamiento de Automoviles Car-park
Estacionamiento Prohibido No parking
Obras Road works
Paso Prohibido No entry
Peatones Pedestrians
Peligro Danger
Salido Exit

ROUTE DIRECTIONS

The following abbreviations are used as prefixes to identify Spanish roads.
A for *Autopistas* and *Autovías*
C for *Comarcal*
N for *Nacional*

SEAT BELTS

Seat belts are compulsory for the driver and front passenger. Middle- and rear-seat passengers must use seat belts if the vehicle is fitted with them.

SPEED LIMITS

Built-up areas 50kph (31mph)
Other roads 90kph (55mph) or
Dual carriageways and roads with overtaking lanes 100kph (62mph)
Motorways 120kph (74mph)

TOLLS

Tolls are payable on many motorways (*autopistas*) in Spain. Tickets are issued on entry, and payment varies according to distance and type of vehicle.

WARNING TRIANGLES

In the event of accident or breakdown, the use of two warning triangles is compulsory for vehicles over 3,500kg (3 tons, 8cwt, 100lb) and passenger vehicles with more than nine seats (including the driver's). These must be placed on the road 30m (33 yards) in front of and behind the vehicle and be visible from at least 100m (110 yards). It is strongly recommended that all vehicles (except those with two-wheels) carry triangles to avoid any misunderstandings with the local authorities.

ACCOMMODATION & RESTAURANTS

On the following pages is a selection of hotels (⊞) which can be found along the routes of each tour, along with suggestions for restaurants (❙❙❙) where you can take a break.

Hotel Prices

The hotels listed are grouped into three price categories based on a nightly rate for a double room with breakfast:
€ up to €60
€€ €60–120
€€€ over €120

Restaurant Prices

The restaurants are also in three price categories, based on a three-course meal with house wine, for one person. Some are located in the hotels listed:
€ up to €12
€€ €12–30
€€€ over €30
Unless otherwise stated, restaurants are open daily for lunch and dinner.

TOUR 1
BARCELONA, Barcelona
🏨 **Astoria €€€**
París 203, 08036 Barcelona
(tel: 932 09 83 11).
🏨 **Claris €€€**
Carrer de Pau Claris 150, 08009
Barcelona (tel: 934 87 62 62).
🏨 **Continental €**
Rambla de Canaletes 138, 08002
Barcelona (tel: 933 01 25 70).
🏨 **Oriente €€**
Ramblas 45, 08002 Barcelona
(tel: 933 02 25 58).
🍴 **Agut d'Avignon €€€**
Trinitat 3, Barcelona (tel: 933
02 60 34).
🍴 **Los Caracoles €€**
Escudellers 14, Barcelona
(tel: 933 02 31 85).

MONTSERRAT, Barcelona
🏨 **Abat Cisneros €€**
Plaça del Monestir, 08691
Montserrat (tel: 938 77 77 01).

CARDONA, Barcelona
🏨 **Parador de Cardona €€**
Castell de Cardona s/n, 08261
Cardona (tel: 938 69 12 75).
Also 🍴 **€€**.

TOUR 2
BARCELONA, Barcelona
🏨 **Mesón de Castilla €€**
Valldonzella 5, 08002 Barcelona
(tel: 933 18 21 82).
🏨 **San Agustín €€**
Plaça de San Agustín 3,
08001 Barcelona (933 18
16 58).
🍴 **Els Quatre Gats €€**
Montsió 3-bis, Barcelona (tel:
933 02 41 40). Closed Aug.
🍴 **La Lubina €€**
Viladomat 257, Barcelona
(tel: 934 30 03 33). Closed Sun
dinner & Aug.

TOSSA DE MAR,
Girona/Gerona
🏨 **Diana €**
Plaça de Espanya 6, 17320
Tossa de Mar (tel: 972 34 18 86).
🏨 **Pensión Cap d'Or €**
Passeig de Vila Vella 1, 17320
Tossa de Mar (tel: 972 34 00 81).

GIRONA, Girona/Gerona
🍴 **Condal €**
Joan Maragall 10, 17002 Girona
(tel: 972 20 44 62).

🏨 **Peninsular €**
Carrer Nou 3, 17001 Girona
(tel: 972 20 38 00).
🍴 **Llegendes €€**
Riera Can Camaret 3, Pont
Major, Girona (tel: 972 22 07 09).

TOUR 3
BARCELONA, Barcelona
🏨 **Turin €€**
Carrer Pintor Fortuny 9–11, 08
001 Barcelona (tel: 933 02 48 12).
🍴 **7 Portes €€**
Passeig Isabel II 14, Barcelona
(tel: 933 19 30 33).

SITGES, Barcelona
🏨 **El Cid €**
Sant Josep 39 bis, 08870 Sitges
(tel: 938 94 18 42).
🏨 **Sitges Park Hotel €**
Carrer Jesús 16, 08870 Sitges
(tel: 938 94 02 50).
🍴 **Fragata €€**
Passeig de la Ribera 1, Sitges
(tel: 938 94 10 86).

TARRAGONA, Tarragona
🏨 **Astari €€**
Via Augusta 95, 43003
Tarragona (tel: 977 23 69 00).
🏨 **Núria €**
Via Augusta 217, 43007
Tarragona (tel: 977 23 50 11).
🍴 **Merlot €€**
Cavallers 6, Tarragona (tel: 977
22 06 52).

TOUR 4
VALENCIA, Valencia
🏨 **Bisbal €**
Pie de la Cruz 9, 46001 Valencia
(tel: 963 91 70 84).
🏨 **Sorolla €**
Convento Santa Clara 5, 46002
Valencia (tel: 963 52 33 92).
🍴 **El Gourmet €€**
Marti 3, Valencia (tel: 963 95 25
09). Closed Sun, Holy Week, &
Aug.

BENIDORM, Alicante
🏨 **Canfali €€**
Plaza de San Jaime 5, 03500
Benidorm (tel: 965 85 08 18).
No credit cards.
🏨 **Cimbel €€**
Europa 1, 03500 Benidorm
(tel: 965 85 21 00).
🍴 **El Pulpo Pirata €**
Tomás Ortuño s/n, Benidorm
(tel: 966 80 32 19).

The view from a look-out point
near Ronda (see Tour 9)

TOUR 5
ALICANTE, Alicante
🏨 **Meliá Alicante €€€**
Playa del Postiguet s/n, 03002
Alicante (tel: 965 20 50 00).
🏨 **Sol Inn Alicante €€€**
Gravina 9, 03002, Alicante
(tel: 965 21 07 00).
🍴 **La Goleta €€**
Esplanada de España 8,
Alicante (tel: 965 20 03 38).

ELCHE O ELX,
Alicante
🏨 **Huerto del Cura €€**
Porta de la Morera 14, 03203
Elche (tel: 966 61 00 11)
🍴 **Mesón el Granaíno €€**
Josep Ma Bucch 40, Elche
(tel: 966 66 40 80). Closed Sun
& middle 2 weeks of Aug.

MURCIA, Murcia
🏨 **Hotel Residencia Hispano
2 €**
Calle Radio Murcia 3 (tel: 968
21 61 52).

Pensión Hispano I €
Trapería 8, 30001 Murcia
(tel: 968 21 61 52).

La Onda €€
Bando de la Huerta 8, Murcia
(tel: 968 24 78 82). Closed Sun.

TOUR 6
PALMA, Mallorca
Meliá Victoria €€€
Avenida Joan Miró 21, 07014
Palma (tel: 971 73 25 42).

Palacio Ca Sa Galesa €€€
Miramar 8, 07001 Palma (tel:
971 71 54 00).

San Lorenzo €€
Carrer Sant Lorenc 14, 07012
Palma (tel: 971 72 82 00).

Casa Eduardo €€
Travessia Pesquera 4, Palma
(tel: 971 72 11 82).

La Lubina €€
Muella Viejo, Palma (tel: 971
72 33 50).

DEIÀ, Mallorca
Costa d'Or €€
Lluch Alcari s/n, 07179 Deià
(tel: 971 63 90 25). Closed
Nov–Apr.

PORT DE POLLENÇA,
Mallorca
Sis Pins €€
Avinguda Anglada Camarasa
77, 07470 Port de Pollença
(tel: 971 53 40 13).

Lonja del Pescado €€
Muelle Viejo, Port de Pollença
(tel: 971 86 65 04).

TOUR 7
ALMERIA, Jaén
Torreluz II €€
Plaza Flores 3, 04001 Almeria
(tel: 950 23 43 99). Also €.

ÚBEDA, Jaén
Hotel la Paz €
Calle Andalucía 1, 23400
Úbeda (tel: 953 75 21 46).

Parador de Úbeda €€€
Plaza Vázquez Molina 1, 23400
Úbeda (tel: 953 75 03 45) Also
€€.

TOUR 8
MÁLAGA, Málaga
Los Naranjos €€
Paseo de Sancha 3, 29016
Málaga (tel: 952 22 43 19).

**Parador de Málaga-
Gibralfaro €€€**
Castillo de Gibralfaro, 29016
Málaga (tel: 952 22 19 02).

El Chinitas €€
Moreno Monoy 4, Málaga
(tel: 952 21 09 72).

NERJA, Málaga
Balcón de Europa €€
Paseo Balcón de Europa 1,
29780 Nerja (tel: 952 52
08 00).

Parador de Nerja €€€
Almuñecar 8, 29780 Nerja
(tel: 952 52 00 50).

Casa Luque €€
Plaza Cavana 2, Nerja (tel: 952
52 10 04).

GRANADA, Granada
Alhambra Palace €€€
Peña Partida 2, 18009 Granada
(tel: 958 22 14 68).

Dauro II €€
Navas 5, 18009 Granada
(tel: 958 22 15 81).

Macía Plaza €
Plaza Nueva 4, 18010 Granada
(tel: 958 22 75 36).

¶¶ Sevilla €€
Oficios 12, Granada (tel: 958 22 12 23). Closed Mon & Sun eve.

TOUR 9
MÁLAGA, Málaga
🏨 Don Curro €€
Sancha de Lara 7, Málaga (tel: 952 22 43 19).
¶¶ Antonio Martín €€
Plaza de la Malagueta, Málaga (tel: 952 22 73 98).

TORREMOLINOS, Málaga
🏨 Hotel Cervantes €€€
Las Mercedes s/n, 29620 Torremolinos (tel: 952 38 40 33).
🏨 Miami €
Aladino 14, 29620 Torremolinos (tel: 952 38 52 55).
¶¶ El Bodegón €€
Cauce 4, Torremolinos (tel: 952 38 20 12).

MIJAS, Málaga
🏨 Mijas €€
Urbanización Tamisa 2, 29650 Mijas (tel: 952 48 58 00).
¶¶ El Mirlo Blanco €€
Plaza de la Constitución 2, Mijas (tel: 952 48 57 00).

MARBELLA, Málaga
🏨 Andalucia Plaza €€€
Apartado 21, Nueva Andalucia, 29600 Nueva Andalucia, Marbella (tel: 952 81 20 00).
🏨 El Rodeo €
Victor de la Serna s/n, 29600 Marbella (tel: 952 77 51 00).
🏨 Hostal El Castillo €
Plaza San Bernabé 2, 29600 Marbella (tel: 952 77 17 39).
¶¶ Gran Plaza €€€
Plaza de los Naranjos, Marbella (tel: 952 82 48 60).

PUERTO BANÚS, Málaga
🏨 Pyr Marbella €€€
Puerto Banús (tel: 952 81 73 53).
¶¶ Antonio €€€
Muelle Rivera, Puerto Banús (tel: 952 81 35 36).
¶¶ Caracola Del Puerto €€
Muelle Benabola 5, Puerto Banús (tel: 952 81 16 84). Closed Tue.

RONDA, Málaga
🏨 Hotel Don Miguel €€
Villanueva 8, 29400 Ronda (tel: 952 87 77 22).

🏨 Parador de Ronda €€€
Plaza de España, 29400 Ronda (tel: 952 87 75 00).
🏨 Reina Victoria €
Paseo Dr. Fleming 25, 29400 Ronda (tel: 952 87 12 40).

TOUR 10
SEVILLA, Sevilla
🏨 Bécquer €€
Calle Reyes Católicos 4, 41001 Sevilla (tel: 954 22 89 00).
🏨 Hostal Goya €
Mateus Gago 31, 41004 Sevilla (tel: 954 21 11 70).
🏨 Hotel Amadeus €€
Calle Farnesio 6, 41004 Sevilla (tel: 954 50 14 43).
¶¶ Doña Elvira €€
Plaza de Doña Elvira 6, Sevilla (tel: 954 21 54 83).

CARMONA, Sevilla
🏨 Parador de Carmona €€€
41410 Carmona (tel: 954 14 10 10).

CÓRDOBA, Córdoba
🏨 Hotel Conquistador €€€
Magistral González Francés 15–17, 14003 Córdoba (tel: 957 48 11 02).
🏨 Mezquita €€
Plaza Santa Catalina 1, 14003 Córdoba (tel: 957 47 58 85).
¶¶ El Churrasco €€/€€€
Romero 16, Córdoba (tel: 957 29 08 19).

TOUR 11
SEVILLA, Sevilla
🏨 Hostería del Laurel €€
Plaza de los Venerables 5, 41004 Sevilla (tel: 954 22 02 95).
🏨 Residencia Murillo €
Calle Lope de Rueda 7–9, 41001 Sevilla (tel: 954 21 60 95).

HUELVA, Huelva
🏨 Los Condes €€
Alameda Sundheim 14, 21003 Huelva (tel: 959 28 24 00).
¶¶ Portichuelo €
Gran Vía 1, Huelva (tel: 959 24 57 68). Closed Sun in summer; Sun dinner rest of year.

TOUR 12
SEVILLA, Sevilla
🏨 América €€
Jesús del Gran Poder, 2, 41002 Sevilla (tel: 954 22 09 51).

¶¶ Casa Robles €€/€€€
Calle Alvarez Quintero 58, Sevilla (tel: 954 56 32 72).

ARCOS DE LA FRONTERA, Cádiz
🏨 Parador de Arcos de la Frontera €€
Plaza del Cabildo, 11630 Arcos de la Frontera (tel: 956 70 05 00).

JEREZ DE LA FRONTERA, Cádiz
🏨 Ávila €
Calle Ávila 3, 11140 Jerez de la Frontera (tel: 956 33 48 08).
🏨 Montecastillo €€€
Carrertera N-342, 11406 Jerez de la Frontera (tel: 956 15 12 00).
🏨 Serit €
Higueras 7, 11402 Jerez de la Frontera (tel: 956 34 07 00).
¶¶ Gaitán €€€
Gaitán 3, Jerez de la Frontera (tel: 956 34 58 59). Closed Sun in summer; Sun dinner rest of year.

TOUR 13
ZARAGOZA, Zaragoza
🏨 Ramiro I €€
Coso 123, 50001 Zaragoza (tel: 976 29 82 00).
🏨 Rey Alfonso I €€
Calle Coso 17–19, 50003 Zaragoza (tel: 976 39 48 50).
¶¶ La Bastilla €€
Coso 177, Zaragoza (tel: 976 29 84 49). Closed Sun & Holy Week.

CALATAYUD, Zaragoza
🏨 Calatayud €
Autovia de Aragón Salida, Km 237, 50300 Calatayud (tel: 976 88 13 23).
¶¶ Bílbilis €€
Madre Puy 1, Calatayud (tel: 976 88 39 55).

TOUR 14
HUESCA, Huesca
🏨 Pedro I de Aragón €€
Avenida del Parque 34, Huesca (tel: 974 22 03 00).
🏨 San Marcos €
San Orencio 10, 22001, Huesca (tel: 974 22 29 31).
¶¶ El Molinero €€
San Orencio 10, Huesca (tel: 974 23 07 31).

JACA, Huesca
🏨 **Hotel Conde Aznar €€**
Paseo Constitución 3, 22700,
Jaca (tel: 974 36 10 50). Also 🍴
€€. Closed Wed, except winter.

TOUR 15
PAMPLONA, Navarra
🏨 **Hotel Residencia La Perla €**
Plaza del Castillo 1, 31001
Pamplona (tel: 948 22 15 19).
🏨 **Residencia Eslava €€**
Plaza Virgen de la O 7, or Calle
Recoletas 20, 31001 Pamplona
(tel: 948 22 22 70).
🍴 **Erburu €**
San Lorenzo 19–21, Pamplona
(tel: 948 22 51 69). Closed Mon
& second half Jul.

OLITE, Navarra
🏨 **Parador de Olite €€**
Plaza de los Teobaldos 2, 31390
Olite (tel: 948 74 00 00).

TUDELA, Navarra
🏨 **Morase €**
Paseo de Invierno 2, 31500
Tudela (tel: 948 82 17 00).
🏨 **Tudela €**
Avenida Zaragoza 60, 31500
Tudela (tel: 948 41 08 02).

TARAZONA, Zaragoza
🏨 **Brujas de Bécquer €**
Carretera Zaragoza s/n 30,
50500 Tarazona (tel: 976 64
04 04).

LOGROÑO, La Rioja
🏨 **Hotel Residencia La Numantia €**
Calle Sagasta 4, 26001 Logroño
(tel: 941 25 14 11).
🏨 **Murrieta €€**
Marqués de Murrieta 1,
26005 Logroño (tel: 941 22
41 50).
🍴 **Cachetero €€**
Laurel 3, Logroño (tel: 941 22
84 63).

TOUR 16
MADRID, Madrid
🏨 **Anaco €€**
Tres Cruces 3, 28013 Madrid
(tel: 915 22 46 04).
🏨 **Hostal Nuevo Gaos €**
Calle Mesonero Romanos 14,
28013 Madrid (tel: 915 32
71 07).

🏨 **Hotel Inglés €**
Echegaray 8, 28014 Madrid
(tel: 914 29 65 51).
🍴 **Botín €€**
Cuchilleros 17, Madrid (tel: 913
66 42 17).

TOLEDO, Toledo
🏨 **Hostal del Cardenal €€**
Paseo de Recaredo 24, 45003
Toledo (tel: 925 22 49 00).
🏨 **Maravilla €**
Plaza de Barrio Rey 7, 45001
Toledo (tel: 925 22 83 17).
🏨 **Maria Cristina €€**
Marqués de Mendigorría 1,
45003 Toledo (tel: 925 21
32 02).
🏨 **Residencia Imperio €**
Calle de las Cadenas 5, 45001
Toledo (tel: 925 22 76 50).
🍴 **Hierbabuena €**
Callejón de San José 17,
Toledo (tel: 925 22 39 24).
Closed Sun evening.

ARANJUEZ, Madrid
🏨 **Hotel Castilla €**
Carretera Andalucia 98, 28300
Aranjuez (tel: 918 91 26 27).

CHINCHÓN, Madrid
🏨 **Parador de Chinchón €€**
Avenida Generalísimo 1,
Chinchón, 28370 Madrid
(tel: 918 94 08 36). Open
summer only.

TOUR 17
MADRID, Madrid
🏨 **Hostal la Macarena €**
Cava de San Miguel 8, 28005
Madrid (tel: 913 65 92 21).
🏨 **Hostal la Perla Asturiana €**
Plaza de Santa Cruz 3, 28012
Madrid (tel: 913 66 46 00).
🏨 **Hostal Residencia Americano €**
Puerta del Sol 11, 28013
Madrid (tel: 915 22 28 22).
No credit cards.
🍴 **Café de Oriente €€**
Plaza de Oriente 2, Madrid
(tel: 915 41 39 74).

CUENCA, Cuenca
🏨 **Hotel Residencia Avenida €**
Avenida Carretería 39, 16002
Cuenca (tel: 969 21 43 43).

🏨 **Hotel Residencia Figón de Pedro €**
Calle Cervantes 17, 16004
Cuenca (tel: 969 22 45 11).
🏨 **Parador de Cuenca €€€**
Convento de San Pablo, Paseo
de la Hoz del Huécar, 16001
Cuenca (tel: 969 23 23 20). Also
🍴 €€/€€€.

TOUR 18
MADRID, Madrid
🏨 **Francisco I €€**
Arenal 15, 28013 Madrid
(tel: 915 48 02 04).
🏨 **Paris €€**
Alcalá 2, 28014 Madrid
(tel: 915 21 6496).
🏨 **Tryp Reina Victoria €€€**
Plaza de Santa Ana 14, 28012
Madrid (tel: 915 31 45 00).
🍴 **Las Cueves de Luis Candelas €€**
Cuchilleros 1, Madrid (tel: 913
66 54 28).

EL ESCORIAL, Madrid
🏨 **Hostal Cristina €**
Juan de Toledo 6, 28200 San
Lorenzo de El Escorial (tel: 918
90 19 61).
🏨 **Miranda Suizo €€**
Calle Floridablanca 18, 28200
San Lorenzo de El Escorial
(tel: 918 90 47 11).

ÁVILA, Ávila
🏨 **Hostería Bracamonte €€**
Bracamonte 6, 05001 Ávila
(tel: 920 25 12 80).
🏨 **Parador de Ávila €€€**
Marqués Canales de Chozas 2,
05001 Ávila (tel: 920 21 13 40).

TOUR 19
MADRID, Madrid
🏨 **Liabeny €€€**
Salud 3, 28013 Madrid (tel: 915
31 90 00).
🏨 **Residencia Lisboa €**
Ventura de la Vega, 17, 28014
Madrid (tel: 914 29 98 94).
🍴 **Casa Paco €**
Puerta Cerrada 11, Madrid (tel:
913 66 31 66). Closed Sun, Aug.

SEGOVIA, Segovia
🏨 **Los Arcos €€**
Paseo de Ezequiel González
26, 40002 Segovia (tel: 800
528 1234 in the US, or 921 43
74 62).

🏨 **Los Linajes €€**
Dr. Velasco 9, 40003 Segovia
(tel: 921 46 04 75).

🏨 **Parador de Segovia €€€**
Carretera Valladolid, La
Lastrilla s/n, 40003 Segovia
(tel: 921 44 37 37).

🍽 **Casa Duque €€/€€€**
Cervantes 12, Segovia (tel: 921
46 24 87).

TOUR 20
CÁCERES, Cáceres
🏨 **Extremadura €€**
Avenida Virgen de Guadalupe 5,
10001 Cáceres (tel: 927 22
16 04).

🏨 **Meliá Cáceres €€€**
Plaza San Juan 11, 10003
Cáceres (tel: 927 21 58 00).

🏨 **Parador de Cáceres
€€€**
Calle Ancha 6, 10003 Cáceres
(tel: 927 21 17 59). Also 🍽 **€€**.

TRUJILLO, Cáceres
🏨 **Las Cigüeñas €€**
Avenida de Madrid s/n,
Carretera N-V, 10200 Trujillo
(tel: 927 32 12 50).

🏨 **Parador de Trujillo €€€**
Calle de Santa Beatriz de Silva,
10200 Trujillo (tel: 927 32
13 50). Also 🍽 **€€**.

GUADALUPE, Cáceres
🏨 **Hospedería Real
Monasterio €**
Plaza Juan Carlos 1, 10140
Guadalupe (tel: 927 36 70 00).

🏨 **Parador de Guadalupe
€€€**
Marqués de la Romana 12,
10140 Guadalupe (tel: 927 36
70 75). Also 🍽 **€€**.

MÉRIDA, Badajoz
🏨 **Nova Roma €€**
Suárez Somonte 42, 06800
Mérida (tel: 924 31 12 61).

🏨 **Parador de Mérida €€**
Plaza de la Constitución 3,
06800 Mérida (tel: 924 31
38 00). Also 🍽 **€€**.

🏨 **Tryp Medea €€€**
Avenida de Portugal s/n, 06900
Mérida (tel: 924 37 24 00).

BADAJOZ, Badajoz
🏨 **Barcelo Zurbarán €€€**
Paseo Castelar s/n, 06001
Badajoz (tel: 924 22 37 41).

🏨 **Lisboa €€**
Avenida díaz Ambrona 13,
06006 Badajoz (tel: 924 22 37
41).

🏨 **Río €€**
Avenida Adolfo Díaz Ambrona
13, 06006 Badajoz (tel: 924 27
26 00).

TOUR 21
SALAMANCA, Salamanca
🏨 **Gran Hotel €€€**
Plaza Poeta Iglesias 5, 37002
Salamanca (tel: 923 21 35 00).

🏨 **Hotel las Torres €€**
Plaza Mayor 26 (at the intersec-
tion of Calle Concejo), 37002
Salamanca (tel: 923 21
21 00).

🏨 **Monterrey €€€**
Azafranal 21, 37001 Salamanca
(tel: 923 21 44 00).

🏨 **Parador de Salamanca
€€€**
Teso de la Feria 2, 37008
Salamanca (tel: 923 19 20 82).
Also 🍽 **€€**.

ZAMORA, Zamora
🏨 **Hostal Chiqui €**
Benavente 2, 49002 Zamora
(tel: 980 53 14 80). No credit
cards.

🏨 **Hostería Real de
Zamora €**
Cuesta de Pizarro 7, 49027
Zamora (tel: 980 53 45 45).

🏨 **Parador de Zamora
€€€** Plaza de Viriato 5, 49001
Zamora (tel: 980 51 44 97).
Also 🍽 **€€/€€€**.

VALLADOLID, Valladolid
🏨 **Felipe IV €€**
Calle de Gamazo 16, 47004
Valladolid (tel: 983 30 70 00).

🏨 **Hotel Residencia
Enara €**
Plaza de España 5, 47001
Valladolid (tel: 983 30
02 11).

🏨 **Olid Meliá €€€**
Plaza San Miguel 10, 47003
Valladolid (tel: 983 35 72 00).

🏨 **Parque €€€**
Joaquin Garcia Morato 17,
47007 Valladolid (tel: 983 22
00 00).

🍽 **Mesón La Fragua €€**
Paseo de Zorilla, Valladolid
(tel: 983 33 87 85). Closed Sun
dinner & Aug.

BURGOS, Burgos
🏨 **España €**
Paseo de Espolón 32, 09003
Burgos (tel: 947 20 63 40).
Closed 20 Dec–20 Jan.

🏨 **Mesón del Cid €€€**
Plaza Santa María 8, 09003
Burgos (tel: 947 20 87 15).

🏨 **Norte y Londres €€**
Plaza de Alonso Martínez 10,
09003 Burgos (tel: 947 26
41 25).

🍽 **Casa Ojeda €€/€€€**
Calle Vitoria 5, Burgos (tel: 947
20 90 52).

TOUR 22
A CORUÑA, La Coruña
🏨 **España €**
Juana de Vega 7, 15004 La
Coruña (tel: 981 22 45 06).

🏨 **Finisterre €**
Paseo del Parrote 2, 15001 A
Coruña (tel: 981 20 54 00).

🏨 **Residencia Riazor €**
Barrie de la Maza 29, 15004 La
Coruña (tel: 981 25 34 00).

🍽 **El Coral €€**
Callejón de la Estacada 9, A
Coruña (tel: 981 20 05 69).

LUGO, Lugo
🏨 **Gran Hotel Lugo €€€**
Avenida Ramón Ferreiro 21,
27002 Lugo (tel: 982 22 41 52).

🏨 **Méndez Núñez €**
Reiña 1, 27002 Lugo (tel: 982
23 07 11).

PONTEVEDRA, Pontevedra
🏨 **Parador de Pontevedra
€€€**
Barón 19, 36002 Pontevedra
(tel: 986 85 58 00). Also 🍽
€€/€€€.

🏨 **Rías Bajas €€**
Daniel de la Sota 7, 36001
Pontevedra (tel: 986 85 51 00).

🏨 **Virgen del Camino €**
Virgen del Camino 55, 36001
Pontevedra (tel: 986 85 59 04).

**SANTIAGO DE
COMPOSTELA,** A Coruña
🏨 **Gelmírez €**
Hórreo 92, 15702 Santiago de
Compostela (tel: 981 56 11 00).

🏨 **Hostal Residencia
Alameda €**
San Clemente 32, 15705
Santiago de Compostela (tel:
981 58 81 00).

The magnificent Alcázar (Citadel) stands guard over Toledo

🏨 Parador Hostal de los Reyes Católicos €€€
Placa do Obradoiro 1, 15705 Santiago de Compostela (tel: 981 58 22 00).

🏨 Universal €€
Plaza de Galicia, 2, 15706 Santiago de Compostela (tel: 981 58 58 00).

🍽 Don Gaiferos €€
Rua Nova 23, Santiago de Compostela (tel: 981 58 38 94). Closed Sun.

TOUR 23
OVIEDO, Asturias
🏨 De La Reconquista €€€
Gil de Jaz 16, 33004, Oviedo (tel: 985 24 11 00).

🏨 La Gruta €€
Alto de Buenavista, s/n, 33006 Oviedo (tel: 985 23 24 50).

🍽 El Raitán €
Plaza de Trascorrales 6, Oviedo (tel: 985 21 42 18). Closed Sun evening.

LEÓN, León
🏨 Guzmán El Bueno €
López Castrillón 6, 24003 León (tel: 987 23 64 12). No credit cards.

GIJÓN, Asturias
🏨 Begoña €€
Carretera de la Costa 44, 33205 Gijon (tel: 985 14 72 11).

🏨 Hernán Cortés €€€
Fernández Vallín 5, 33205 Gijón (tel: 985 34 60 00).

🏨 Parador de Gijón €€€
Parque de Isabel la Católica, 33203 Gijón (tel: 985 37 05 11).

🍽 El Puerto €
Claudio Alvargonzaález, Gijón (tel: 985 35 13 37). Closed Sun evening & Holy Week.

TOUR 24
SANTANDER, Santander
🏨 Ciudad de Santander €€€
Menéndez Pelayo 13–15, 390-06 Santander (tel: 942 22 79 65).

🏨 México €€
Calderón de la Barca 3, 39002 Santander (tel: 942 21 24 50).

🍽 Zacarîas €€
General Mola 41, Santander (tel: 942 21 23 33).

SANTILLANA DEL MAR, Santander
🏨 Parador de Santillana €€€
Plaza de Ramón Pelayo 8, 39330 Santillana de Mar (tel: 942 81 80 00).

LAREDO, Santander
🏨 Risco €€
La Arenosa 2, 39770 Laredo (tel: 942 60 50 30).

TOUR 25
SAN SEBASTIÁN, Guipúzcoa
🏨 Londres y de Inglaterra €€€
Zubieta 2, 200007 San Sebastián (tel: 943 44 07 70).

🏨 Monte Igueldo €€
Paseo del Faro 134, Monte Igueldo, 20008 San Sebastián (tel: 943 21 02 11).

🏨 Niza €€
Zubieta 56, 20007 San Sebastian (tel: 943 42 66 63).

🍽 Juanito Kojua €€
Portu 14, San Sebastían (tel: 943 42 01 80).

BILBAO, Vizcaya
🏨 Barcelo Hotel Avenida €€
Zumalacárregui 40, 48007 Bilbao (tel: 944 12 43 00).

🏨 Carlton €€€
Plaza Federico Moyua 2, 48009 Bilbao (tel: 944 16 22 00).

🏨 Ercilla €€€
Ercilla 37–39, 48011 Bilbao (tel: 944 70 57 00).

🍽 Casa Vasca €€
Avenida Lehendakari Aguirre 13, Bilbao (tel: 944 48 39 80).

VITORIA-GASTEIZ, Alava
🏨 Parador Argómanix €€€
Carretera N-1, Km 363 (15km from Vitoria), 01192 Vitoria (tel: 945 29 32 00).

FUENTERRRABÍA/ HONDARRIBIA, Guipúzcoa
🏨 Jauregui €€
Zuloaga 5, 20280 Fuenterrabía (tel: 943 64 14 00).

🏨 Parador de Hondarribia €€€
Plaza de Armas 14, 20280 Fuenterrabía (tel: 943 64 55 00).

Practical information

[i] Tourist Information Office
[12] Number on tour

TOUR 1

[i] Plaça de Catalunya 17–S, Barcelona. Tel: 933 04 31 35 or 906 30 12 82.

[i] Avenida Valls d'Andorra 33. La Seu d'Urgell. Tel: 973 35 15 11.

[i] Querol 1, Puigcerdá. Tel: 972 88 05 42.

[i] Plaça de l'Ajuntament 3, Ribes de Freser. Tel: 972 72 72 28.

[i] Plaça Abat Oliba, Ripoll. Tel: 972 70 23 51.

[i] Plaça de lAbadia 9, Sant Joan de les Abadesses. Tel: 972 72 05 99.

[i] Plaça d'Espanya 1, Camprodón. Tel: 972 74 00 10.

[i] Lorenzana 15, Olot. Tel: 972 26 01 41.

[i] Ciutat 4, Vic. Tel: 938 86 20 91.

1 Montserrat
Monestir de Montserrat
Sierra de Montserrat.
Tel: 938 35 02 51 (Basílica).
Open daily 7am–7.45pm (closes 8.15pm Sat, Sun).

2 Cardona
Colegiata de Sant Vincenc
Castillo de Cardona.
Tel: 938 68 41 69.
Open Tue–Sat 10–1, 3–5.30 (6.30 Jul–Sep), Sun 10–1.30.

3 Solsona
Museu Diocesano y Comarcal
Palau Episcopa, Solsona.
Tel: 937 48 21 01.
Open Tue–Sat 10–1, 4–6 (10–1, 4.30–7 May–Sep), Sun 10–2.

4 La Seu d'Urgell
Museu Diocesà
Plaça del Degenat, La Seu de Urgell. Tel: 937 26 86 28.
Open Jun–Sep, Mon–Sat 10–1, 4–7, Sun 10–1; Oct–May Mon–Fri noon–1, 4–6. Sat, Sun 11–1.

7 Ripoll
Antiguo Monestir de Santa Maria
Ripoll.
Tel: 972 70 02 43.
Open daily 8–1, 3–8; cloisters open daily 10–1, 3–7.

8 Sant Joan de les Abadesses
Sant Joan de les Abadesses
Tel tourist office:
972 72 05 99.
Open Mar–Apr & Oct, daily 10–2, 4–6; May–Jun & Sep 10–2, 4–7; Jul–Aug 10–7; Nov–Feb 10–2 (also 4–6 Sat, Sun)

10 Olot
Museu Comarcal de la Garrotxa
Carrer Hospici, 8, Olot.
Tel tourist office:
972 26 01 41.
Open Mon–Sat 11–2 ,6–8.

Jardí Botànic i Casal dels Volcans
Avinguda Santa Coloma de Farners, Olot.
Tel: 972 26 62 02.
Open daily in winter 10–2, 5–6 (7 in summer).

11 Vic
Museu Episcopal
Adjoining cathedral.
Tel: 938 86 22 14.
Open daily 10–1 (mid-May–mid-Oct, Mon–Sat 10–1, 4–6).

Back to nature
Parc Natural del Cadi-Moixeró
Information Centre.
Tel: 938 24 41 51.

TOUR 2

[i] Plaça de Catalunya 17–S, Barcelona. Tel: 933 04 31 35 or 906 30 12 82.

[i] Plaça Catalunya s/n, Blanes. Tel: 972 33 03 48.

[i] Avenida del Pelegrí 25, Edif Terminal, Tossa de Mar. Tel: 972 34 01 08.

[i] Plaça Monestir 54, Sant Felio de Guíxols. Tel: 972 82 00 51.

[i] Passeig del Mar s/n, Palamós. Tel: 972 60 05 00.

[i] Carrilet 2, Palafrugell. Tel: 972 30 02 28.

[i] Aigüeta 17, La Bisbal d'Empordà. Tel: 972 64 25 93.

[i] Rambla de la Llibertat 1, Girona. Tel: 972 22 65 75.

[i] Plaça del Sol, Figueres. Tel: 972 50 31 55.

[i] Plaça de la Llibertat 1, Besalú. Tel: 972 59 12 40.

[i] Passeig Industria 25, Banyoles. Tel: 972 57 55 73.

5 Tossa de Mar
Museu de la Vila Vela
Plaça Roig y Soler 1.
Open Jun–Sep, Tue–Sun 10–7; Oct–May 10–1, 3–6.

6 Girona
Museu d'Art
Tel: 972 20 38 34.
Open Mon–Sat 10–6 (to 7pm Mar–Sep), Sun 10–2.

Banys Àrabs
Tel: 972 21 32 62.
Open Mon–Sat 10–2 (to 7pm Apr–Sep), Sun 10–2.

9 Empúries
The Site
Tel: 972 77 02 08.
Open daily 10–6 (to 8pm Apr–Sep).

10 Figueres
Museu de l'Empordà
Rambla 1.
Tel: 972 50 23 05.
Open Tue–Sat 11–1, 3–7, Sun 11–1.30; Jun–mid-Sep 10–1, 3–7, Sun 3–7.

Teatre–Museu Dalí
Plaça Gala i Salvador Dali.
Tel: 972 51 18 00.
Open 10.30–5.15; Jul–Sep 9–7.15 (Aug also 10pm–0.15am). Closed Mon except Jul–Sep.

11 Besalú
Monestir de Sant Pere
El Prat de Sant Pere.
For opening times enquire at Tourist Office.

12 Banyoles
Museu Arqueològic Comarcal
Plaxa de la Font, Banyoles.
Open Tue–Sat: Jul–Aug, 11–1.30, 4–8; Sep–Jun, 10.30–1.30, 4–6.30; Sun 10.30–2.

Back to nature
Jardí Botànic Mar i Murtra
Blanes.
Tel: 972 33 08 26
Open Jun–Sep, daily 8–8; Oct–May 9–6.

For children
Water World
Carretera de Vidreres, km 1.2, Lloret de Mar.
Tel: 972 36 86 13.
Open 15 May–30 Sep 10am to sunset.

Back to nature
Jardí Botànic Cap Roig
Castell Cap Roig. Calella de Palafrugell.
Tel: 972 61 45 82.
Open summer, daily 8am–9pm (to 6pm in winter).

For children
Museu de Joguets
La Rambla, Figueres.
Tel: 972 50 45 85.
Open Jul–Sep, Mon–Sat 10–1, 4–7, Sun 11–1.30, 5–7.30; Oct–Jun closed Tue.

TOUR 3

[i] Plaça de Catalunya 17–S, Barcelona. Tel: 933 04 31 35 or 906 30 12 82.

[i] Sínia Morera 1, Sitges. Tel: 938 94 42 51.

[i] Passeig del Carme (Parc de Ribes Roges), Vilanova i la Geltrú. Tel: 938 15 45 17.

[i] Fortuny 4, Bajos, Tarragona. Tel: 977 23 34 15.

[i] Plaça del Bimil, Tortosa. Tel: 977 51 08 22.

[i] Major 31 bis, Lleida (Lérida). Tel: 973 70 03 19.

1 Sitges
Museu Cau Ferrat
Carrer del Fonollar, Sitges.
Tel: 938 94 03 64.
Open Apr–Sep, Tue–Fri

9.30–2, 4–6, Sat 9.30–8,
Sun 11–2, 5–7; Oct–Mar,
Sat, Sun noon–2, 4.30–6.

[2] Vilanova i la Geltrú
Museu Romàntic Can
Papiol
Calle Major 32, Vilanova
y la Geltrú.
Open Tue–Sat 10–2, 4–6,
Sun 10–2.

Biblioteca Museu Balaguer
Vilanova i la Geltrú. Tel
tourist office: 938 15 45 17.
Open Tue–Sat 10–1.30,
4.30–7 (closes 8.30pm
Wed), Sun 10–1.30.

[4] Tarragona
Museu Nacional
Arqueològic
Plaça del Rei, 5, Tarragona.
Tel: 977 23 62 09.
Open Tue–Sat 10–1.30,
4–7; mid-Jun–mid-Sep
10.30–2, 4–7, Sun 10–2.

Museu y Necrópolis
Paleocristina
Paseo de la Independencia,
15, Tarragona.
Tel: 977 21 11 75.
Open Tue–Sat 10–1.30,
4–7; mid-Jun–mid-Sep
10.30–2, 4–7, Sun 10–2.

[8] Lleida
Museu Arquelògic
Avenida del Blondel, Lleida.
Tel tourist office:
973 70 03 19.
Open Tue–Sat noon–2, 6–9.

[9] Monestir de Poblet
Plaça Corona d'Aragó,
Poblet.
Tel: 977 87 02 54.
Guided tours 10–12.30,
3–5.30; Mar–Oct
10–12.30, 3–6.

[11] Monestir Santes Creus
Santes Creus.
Tel: 077 63 83 29.
Open Tue–Sat 10–1.30,
3–6 (to 7pm Jun–Sep).

Special to...
Museu del Vi (Wine
Museum)
Plaça Jaume 1, Vilafranca
del Penedès.
Tel tourist office:
93 892 03 58.
Open Tue–Sat 10–2, 4–7,
Sun 10–2; summer 9–9.

For children
Port Aventura
Autovía Salou/Vila–Seca,
Km 2.
Tel: 977 77 90 90.
Open Mon–Fri 10–7, Sat,
Sun 10–8. (late Jun–mid-
Sep, daily 10am–midnight)

Back to nature
Parc Natural del Delta de
l'Ebre.
Information Centre
Tel: 977 48 96 79.

TOUR 4

[i] Calle de la Paz, 48,
Valencia. Tel: 963 99 64 22.

[i] Plaza Cronista Chabret,
Sagunto. Tel: 962 66 22 13.

[i] Carrer del Riu, 38,
Cullera. Tel: 961 72 09 74.

[i] Avenida Marqués del
Campo s/n, Gandía. Tel: 962
87 77 88.

[i] Plaza Oculista Buiges, 9,
Dénia. Tel: 966 42 23 67.

[i] Plaza Almirante
Bastarreche, 11, Jávea
(Xàbia). Tel: 965 79 07 36.

[i] Avenida Ejércitos
Españoles, 66, Calpe/Calp.
Tel: 965 83 69 20.

[i] Martínez Alejos, 16,
Benidorm. Tel: 965 85 32
24.

[i] Ayuntamiento, Alcoy
(Alcoi). Tel: 965 54 52 11.

[i] Alameda Jaume 1–50,
Xátiva. Tel: 962 27 33 46.

[1] Sagunto
Teatro Romano
Sagunto. Tel: 962 66 22 13.
Open Tue–Sat 10–2, 4–6,
Sun 10–2.

[4] Gandía
Palacio de los Duques
Signposted from the
centre, Gandía.
Tel: 962 87 12 03.
Guided tour Sat 11am;
Oct–Mar, Mon–Fri 11am,
5pm; Apr–Sep 11am, 6pm.

[6] Xàbia (Jávea)
Lighthouse
Cabo de San Antonio
Tel tourist office:
965 79 07 36.

---

[10] Alcoy o Alcoi
Museu Arqueológico
Placeta del Carbó, s/n,
Alcoy. Tel: 965 54 03 02.
Opening times. Enquire at
local tourist office.

[11] Xátiva
Museo Municipal
Uphill from the Almeda
Jaume 1, Xátiva.
Tel: 962 27 65 97.
Open weekends 10–2,
Tue–Fri 10–2 , 4–6;
mid-Jun–mid-Sep, Tue–Fri
9.30–2.30.

Back to nature
L'Albufera
Visitors Centre Tel: 961
62 73 45.

For children
Safari Park Vergel
Between Ondarra and
Oliva.
Tel: 965 75 02 85.
Open daily 11–7.

For children
Terra Mítica
Camino al Moralet, s/n
Tel: 902 02 02 20.
Open daily 10–6 (closes
8pm mid-Mar–mid-Jun;
midnight mid-Jun–mid-Sep).

TOUR 5

[i] Rambla Méndez
Núñez 23, Alicante. Tel: 965
20 00 00.

[i] Parque Municipal,
Paseo de la Estación, Elche
(Elx). Tel: 965 45 27 47.

[i] Francisco Díaz 25,
Orihuela. Tel: 965 30 27 47.

[i] San Cristóbal, 6,
Murcia. Tel: 968 36 61 30.

[i] Lope Gisbert, 12
(Palacio Guevara), Lorca.
Tel: 968 46 61 57.

[i] Avenida Doctor Meca,
47, Mazarrón. Tel: 968 59
44 26.

[i] Plaza Bastarrache s/n,
Cartagena. Tel: 968 50
64 83.

[1] Elche (Elx)
Museo Arqueológico
Tel: 965 45 36 03.
Open Tue–Sat 10–1, 4–7,
Sun 10–1.

Huerta del Cura
Tel: 965 45 19 36.
Open daily 9–6 (to 8.30pm
May–Sep).

[3] Murcia
Museo Salzillo
Plaza San Agustín, Murcia.
Tel: 968 29 18 93.
Open Tue–Sat 9.30–1, 3–6
(to 7pm Apr–Sep), Sun
11–1. (Jul–Aug closed Sat &
Sun, but open Mon.)

[4] Alhama de Murcia
Museu de Tradiciones y
Artes Populares de la
Región de Murcia
Alcantarilla. Tel: 968 80
03 40.
Open summer, Tue–Sun
10–8; winter 10.30–6.

For history buffs
Santuario de la Fuensanta
Tel tourist office:
968 36 61 30.

Back to nature
Parque Natural de Sierra
Espuña.
Tel tourist office:
968 36 61 30.

TOUR 6

[i] Plaça de la Reina, 2,
Palma. Tel: 971 71 22 16.

[i] Canonge Oliver 10,
Port de Sóller. Tel: 971 63
30 42.

[2] Valldemossa
Reial Cartuoxa de
Valldemossa.
Tel: 971 61 21 06.
Open Mon–Sat 9.30–1,
3–6.30 (closes 6pm Mar &
Oct; 5.30pm Nov–Feb).

[5] Monestir de Lluc
Monestir de Lluc.
Tel: 971 87 15 25
Open daily 10–5.30.

[8] Coves d'Artà.
Tel: 971 56 32 93.
Guided tours daily 10–5;
Jul–Sep 10–7 (last visit of
the day 30 minutes before
closing time).

[9] Manacor
Museo Arqueológico
Torre dels Enegistes, Ctra.
Cales de Mallorca, s/n.
Tel: 971 84 30 65.
Open Tue, Wed, Thu 9–1.

[11] Coves del Drac
Tel: 971 82 16 17.
*Guided tours daily
10.45–4.30; Apr–Oct 10–5.*

Castell de Bellver
West of Avinguda Joan
Miró, Palma.
Tel: 971 73 06 57.
*Open daily 8–6 (to 8pm
Apr–Sep).*

For children
Marineland
Costa d'en Blanes, Calvià.
Tel: 971 67 51 25.
*Open Apr–Sep, daily
9.30–6; Oct–Mar 9.30–5.*

Aquapark
Carretera Cala
Figuera–Magaluf.
Tel: 971 13 08 11.
*Open May–Oct, daily 10–5
(to 6pm Jun–Sep).*

Wester Park
Carretera Cala-Figuera-Sa
Porrassa, 12–22, Magaluf.
Tel: 971 13 16 27
Open May–Oct, daily 10–6.

Aquacity Park
Autovía Palma–El Arenal,
Km .15.
Tel: 971 44 00 00.
*Open May–Sep daily 10–5;
Oct, Sun–Fri 10–5.*

Acuario de Mallorca
Near the Coves del Drac.
Tel: 971 82 09 71.
*Open Apr–Oct daily
10.30–5; Nov–Mar 11–3.*

Autosafari Park
Carretera Portocristo–Son
Servera, Km.5.
Tel: 971 81 09 09.
*Open daily 9–5 (to 7pm
Apr–Sep).*

For history buffs
Museu and Casa Junípero
Serra
Carrer de Junípero Serra,
Petra.
Tel: 971 56 11 49.
Open daily 9–8.

Back to nature
Parc Natural Mondragó
Santinyi.
Tel: 971 18 10 22.
*Open summer daily 9–1,
2–5; winter Mon–Fri
8.30–1.30, Sat, Sun 10–1.*

TOUR 7

[i] Parque de Nicolás
Salmerón Esq Martínez
Campos, Almeria. Tel: 950
27 43 55.

[i] Plaza Nueva s/n,
Mojácar. Tel: 950 47 51 62.

[i] Juan Domingo 2.
Cazorla. Tel: 953 72 01 15.

[i] Avenida Mariana
Pineda s/n, Guadix. Tel: 958
66 26 65.

[6] Vélez Blanco
Cueva de los Letreros.
Vélez Blanco. Tel: 950 41
50 01.
*Visits by arrrangement with
town hall (Ayuntamiento).*

Back to nature
Parque Natural de Cabo
de Gata-Nijar.
Tel Information Centre:
950 25 12 52.

Back to nature
Parque Natural de
Cazorla.
Carretera del Tranco, Km
18. Torre de Vinagre Visitor
Centre. Tel: 953 72 01 02.

TOUR 8

[i] Pasaje de Chinitas, 4,
Málaga. Tel: 952 21 34 45.

[i] Puerta del Mar, 2,
Nerja. Tel: 952 52 15 31.

[i] Avenida Europa
Palacete La Najarra, Almuñecar Tel: 958 63 11 25

[i] Plaza de Mariana
Pineda, 10, Granada.
Tel: 958 22 66 88.

[i] Plaza San Sebastian 7,
Antequera. Tel: 952 70
25 05.

[2] Nerja
Cuevas de Nerja
4km east. Tel: 952 52 95 20.
*Open daily summer 10–2,
4–8; winter 10–2, 4–6.30.*

[6] Granada
Alhambra and Generalife
Tel: 958 22 15 03.
*Open Apr–Sep, Mon–Sat
8.30–8; Sun 9–6 ; floodlit
visit Tue, Thu, Sat 10–
11.30pm; Oct–Mar, daily
9–6, floodlit Sat 8–10pm.*

Museo de Bellas Artes
Palacio Carlos V. Tel: 958
22 48 43.
*Open Tue 2.30–6, Wed–Sat
9–6. Sun 9–2.30 (closes
8pm Apr–Sep, except Sun).*

Museo Hispano–
Musulmán
Casa Real de la Alhambra.
Tel: 958 22 62 79.
Open Tue–Sat 9–2.30.

Museo Arqueológico
Provincial
Carrer del Darro 41. Tel:
952 22 56 40.
*Open Tue–Fri 9.30–2, Sat,
Sun 10–2.*

[8] Antequera
Los Dólmenes (Dolmen
Caves)
1km east of Antequera.
Tel: 952 70 25 05.
*Open Tue–Fri 10–2, 3–5,
Sat, Sun 10–2.*

For children
Parque Acuático Aquavelis
Urb. el Tomillar-Carr. Vélez.
Tel: 952 54 25 92.
Open daily 10–6.

For history buffs
Museo Federico García
Lorca
Fuente Vaqueros. Tel: 958
51 64 53.
*Open Tue–Sun 10–1, 6–8
(5–7pm Apr–Jun; 4–6pm
Oct–Mar).*

Back to nature
Parque Nacional El Torcal
1.5km south of Antequera.
Tel: 952 03 13 89
*Open 10–2, 4–6 (3–5
winter).*

TOUR 9

[i] Pasaje de Chinitas 4,
Málaga. Tel: 952 21 34 45.

[i] Plaza Blas Infante, 1,
Torremolinos. Tel: 952 37
95 12.

[i] Antonio Machado, 12.
Benalmádena. Tel: 952 44
24 94.

[i] Plaza de la Virgen,
Mijas. Tel: 952 48 59 00.

[i] Avenida Jesús Santos
Rein, 6, Fuengirola. Tel: 952
46 76 25.

[i] Plaza de la Fontanilla,
Marbella. Tel: 952 77 14 42.

[i] Plaza de España, 1,
Ronda. Tel: 952 87 12 72.

For history buffs
Cueva de la Pileta
20km southwest of Ronda.
Tel: 952 16 73 43.
*Guided tours daily 10–1,
4–5 and by arrangement.*

Special to...
Museo Taurino
Calle Virgen de la Paz,
Ronda. Tel: 952 87 41 32.
*Open daily 10–6 (to 8pm in
summer). Closed day of bull-
fight and day before.*

For children
Tivoli World
Carretera de Benalmá-
dena, Arroyo de la Miel.
Tel: 952 57 70 16.
*Open Apr–Oct, daily 4pm–
1am (Jun–Aug 6pm–3am);
Nov–Mar, Sat, Sun 1–10pm.*

Sea Life Parque Submarino
Puerto Marina,
Benalmádena. Tel: 952 44
50 00.
Open daily 10–6.

Jardín de las Aguilas
Castilo de Aguilas,
Benalmádena Pueblo.
Tel: 952 56 82 39
*Open Tue–Sun. Perform-
ances subject to weather.*

Prado World
Carretera de Cádiz.
(Marbella–Estepona road).
Tel: 952 79 11 74.
*Open summer daily from
10am; winter weekends
from 11am.*

Aquapark
Carretera de Circun-
valación, Torremolinos.
Tel: 952 38 88 88.
Open May–Sep, daily 10–6.

TOUR 10

[i] Avenida de la
Constitución, 21B, Sevilla.
Tel: 954 22 14 04.

[i] Torrijos 10, Córdoba.
Tel: 957 47 12 35.

[i] Río s/n, Priego de
Córdoba. Tel: 957 70 06 25.

Practical information

Alcázar
Plaza del Triunfo, s/n, Sevilla.
Tel: 954 50 23 23.
*Open Tue–Sat 9.30–6, Sun
9.30–2.30.*

3 Córdoba
Mezquita–Catedral
Torrijos, s/n, Córdoba.
Tel: 957 47 105 12.
*Open Apr–Sep daily 10.30,
4–7; Oct–Mar 10.30–1.30,
3.30–5.30.*

Museo Arqueológico
Plaza Jerónimo Páez.
Tel: 957 47 40 11.
*Open Wed–Sat 9–8, Tue
3–8, Sun 9–3.*

Museo de Bellas Artes
Plaza del Potro.
Tel: 957 47 33 45.
*Open Wed–Sat 9–8, Tue
3–8, Sun 9–3.*

Museo Municipal Taurino
Plaza Maimónides, 5.
Tel: 957 20 10 56.
*Open Tue–Sat 10–2,
4.30–6.30, Sun 9.30–2.30.
Closed Mon.*

5 Priego de Córdoba
Museo Casa Natal de D
Niceto Alcalá Zamora
Río, 33, Priego de Córdoba.
Tel: 957 70 06 25.
Open Mon–Sat 10–1.

The charming village of Le Granja, Mallorca

9 Osuna
Museo Arqueológico
Torre del Agua, Osuna.
Tel: 954 81 04 44.
*Open daily, summer
10–1.30, 4.30–7.–7.30; winter
10–1.30, 3.30–6.30..*

For children
Parque Zoológico de
Hosé Cruz Conde
Avenida Linneo, Córdoba.
Tel: 957 29 37 59.
Ask locally for opening hours.

Guadalpark
Polígono Aeropuerto-
Sevilla-Este. Tel: 954 51 66
22. *Open May–Sep.*

Aquasierra
Villafranca de Córdoba.
Tel: 957 47 24 37.
Ask locally for opening hours.

TOUR 11

i Avenida de la
Constitución, 21B, Sevilla.
Tel: 954 22 14 04.

i Avenida de Alemania
12, Huelva. Tel: 959 25
74 03.

2 Itálica
Roman Ruins
9km northwest of Sevilla
on N630.
Tel: 955 99 73 76.

*Open Tue–Sat 9–5, Sun
10–4; Apr–Sep 9–9, Sun
9–3.*

5 Zalamea la Real
Mining Museum
Plaza del Museo, s/n, Mines
del Río Tinto (call Nerva
Turismo Tel: 959 59 00 25).
*Museum open 10–3 (closes
6 Sat, Sun).*

8 Huelva
Museo Provincial
Calle Alameda Sundheim
13, Huelva.
Tel: 959 25 93 00.
Open Tue–Sat 9–8; Sun 9–3.

9 Monasterio de la
Rábida
4km southwest of Palos de
la Frontera.
*Tel: 959 35 04 11.
Open daily, summer 10–1,
4.45–8; winter 10–1, 4–6.*

Back to nature
Parque Nacional de
Doñana
Reception and
Interpretation Centre.
Tel: 959 44 87 11.
Pre-booked guided tours only.

For children
Carabelas Quay
Huelva.
Tel: 959 53 05 97.
*Open Apr–Sep, Tue–Sun
10–7; Oct–Mar, Tue–Sun
10–5.*

TOUR 12

i Avenida de la
Constitución, 21B, Sevilla.
Tel: 954 22 14 04.

i Avenida Ramón de
Carranza, s/n, Cádiz. Tel:
956 25 86 46.

i Luna 22, El Puerto de
Santa María. Tel: 956 54 24
75.

i Calle Larga, 39, Jerez de
la Frontera. Tel: 956 33 11 50.

6 Cádiz
Museo de Cádiz
Plaza de la Mina s/n, Cádiz.
Tel: 956 21 22 81.
*Open Tue 2.30–8, Wed–Sat
9–8, Sun 9.30–2.30.*

Museo Históric Municipal
Calle Santa Inés, s/n, Cádiz.
Tel: 956 22 17 88.
*Closed for work in progress
at time of going to print.*

11 Jerez de la Frontera
Alcázar
South of the Plaza del
Arenal. Tel: 956 33 73 06.
*Open daily 10–6 (8pm in
summer*

For children
Real Escuela Andaluza de
Arte Ecuestre
Avenida Duqie de

Practical information

Abrantes, s/n, Jerez de la Frontera.
Tel: 956 31 11 11/956 31 80 08.
Guided tours including a visit to facilities and training sessions Mon, Wed, Fri 11–1. Weekly performances Thu at noon (also Tue Mar–Oct).

TOUR 13

ⓘ Torreón de la Zuda, Glorieta Pio XII, s/n, Zaragoza. Tel: 976 39 35 37.

ⓘ Plaza del Fuerte, Calatayud. Tel: 976 88 63 22.

ⓘ Plaza Mayor, Albarracín. Tel: 978 71 02 51.

ⓘ Tomás Nogués, 1, Teruel. Tel: 978 60 22 79.

ⓘ Calle Mayor, 1, Alcañiz. Tel: 978 83 12 13.

❷ Monasterio de Piedra
3.2km from Nuévalos.
Tel: 976 84 90 11.
Open daily 9–8 (to 5pm in winter).

History buffs
Casa–Museo de Goya
Fuendetodos.
Tel: 976 14 38 30.
Open Tue–Sun 11–2, 4–7.

Recommended walks
National Game Reserve
Montes Universales.
Tel tourist office:
978 71 02 51.

TOUR 14

ⓘ Plaza de la Catedral, Huesca. Tel: 974 29 21 70.

ⓘ Avenida Regimiento de Galicia, 2–local 1, Jaca. Tel: 974 36 00 98.

❶ Castillo de Loarre
Northeast of Ayerbe.
Tel: 947 38 26 27.
Open Apr–Sep, Wed–Sun 10–1.30, 4–7; Oct–Mar 11–2.30 (also open Mon, Tue in Aug).

❹ San Juan de la Peña
Monasterio
4km from Santa Cruz de los Seros.

Tel: 947 34 80 99.
Open mid-Mar–mid-Oct, Tue–Sun 10–1.30 (also 4–8pm Jun–Aug) mid-Oct–mid-Mar, Wed–Sun 11–2.30.

❺ Jaca
Museo Diocesano
Housed in the cathedral.
Tel: 974 35 51 30.
Open Tue–Sun 11–2. Closed Nov.

❻ Sabiñanigo
Museo Etnológico de Artes Populares
Sabiñanigo.
Tel tourist office: 974 36 00 98.
Enquire at Tourist Office for opening times.

❾ Parque Nacional de Ordesa y Monte Perdido
2km northeast of Brotó.
Visitors' centre.
Tel: 974 24 33 61.

TOUR 15

ⓘ Eslaba, , Pamplona. Tel: 948 20 65 40.

ⓘ Plaza de Carlos III el Noble, s/n, Olite. Tel: 948 74 17 03.

ⓘ Iglesias, 5, Tarazona. Tel: 976 64 00 74.

ⓘ Plaza Ramón y Cajal s/n, Soria. Tel: 975 21 20 52.

ⓘ Paseo de Espolón, s/n, Logroño. Tel: 941 29 12 60.

ⓘ San Nicolás, 1, Estella. Tel: 948 55 63 01.

❹ Olite
Castillo de los Reyes de Navarra
Tel: 948 74 00 35.
Open Oct–Apr 10–2, 3.30–5.30; May–Sep 10–2, 4–7 (8 Jul–Aug).

❽ Soria
Monasterio de San Juan de Duero
Soria (just outside centre)
Tel: 975 22 13 97.
Open Nov–Mar, Tue–Sat 10–2, 3.30–6; Apr–May and Sep–Oct 10–2, 4–7; Jun–Aug 10–2 and 5–9, Sun 10–2.

Ruinas de Numancia
8km north of Soria.
Tel: 975 21 20 52.
Open Nov–Mar, Tue–Sat 10–2, 3.30–6; Apr–May and Sep–Oct 10–2, 4–7; Jun–Aug 10–2, 5–9, Sun 10–2.

Special to...
The Sanfermines (Fiesta of San Fermín)
Held from 6–14 July annually.

TOUR 16

ⓘ Plaza Mayor, 3, Madrid. Tel: 915 88 16 36.

ⓘ Puerta de Bisagra s/n, Toledo. Tel: 925 22 08 43.

ⓘ Plaza San Antonio, 9, Aranjuez. Tel: 918 91 04 27.

❷ Toledo
Museo de Santa Cruz
Calle Miguel Cervantes, 3, Toledo.
Tel: 925 22 10 36.
Open Tue–Sat 10–6.30, Sun 10–2, Mon 10–2, 4–6.30.

Hospital de Tavera
Tel: 925 22 04 51.
Guided tours Tue– Sun 10.30–1.30, 3.30–6.

Casa y Museo de El Greco
Calle Samuel Leví 3, Toledo.
Tel: 925 22 40 46.
Open Tue–Sat 10–2, 4–6, Sun 10–2.

Alcázar
Calle General Moscardó, 4, Toledo.
Tel: 925 22 30 38.
Open Tue–Sun 10–1.30, 4–5.30 (to 6.30pm in summer).

❹ Aranjuez
Palacio Real
Plaza Parejas, Aranjuez.
Tel: 918 91 07 40.
Guided tours Apr–Sep 10–6.15; Oct–Mar, Tue–Sun 10–5.15.

Casa del Labrador
Guided tours Apr–Sep 10–6.15; Oct–Mar, Tue–Sun 10–5.15.

For children
Tren de las Fresas
Tel: 902 228 822.
Open Apr–Oct.

TOUR 17

ⓘ Plaza Mayor, 3, Madrid. Tel: 915 88 16 36.

ⓘ Callejón de Santa Maria, Alcalá de Henares. Tel: 918 89 26 94.

ⓘ Plaza de los Caídos, 6, Guadalajara. Tel: 949 21 16 26.

ⓘ Glorieta González Palencia, 2–3. Cuenca. Tel: 969 17 88 00.

❶ Alcalá de Henares
Museo Casa Natal de Cervantes
Calle Imagen, 2, Alcalá de Henares.
Tel: 918 89 96 54.
Open Tue–Sun 10.15–1.30, 4.15–6.30.

❷ Guadalajara
Palacio del Infantado
Plaza de los Caídos, 1, Guadalajara.
Tel: 949 21 33 01.
Open Tue–Sun 10.30–2 , 4.15–7; Jul–Aug 9–2.30, Sun 10.30–2.

❸ Sigüenza
Museo Diocesano de Arte Sacro
Adjacent to cathedral's west façade, Siguenza.
Tel: 949 39 10 23.
Open summer Tue–Sun 11.30–2 , 4–7.30; winter 4–6.

❺ Cuenca
Museo de Arte Abstracto Español
Casas Colgadas, Cuenca.
Tel: 969 21 29 83.
Open Tue–Fri 11–2, 4–6, Sat 11–2, 4–8, Sun 10–2.30.

❼ Belmonte
Castillo de Belmonte
Belmonte.
Tel: 967 17 00 08.
Open daily, summer 10–1, 4–8; winter 10–1, 3.30–6.

A bird's-eye view of the ancient hill town of Valldemossa

Practical information

ⓘ Tourist Information Office
🔢 Number on tour

9 Ruinas de Segóbriga
Ruinas de Segóbriga,
Saelices–Museum
Tel: 969 13 20 64.
Open Tue–Sun. Enquire for opening times.

10 Uclés
Monasterio de Uclés
Tel: 969 13 50 58.
Open daily 9.30–8.

Recommended walks
Serranía de Cuenca,
La Ciudad Encantada
35km north of Cuenca
Tel: 969 23 21 19.
Open daily 9am–sunset.

TOUR 18

ⓘ Plaza Mayor, 3, Madrid.
Tel: 915 88 16 36.

ⓘ Floridablanca, 10, El
Escorial. Tel: 918 90 15 54.

ⓘ Plaza de la Catedral, 4,
Ávila. Tel: 920 21 13 87.

ⓘ Paseo de Cervantes, 6,
Béjar. Tel: 923 40 30 05.

ⓘ Ronda del Cañillo,
Talavera de la Reina.
Tel: 925 82 63 22.

1 Valle de los Caídos
Valle de los Caídos.
Tel: 918 90 56 11.
Basílica and La Cruz open Tue–Sun 10–6 (Apr–Sep 9.30–7).

2 El Escorial
Monasterio de El Escorial.
Tel 919 80 59 02
Open Tue–Sun 10–5 (to 6pm Apr–Sep).

6 Béjar
Palacio Ducal
Béjar. Tel tourist office: 923 40 30 05.
For opening times contact Tourist Office.

8 Monasterio de Yuste
1.8km from Cuacos de Yuste. Tel: 927 17 21 30.
Open summer, daily 9.30–12.30, 3.30–6.30 (to 6pm in winter).

9 Talavera de la Reina
Museo Ruiz de Luna
Near Plaza de San Pedro,
Talavera de la Reina

Open Tue–Sat 10–2, 4–6.30, Sun 10–2.

For children
Safari Madrid
Aldea del Fresno, near
Navalcarnero (Madrid).
Tel: 918 62 23 14.
Open Mon–Fri 10.30–6, weekends 10.30–7.

TOUR 19

ⓘ Plaza Mayor 3, Madrid.
Tel: 915 88 16 36.

ⓘ Plaza Mayor 10,
Segovia. Tel: 921 46 03 34.

1 El Pardo
Palacio Real El Pardo
Tel: 913 76 15 00.
*Guided tours Mon–Sat 10–5, Sun 10–1.40;
Apr–Sep, Mon–Sat 10.30–6, Sun 9.25–1.40.*

3 Manzanares el Real
Castillo de los Mendoza
Manzanares el Real.
Tel tourist office: 918 53 00 09.
Open Tue–Sun 10–2, 4–7 (10–5 in winter).

5 El Paular
Monasterio de Santa
Maria de El Paular
El Paular. Tel: 918 69 14 25.
Guided tours Fri–Wed at noon, 1 & 5.

6 La Granja
Palacio
La Granja. Tel: 921 47 00 19.
*Open Jun–Sep, Tue–Sun 10–6; Oct–May, Tue–Sat 10–1.30, 3–5, Sun 10–2.
Guided tours.*

7 Segovia
Alcázar
Plaza del Alcázar
Tel: 921 46 07 59.
Open daily 10–6 (to 7pm Apr–Sep).

For children
Parque del Riofrío
10km south of Segovia.
Tel: 921 50 98 17 (Palacio de Riofrío).
Enquire locally for opening times.

TOUR 20

ⓘ Plaza Mayor, 10,
Cáceres. Tel: 927 24 63 47.

ⓘ Plaza Mayor s/n, Trujillo.
Tel: 927 32 26 77.

ⓘ Plaza Mayor s/n,
Guadalupe. Tel: 927 15 41 28.

ⓘ Avenida J Alvarez
Saenz de Buruaga s/n,
Mérida. Tel: 924 31 53 53.

ⓘ Plaza de la Libertad, 3,
Badajoz. Tel: 924 22 27 63.

1 Trujillo
Palacio de los Duques de
San Carlos
Plaza Mayor, Trujillo.
Tel tourist office:
927 32 26 77.
Open summer daily 9–1, 4.30–6.30; winter 9–1, 4–6.

Palacio de
Orellana–Pizarro
Plaza de Don Juan Tena
Tel: 927 32 11 62.
Open daily 10–2, 4–7.

2 Guadalupe
Monasterio de Guadalupe
Plaza de Guadalupe,
Tel: 927 36 70 00.
Guided tours daily 9.30–1, 3.30–8.45.

3 Mérida
Teatro Romano and
Anfiteatro
Mérida.
Tel: 924 31 20 24.
Open Oct–Mar, daily 9–1.45, 4–6; Apr–Sep 9–1.45, 5–7.

Museo de Arte Romano
Tel: 924 31 16 90.
Open Tue–Sat 10–2, 4–6; Jun–Sep 10–2, 5–7, Sun 10–2.

Alcazaba
Tel: 924 31 53 53.
Open Oct–Mar, daily 9–1.45, 4–6; Apr–Sep 9–1.45, 5–7.

4 Badajoz
Museo Arqueológico
Provincial
Plaza José Alvarez y Saenz
de Buruaga, Badajoz.
Tel: 924 22 23 14.
Open Tue–Sun 10–3.

Back to nature
Parque Natural de
Monfragüe
Tel: 927 45 51 04.

For children
Zoológico Almendralejo
261km south of Mérida.
Tel tourist office: 924 31 53 53.

TOUR 21

ⓘ Casa de las Conchas,
Rua Mayor, Salamanca.
Tel: 923 26 85 71.

ⓘ Calle Santa Clara, 20,
Zamora. Tel: 980 53 18 45.

ⓘ Santiago 19, bajo,
Valladolid. Tel: 983 35 18 01.

ⓘ Calle Mayor, 105,
Palencia. Tel: 979 74 00 68.

ⓘ Plaza Alonso Martínez,
7, Burgos. Tel: 947 20 31 25.

ⓘ La Sal, Aranda de
Duero. Tel: 947 51 04 75.

2 Zamora
Museo Catedrálico
Cathedral, Zamora.
Tel: 980 52 03 74.
Open Mon 4–6, Tue–Sat 9–2, 4–6 (5–8 Apr–Sep), Sun 9–2.

Museo de la Semana Santa
About 1km northeast of
old town, Zamora.
Tel: 980 53 22 95.
Open Mon–Sat 10–2, 4–7 (to 8pm in summer), Sun 10–2.

3 Valladolid
Museo Nacional de
Escultura Policromada
Colegio de San Gregorio,
calle Cadenas de San
Gregorio, Valladolid.
Tel: 983 25 03 75.
Open Tue–Sat 10–2, 4–6, Sun 10–2.

Museo Oriental
Paseo de Filipinos, 7,
Valladolid.
Tel: 983 30 68 00.
Open Mon–Sat 4–7, Sun 10–2.

4 Palencia
Museo
Cathedral Cloister, Plaza
Santa. Tel: 979 70 13 47.
Open Mon–Sat 10.30–1.30, 4–6 (7.30 Jul–Sep), Sun one visit at 11.15.

5 Burgos
Real Monasterio de las Huelgas
Calle Compás de Adentro, Burgos.
Tel: 947 20 16 30.
Guided tours Mon–Sat 11–1.15, 4–5.15 (5.45 Sat), Sun 10.30–2.15.

Cartuja de Miraflores
Carretera de San Pedro Cardeña, about 4km southeast of Burgos.
Tel tourist office: 947 20 31 25.
Open daily 10.15–3, 4–6.

9 Tordesillas
Real Monasterio de Santa Clara
Tordesillas.
Tel: 983 77 00 71.
Open Tue–Sat 10–1, 3.30–6.30 (Apr–Sep 10–1, 3.30–6.30); Sun 10.30–1.30, 3.30–5.30.

For history buffs
Casa de Cervantes
Calle del Rastro, s/n, Valladolid.
Tel: 983 30 88 10.
Guided tours Tue–Sat 9.30–3.30, Sun 10–3.

For children
Valwo Safari Park
Carretera Mojados a Matapozuelos, s/n. Tel: 983 83 27 59.
Open daily 11–dusk.

Back to nature
Monasterio de Santo Domingo de Silos
Tel: 947 39 00 68.
Open Tue–Sun 10–1, 4.30–6 (Mon 4.30–6).

TOUR 22

i Dársena de la Marina s/n, La Coruña.
Tel: 981 22 18 22.

i Plaza Constitución, Betanzos. Tel: 981 77 29 08.

i Plaza de España, Galería 27–29, Lugo.
Tel: 982 23 13 61.

i Curros Enríquez, 1, Orense. Tel: 988 37 21 20.

i Estación Marítima de Trasatlánticos s/n, Vigo.
Tel: 986 43 05 77.

i General Gutiérrez Mellado 1, Pontevedra.
Tel: 986 85 08 14.

i Rua del Villar, 43, Santiago de Compostela.
Tel: 981 58 40 81.

4 Orense
Museo Arqueológico y de Bellas Artes
Plaza Mayor. Tel: 988 22 38 84.
Open Tue–Sat 9.30–2.30, 5–9; Sun mornings only.

6 Pontevedra
Museo Provincial
Calle Pasantería, 10. Tel: 986 85 14 55.
Open Jun–Sep, Tue–Sat 10–2.15, 5–8.45; Oct–Mar, Tue–Sat 10–1.30, 4.30–8; Sun all year 11–1,

Back to nature
Parque de Ancares
Tel tourist office:
982 23 13 61.

For children
Parque Infantil 'La Selva'
Fernando III El Santo 33 Santiago de Compostela.
Tel: 981 59 77 22.
Open daily 4.30–9.15.

TOUR 23

i Plaza de Alfonso II El Casto, 6, Oviedo. Tel: 985 21 33 85.

i Plaza de Regla, 4, Léon.
Tel: 987 23 70 82.

i Plaza la Basílica, Covadonga. Tel: 985 84 60 35.

i Jardines del Ayuntamiento 2, Cangas de Onís. Tel: 985 84 80 05.

i Marqués de San Estéban, 1, Gijón. Tel: 985 34 60 46.

3 Potes
Monasterio de Santo Toribio de Liébana.
3km west of Potes.
Tel tourist office: 985 84 60 35.
Open daily 10–2, 4–8.

5 Covadonga
La Santa Cueva (Holy Cave

Tel tourist office: 985 84 60 35.
Open daily 8–8.

7 Gijón
Palacio de Revillagigedo
Plaza Marqués, Gijón.
Tel: 985 34 69 21.
Open Tue–Sat summer 11–1.30, 4–9; winter 10–1, 4–8; Sun all year noon–2.30.

Back to nature
Parque Nacional de los Picos de Europa
Tel: 985 84 91 54.

TOUR 24

i Plaza Porticada, 5, Santander. Tel: 942 31 07 08.

i Bajo Casas Aguila y Parra, Santillana de Mar.
Tel: 942 81 82 51.

2 Cuevas de Altamira
3km from Santillana del Mar.
For permission to visit the caves apply well in advance to the Centro de Investigación de Altamira, Santillana de Mar:
Tel: 942 81 80 05.
Open Tue–Sun 9.30–7.30.

Museo
Altamira Caves.
Tel: 942 81 80 05.
Open Tue–Sun 9.30–2.30.

TOUR 25

i Paseo de los Fueros, 1–bajo, San Sebastian.
Tel: 943 02 31 50.

i Nafarroa, Zarautz.
Tel: 943 83 02 02.

i Artekale, 8, Guernika-Lumo. Tel: 946 25 58 92.

i Paseo del Arenal, 1, Bilbao. Tel: 944 79 57 60.

i Parque de la Florida s/n, Vitoria-Gasteiz. Tel: 945 13 13 21.

2 Zumaia
Villa Zuloaga
Behind the beach across the river.
Open 6 Jun–mid-Sep, Wed–Sun 4–8.

Opening times of museums and other attractions are subject to change and, in addition to opening and closing times given in the text, are usually closed on some public holidays, so visitors are advised to check locally.

6 Gernika Lumo
Casa de Juntas
Calle Karmelo Etxegarai, Gernika–Lumo.
Tel: 946 25 11 38.
Open Mon–Sat 10–2, 4–6 (7 in summer), Sun 10–1.30.

Cuevas de Santimamiñe
Barrio Basondo, Kortézubi.
Tel: 946 25 29 75.
Guided tours Mon–Fri at 10, 11.15, 12.30, 4.30 & 6.

7 Bilbao (Bilbo)
Museo Guggenheim
Alameda Mazarredo 63–4, Bilbao.
Tel: 944 35 90 80/00.
Open Jul–Aug, Tue–Sun 9–9; Sep–Jun 10–8.

Museo Arqueológico, Etnográfico e Histórico Vasco
Cruz, 4, Bilbao.
Tel: 944 15 54 23.
Open Tue–Sat 10.30–1.30, 4–7, Sun 10.30–1.30.

Museo de Bellas Artes
Plaza del Museo, 2, Bilbao.
Tel: 944 41 01 54.
Open Tue–Sat 10–1.30, 4–7.30, Sun 10–2; 17–24 Aug, Tue–Thu, Sat 10–1.30.

8 Vitoria-Gasteiz
Museo de Arqueología
Correría, 116, Vitoria.
Tel: 945 18 19 18.
Open Tue–Fri 10–2, 4–6.30, Sat 10–2, Sun 11–2.

For children
Funicular de Artxanda
Plaza Funicular s/n, Bilbao.
Tel: 944 45 49 66.

For information on Ecuestrian Centres: Tel Tourist Office: 944 79 57 60.

INDEX

Index & Acknowledgements

The Automobile Association

would like to thank the following libraries and photographers for their assistance in the preparation of this book:

Michael Buselle Photolibrary 4, 25, 54, 79, 82/3, 83; Pictures Colour Library 63b, 64/5, 122/3; Spectrum Colour Library 21b, 24, 26, 38, 78, 96, 145, 151, 150/1, 154/5, 156/7; The Travel Library 2, 44, 77, 117, 118/9, 133, 136/7, 149, 153.

The remaining pictures are held in the Association's own library (AA PHOTO LIBRARY) and were taken by:
P Baker 7, 34, 35a, 35b, 36/7, 37, 39a, 39b, 152; J Edmunson 6, 27, 28/9, 30, 31a, 31b, 32, 33, 45, 47, 50b, 51, 52/3, 55, 56, 57, 58, 59, 62, 68b, 73a, 99, 100, 101, 102, 103, 104, 105, 106, 106/7, 108, 113, 115, 116, 120, 121, 124, 125, 165; P Enticknap 8, 9, 9a, 10a, 10b, 12/13, 14, 15, 16/17, 17, 18, 19, 20, 21a, 22/3, 48, 80, 81, 84/5, 85,86/7, 87, 88, 89, 90, 91, 923/3, 93, 94, 95, 110, 110/1, 126, 127a, 127b, 129, 130/1, 130, 132, 134, 135, 138, 139, 140/1, 142/3, 143, 144/5, 146, 147, 148; A Molyneux 40, 60, 61, 64; K Paterson 169; J Poulsen 49a, 53; D Robertson 41, 42, 43, 46/7, 49a, 50a, 63a, 66, 67, 68a, 69, 70, 71, 72, 73b, 74, 75; R Strange 97, 98, 109; J A Tims 114, W Voysey 161, 171.

Author's acknowledgements:

Mona King thanks the following for their help: Turespaña, Madrid; TurMadrid, Madrid; The Spanish Tourist Office, London and Iberia Airlines of Spain.

Contributors
Verifier: Mona King **Original copy editor:** Helen Douglas-Cooper **Indexer:** Marie Lorimer